THE JOY OF WALKING BY FAITH

The Joy of Walking by Faith

A brother's gift of faith.
A sister's extraordinary journey.

Aster Bato Mohamed

Published by:
Redwood Publishing, LLC
www.redwooddigitalpublishing.com
Orange County, California

ISBN: 978-1-966333-10-4 (hardcover)
ISBN: 978-1-966333-11-1 (paperback)
ISBN: 978-1-966333-12-8 (e-book)
Library of Congress Control Number: 2025907723

Interior Design: Ghislain Viau, Creative Book Publishing Design
Cover & Interior Photos: All photos were taken by the author and are owned expressly by her and may not be reproduced

I DEDICATE *THE JOY OF WALKING BY FAITH*
TO OUR ELDEST BROTHER

Who raised me (the youngest of six siblings) since I was nine years old. Whose strict yet nurturing Christian environment constantly guided and inspired me with his own faith,

which became a model of my Christian faith to this day. A brother, who had a spiritual discernment to name me Aster አስቴር (Esther in the Bible) after reading the entire Bible from cover to cover. He believed that I find favor with God and the people He placed in my path. This was evident throughout my life's journey. Although he never had a formal education, he chronicled my life's story from birth to my adulthood and mailed it to me three years before the angels took him to heaven at the age of ninety-two. He was an example of walking by faith for the villagers as well for the missionaries.

I extend my gratitude to you, Obo.

Your legacy lives on through my story, *The Joy of Walking by Faith*.

"For we walk by faith, not by sight."
(2 Corinthians 5:7)

TABLE OF CONTENTS

FOREWORD

May I introduce you to my very dear and long-time friend, Aster Mohamed?

Aster is such a reserved person that her friends will appreciate what an effort it was for her to have opened up as she did in this book. She is not naturally prone to being the topic of conversation.

We were both young stay-at-home mothers when Aster and I met at our Miami neighborhood pool. While watching or waiting for our children, we talked. Like most Miami residents, we were both from elsewhere, so eventually our "elsewhere" and other experiences of one another's past lives were shared in our conversations. The more Aster told me, however, in small revelations, the more interesting I found her story to be. Aster simply loves meeting people, helping people, making them feel comfortable and cared about; she is a natural altruist. As our children grew up, we both became community activists, often working together. While my contributions were writing, promotions, and statistics, Aster's were her considerable people skills. She generously opened her home to gatherings and record-keeping, she recruited volunteers, conducted door-to-door interviews, telephone calls, and did whatever else was needed.

Aster and I soon joined ranks with a renowned Miami-born altruist, the late Dorothy Cissel, for a number of civic and charity projects. For years, the three of us (Aster, Dorothy, and I) talked each other into joining and participating in various causes and organizations.

Through the decades of our friendship, Aster has remained an example, an inspiration, a helper, and a spearhead for great ideas and genuine Christian practices. Little by little, over the years, I thought I had put the pieces of her story together. I wanted to write it, but a thorough and truthful biography takes a lot of time and is an all-consuming task that would have been a major interruption to both our very purpose-driven lives. Only a while after I moved away from Miami did she tell me she had finally decided to write and share her story with discerning readers.

Not until I read this manuscript did I know nearly as much about Aster as I thought I did. This book, in your hands, is the key to a very compelling life story that took me decades to learn. It will be difficult to find a purer heart and a more honest person.

—Marie Grime

PREFACE

My personal story begins as a cattle tender girl from Aira village, Ethiopia, a girl in a country with lots of love but little opportunity. My eldest brother, who is a model of my faith to this day, named me Aster አስቴር (Esther) in the Bible, for he believed I, too, would find favor with God.

I hope in my story, *The Joy of Walking by Faith*, I can share with you my culture and inspire you to never despair when faced with challenges. It is said, "When fear knocks at your door send faith to answer it, and you will find that there is no one there." God placed compassionate people in my path to educate me, to guide my talents, to assimilate me into the American culture, and to become an educator in the fourth largest school system in the United States, as well as an advocate for a safe school and community, and a participant in various church and community organizations. As a neighborhood volunteer leader for the first African American presidential reelection, I was even privileged to meet President Obama.

I was motivated to write my story to leave a legacy for my three children, two grandchildren, and all of my younger generation of relatives who know so little about how I got to where I am in my life. It may also comfort not only other immigrants but all those who struggle with what seem like insurmountable obstacles.

I encourage you, too, to walk by faith.

INTRODUCTION

In my memoir, you will discover how my eldest brother's faith in God and the significance of my name have blessed me throughout my life's journey. I first started writing my memoir in 2003, as a result of attending an author's showcase, in order to leave a legacy for my three children (no grandchildren yet at that time) who had never visited my birthplace in a remote village in Ethiopia. In addition, I wanted to share my past success with the many younger-generation relatives who knew little about the home I grew up in, and how I became the person I am today.

As I interacted with individuals in my community, they, too, were curious about what brought me to Miami, which often was followed by unending questions. To this date, it is overwhelming and cumbersome to initiate a conversation about my upbringing, my accomplishments, and about my extended families at my birthplace with my children or the individuals I meet. Although I am grateful to God for His countless blessings in my life, culturally we do not openly or easily speak of our accomplishments. However, I dared to circumvent this custom and share my story of how I became who I am today because of my two devoted Christian brothers and the people God placed in my path.

Those I shared my story with encouraged me to write my story for others to read. There were painful cultural practices I experienced in my life in Ethiopia that discouraged me from sharing my story verbally because revealing these painful practices were humiliating and cumbersome for me. "Maybe I could express them through writing," I thought. I drew strength to write about these practices by reading online that these practices in Ethiopia, as well as in different parts of the world, are now considered a human rights violation.

Furthermore, I was extremely excited and encouraged to write my autobiography after reading former President Barack Obama's memoir, *Dreams from My Father*. His dad, who was from Kenya, a neighboring country of Ethiopia, had a humble background similar to my own upbringing in the village. If our former president with national recognition could share his dad's humble story, I had more courage to write my own story.

My educational journey involved four languages: First, I spoke my tribal language Oromifa. Once I enrolled in first grade, I learned and memorized the 231 letters of the Ethiopian alphabet (Fidel). Next, I studied Amharic, which was the national language at that time which shared the same letters with my tribal language with a few exceptions; however, the grammar was very different. By the third grade, the English language was introduced and eventually became an academic language during the latter part of elementary grades and most of high school years. During the elementary school years, we had access to English-English dictionaries only. We learned most subjects through memorization. Therefore, I had never studied any academic subject in my tribal language Oromifa, except the Bible. However, in the last fifty years it has been changed to Quibee, which uses the Roman letters, and, in recent years, has become the most widely spoken language in Ethiopia. Although I can read the words and understand, I cannot write in Quibee with accuracy.

Throughout my story, you will encounter the Oromifa words, "Obo" or "Ade" in front of my brother or sisters' names. Growing up, I did not call my elder siblings or anyone in the village older than I by their names. I called my eldest brother "Obo" and our second elder brother, "Obosha," an endearment form to differentiate between the two brothers. Obo was a form showing general respect for older men. Likewise, I called my older sisters and any female older than I, "Ade." These forms of respect were commonly used during my youth and I still use them today. Yet in the larger cities, Gashe, for a male, and Itiye, for a female were used. I am surprised to hear the young generation, including my own relatives, calling their parents by their first names.

When I began writing my memoir in 2003, I chronicled it from my childhood to the end of elementary school, based on my memories. That year, I joined a writing group that met at the home of one of the members. Each member brought hard copies of their memoir to share with each member. After critiquing and discussing, it was returned to each writer. The group was fascinated by my history and encouraged me to continue. However, I saved the corrected document on floppy disks, printed out hard copies, and stopped writing my story altogether. This was mostly because of my increased involvement at my workplace and within my community.

Fourteen years later, in February 2017, I attended an all-day annual conference hosted by the South Florida Writers' Association at the invitation of one of my community organization's board member. The various speakers were fascinating and inspiring. This included the CEO and founder, Mitchell, of Books and Books of Miami, Inc., an independently owned bookstore in Miami. In addition, there were breakout sessions. I participated in the ghostwriter's group, thinking it was about writing autobiographies. Surprisingly, the group discussed why the members desired to write their stories and who would be interested in reading them. Some members sought to write for additional income by selling their books, while others expressed that they would like to leave a legacy for their families. I, too, wished to leave a lasting legacy for my children, grandchildren, extended families, and friends. Yet, I was conflicted about continuing to write my story because the idea of sharing my gruesome cultural experience still haunted me. With some trepidation, I joined the South Florida Writers' Association.

When I resumed writing my memoir in 2017, I faced an unprecedented dilemma. The floppy disks I had saved my writing on were now obsolete. I was not ready to retype the eighty-five pages. Then, I embarked on what seemed to be an easy solution: searching on Google for an "external device" to transfer my document from floppy disks to my laptop. I discovered that it was available at Staples, a nearby office supply store. I was so excited! Immediately, I printed out the page with the information on it, rushed to the store, and asked for a manager whom I knew was studying computer engineering. After checking on the store computer, he instantly located the external device for floppy disk. I purchased it. The manager promised me that I could return the device to the store if it did not operate. I rushed to my house, read the direction, and connected the external device to my laptop and started downloading. I could not believe my eyes. I thanked God for His guidance. I opened the file and saved it on my laptop and USB. I felt like I invented something new.

Next, I joined a nonfiction critique group led by an accomplished author, and a former University of Minnesota retired professor. What a coincidence! That was the same university where I had received my master's degree. Some of the members had already published articles, and the rest of the member were new, like me. All of the members of the group spoke English as their first language, with the exception of another member who was a Spanish speaker, and me.

Unlike the critique group in 2003, the critique group in 2017, emailed their stories to each other in advance of the monthly critique group meeting to allow extra time to prepare.

Although my memoir was already reviewed in 2003-4, the 2017 group found more errors in my writing style. Nevertheless, the group found my story culturally fascinating, credible and encouraged me to continue writing. This time I was grateful and excited to write.

In 2005 my eldest brother had sent me the very special journal he kept which chronicled my life throughout the years, and he wanted me to include his journal entries in an appendix in my book, which I was excited to do.

However, I became overwhelmed with emotions, grief, and regrets. I was heartbroken because I didn't finish writing the book, or have it published in time to send to him before his passing away in June of 2008. Following my eldest brother's passing, my eldest sister, my second older brother, and several other relatives also passed away. My regret is that I could have written part one of my memoir and shared it with them. However, I am grateful that my two older sisters and my two brothers' spouses are still alive. Since I cannot go back and change the past, I will continue honoring my brother's legacy by sharing my Christian faith, knowledge, and hope with everyone I meet, through my memoir.

Wanting to honor my brother's legacy was being held up by a story I was hesitant to share with the world. Because of this, I stopped participating in the critique group because I was embarrassed to share about the humiliating practice of female circumcision that me and other women were forced to endure in my village and entire country. However, God led me to a friend and member of our church who had been a retired high school English teacher. The other individual is someone I met through volunteerism at school and the community I was involved in. She is a journalist by profession. Although I was comfortable with these two ladies, it took me some time to overcome my fear and let them edit my manuscript.

The people in my autobiography are my immediate relatives and I have used their actual names. The photos that are included in the story were from my eldest brother's collection (given to him by the German Mission since he did not own a camera), from friends, my own collection, as well as professional photos, which are so identified. The cover photo is my college graduation photo.

My story, *The Joy of Walking by Faith*, is the result of my brother's faith in God, his spiritual vision to name me Aster, and the compassionate people God put in my path. My own faith and trust in God has helped me reach my full potential. Therefore, I encourage you to find people in your life that guide and support you to reach your own full potential, regardless of your parents' educational and economic background, nationality, faith, and the obstacles and roadblocks you may face in your life's journey, and then give thanks to God.

CHAPTER ONE

A Glance at My Own Death

My earliest memory was living in a roundhouse my father built in a remote village called Aira, located in the southwest of Ethiopia in the province of Wollega. I was about six years old. The brown wall was covered with a smooth mud mixture. The thatched and fastened roof looked like a perfect mushroom haircut, with many layers. A see-through wooden wall divided the sleeping and cooking areas from the guest section. My mother was cooking on a fireplace, which was supported by three medium size stones. I sat on an elevated floor of the sleeping area right next to the fireplace.

I felt as if I had awakened from a deep sleep. I don't remember what time of day it was. I had just regained consciousness from malaria. I glanced through the wooden wall and was surprised to see a small wooden coffin, made from a trunk of a tree, propped next to a big coffin, which had been draped with a blanket and was used to sit on. It had probably been made for my brother, Obo Deressa, when he suffered a massive stroke several years earlier.

"Who is that for?" I asked my mother pointing to the small coffin. There was silence. Tears rolled down her cheeks. "Why are you crying?" I asked. She kept stirring what seemed to be a porridge with one hand and wiping her tears with the other hand. I hope the porridge is for me, I thought. My mother made porridge when we were sick.

Meanwhile, I recall hearing Obo praying. "Thank you, God, for sparing my sister thus far and I trust in your power to heal her from this deadly disease, if it is Your will," he prayed. Obo is a prayer warrior and a man of great faith. He is to become the model of my own faith. His prayers worked, because I fully recovered from malaria.

My immediate family was large as I was growing up. My parents, Bato Eba and Beshatoo Homa, had eight children in total. The first was a boy, named Deressa (long life); the second was a girl, Gaalitu, the third child was a boy named Lamessa (one more boy). Two girls in a row followed, Dessi (contented) and Terunesh (beautiful). Then two boys came, one died at birth and the other at two. I was the last child to be born. Our eldest brother, "Obo" Deressa, carefully selected my name and named me አስቴር "Aster" after reading the book of Esther in the Bible in our tribal language Oromifa. "Obo" means brother, a title given to the oldest brother out of respect. Likewise, we call our older sister "Ade," which is also a title of respect. Obo read the entire Bible from Genesis to Revelation at least once during his confinement from a stroke he suffered earlier in his life.

In 1994, when I went back to Ethiopia and visited my family back in my village, Obo reminded me of the significance of naming me "Aster" and he said, "I see that God blessed you and favored you with many things."

"Yes, but I don't want to be a queen," I answered. Then he replied, "If God makes you a queen, you've to accept it." I marveled at Obo's response and laugh. This was our first and last personal conversation we had. We never talked casually with each other because of the respect I had for him, which was our custom. In a letter he wrote me in 2005, he outlined my life's story. "At the time you were born on June 4, 1944 (1936 according to Ethiopian calendar), I was again reading the story of Queen Esther. I named you Aster (Ethiopian for Esther), hoping that you will find favor before God with life." I realized that God had favored me with my life, education, physical and spiritual blessings throughout my life's journey. He granted me favor in the eyes of everyone and gave me success in whatever I did. *And Esther won the favor of everyone who saw her*" (Esther 2:15b). In January of 2018, my sister who lives in Addis Ababa, Ethiopia, informed me that all churches in Ethiopia commemorate Queen Esther. "It reminded me of when Obo named you Aster," she added. We laughed, but my eyes welled up with tears.

After I survived my illness, my parents did not give me major house chores to complete. Instead, I would help my sisters and

11

sister-in-law with small tasks like serving coffee. Culturally, all children were expected to help around the house. I frequently begged, "When can I cook and grind grain on a grinding stone like my sisters?" It seemed to me like it was a lot of fun. I could help them only when they asked me to get water from the river. (There was no running water in the homes). Amazingly, my mother seldom asked me to help her but encouraged me to help my siblings and my sister-in-law.

My parents always said, *"One throws a small stone."* It meant that I, the youngest child, had to do the entire running. Whenever they needed small chores to be done, they asked me to complete them. No telephone existed in the village. So, when my mother, sisters, or sister-in-law needed to borrow something from a neighbor, they would beg me, "Aster, please go and get it." I always obeyed them because they cared for me and loved me unconditionally. But it was scary for me to go to a neighbor's house, which was one-eighth of a mile away and surrounded by corn fields during the summer, which was May through September. Sometimes, I had to go to the neighbor's house at night. I was not scared of people because the villagers would never harm the children. They believed that God and His guardian angels protected the young ones. But what if a lion or hyena were waiting for me? I worried. Often wild animals roamed through the neighborhood at night. Frequently, I heard sounds from the hyenas, which resembled the laughter of dozens of women gathered together, chuckling in the evening, or a lion's roar that echoed through the air like thunder.

"Is the lion close by?" I asked my family.

"It is far away, in the forest," they assured me.

At about age seven or eight, I was also permitted to help take care of the cattle along with my cousin. He was the same age as I. Groups of families in the neighborhood took turns watching the cattle from morning to evening. This was called cattle sitting. When we were first allowed to cattle sit by ourselves, my cousin and I were scared of the giant bulls with long horns.

"What if these bulls mistake us for some small wild animals?" We thought. Wow! Their horns were as long as swords. Thankfully, a grown-up from our family accompanied us to guide us before we were left on our own.

By the age of eight, we were on our own. There were about fifteen to twenty cows and bulls from different families. They were dropped off at our house between 2 and 3 am (the equivalent of 9 am. In Ethiopia, we count 12 hours of daylight and 12 hours of nighttime). Cows and bulls had names like kids do. Knowing their names was very helpful when they went places they were not supposed to go. When one of us called their names, most of them stopped. Some of them didn't pay attention. However, my cousin and I took the cattle to green pasture and they grazed until they were full.

This gave my cousin and I great satisfaction. It reminded me of Psalms, *"He makes me lie down in green pastures, and He leads me to still waters"* (Palms 23:2).

Then, we guided them to a river located in the valley surrounded by bushes and trees to drink water. Monkeys would

13

start jumping from tree to tree, making noises, and tormenting the cows. The cows began mooing. We worried. *"What if the lions heard all these noises and came to get the cows as well as both of us?"* Maybe the lions were sound asleep from eating all night. Luckily, the cattle and we were spared.

After the cattle drank water, we directed them up the hill to a giant sycamore tree to rest. They all rested and even slept under that tree. We, too, rested while keeping an eye on some mischievous young cows or bulls. That old oak tree that we had rested under became my landmark when I visited the modernized village twenty-five years later, looking for my family's house.

When we as children misbehaved, our parents didn't raise their voices or scream at us. They just looked at us with stern faces. Immediately, we stopped what we were doing. Otherwise, there were severe consequences.

It is said, *"It takes the whole village to raise a child,"* according to an African proverb. In our culture, neighbors and grown-ups could reprimand or punish us if they saw us doing something unacceptable in the neighborhood. Sometimes we begged our neighbors not to tell our parents because our parents' punishments were more severe. Unfortunately, the missionary took advantage of our culture and took extreme punishment.

My father was a farmer and he also sold fabrics at the marketplaces. He was a handsome six feet tall slender man. My mother was a beautiful and slim woman and a full-time housewife. She also worked on the farm. Like many other people in the village, my parents owned a large farmland. They cultivated various grains, such as corn, wheat, oats, millets, and other grains native to Ethiopia, including teff, a tiny grain the size of a poppy seed. Teff is ground into flour from which injera, a sour flatbread, is made. Similar to other families in the village, my parents were illiterate. However, skills for farming were passed down through generations. During sowing and harvesting, families took turns working on each other's farms. Only the men plowed the fields. Each bull wore a wooden yoke attached to a plow which had sharp metal to penetrate the ground and made it ready for sowing the grains. I was amazed to watch my father making such a straight track for the other men to follow. *"What an imaginary ruler he had in his mind!"* I thought. Later I found out his secret was to look ahead instead of down. Meanwhile, the women had the task of preparing food for the men.

In addition to farming, Ababa (father) also sold white fabrics at various markets or directly from our house. He bought the fabric wholesale from faraway markets. People made clothing for children and adults. There was no standard measurement to measure the fabric when he sold to his customers. Instead, he used his long right arm to measure. (I had never seen anyone using their left hand because children were punished for using our left hands.) I also observed as he invented his own standard measurement by cutting a straight stick, which is three times the length of his arm. It was equivalent to a yard stick. *"What a genius Ababa!"* I thought. I adored him, especially his medium length beard.

I remember my dad had a beautiful bed made from a woven cowhide which stood about three feet above the ground from where the rest of family members slept. As the head of the family, he slept on this special bed. Occasionally, I begged him to sleep too on his special bed. Sometimes, when I had a severe headache, he would hold my head between his two giant palms. His palms became a painkiller and a sleeping pill. Immediately, my headache would be gone and I would fall asleep.

CHAPTER TWO

Dear God, Why Did You Take Away My Father So Soon?

When I wasn't taking care of the cattle, I enjoyed going with my father to the farm. I watched Ababa plow with two oxen. When I accompanied my father during harvesting as he cut the grains, I loved being in his shade. He was about six feet tall, and it was easy to fit in his overarching, giant body.

Sometimes I helped carry the tools home. One time I misplaced one of his tools somewhere in the house. The next day he asked me, "Where did you put it?" I frantically searched for it but couldn't find it. I didn't dare look at his face. Instead, I looked down. He started looking for a thin switch which he hid somewhere in the house just in case he needed it. I melted in fear. I waited patiently for my punishment and he whacked me. I cried uncontrollably for a moment. This was the only spanking that I remember receiving from Ababa.

Most villagers lived primarily on the food they raised on their farms. However, sometimes married women and young men went to various marketplaces, mainly to buy items they didn't have at home, such as salt blocks and spices. They also sold things they had plenty of at home. Women purchased household items while men sold fabrics. The market sites were held at different locations depending on the days of the week: Monday, Wednesday, and Friday afternoons. The Friday market was close to our house where my mother, Hortu shopped. (Hortu is a name given to a wife married to the second brother. Everyone called her "Hortu, " including us children.)

I have never forgotten the one summer when my mother went to the marketplace on a Friday. She came down with some kind of illness a week later after visiting the market. The missionary doctors diagnosed it as typhus. Soon my two sisters became ill, as well. "You brought the disease from the marketplace to kill our family!" my father yelled at her. I didn't know what went on in my mother's mind. I was devastated to hear this from my Ababa. She didn't show any emotion or say anything. Generally, women never showed emotions and didn't talk back to their husbands. Thank God Hortu and my sisters recovered from their illnesses. Miraculously, Obo, my brother's pregnant wife, Soretti (a name given to the first son's wife), and I didn't catch this serious bacterial disease spread by lice or fleas.

However, my father became ill with typhus. His health deteriorated rapidly. He called Obo, our eldest brother, and asked him to document any business and household-related matters, such as paying off debts and dividing his assets among family members. In those days, there were no banks. Money was buried underground in an undisclosed place. According to our culture, the oldest son became the head of the family if the father was incapacitated for some reason or had died. In the villages, the wife was not included in much of the decision-making. Luckily, Obo knew how to read and write. So he would make a record of my father's request.

What will happen to my father? What will I do without him? I wondered. I stopped sleeping with him on his special bed because he was very sick. A father who had been the family's hero now became helpless. Generally, people in Ethiopia are not heavy; my father was tall and slender. He lost so much weight that his bones showed through the blanket as he lay on his side. Ababa was in so much pain that I heard him moaning for the first time. Generally, men try to be tough at all times and hide their pain. Because of this, I understood the extent of his pain. We prayed for my father continuously. I was comforted when I realized that Jesus also cried aloud to His father when he was on the cross because he was in pain.

Obo Deressa, my brother, had been working for the German Mission Grades 1 - 8 school. He had a good rapport with the missionaries. He suggested to Ababa that he would send a messenger to bring doctors. There were two female doctors who worked at a small hospital about two miles walking distance from our house. My father reluctantly agreed to my brother's advice.

Soon, the two female doctors walked to our house. They brought something with them that looked like water. It was in a clear container. I overheard one of the doctors telling my father, "This is water. It will make you feel better." Meanwhile, the second doctor pulled out of her briefcase a giant needle attached to a syringe. I watched as she filled it with the salt-water solution.

"Ato (Mr.) Bato, it will hurt a little," she said as she forced the needle under the dried-up skin on his hip. I was traumatized as my father screamed and moaned.

"Leave me alone," he demanded. "I'd rather die than receive this water," he told the doctors. It was unusual for a man to show emotion when he was in pain. Then one of the doctors said, "Goodbye, Ato Bato, you will die," and walked out. That was the way she treated patients. "Who is she to tell my father that he would die?" I thought to myself. Her statement angered my family.

As soon as the two doctors left him, I went outside to watch the cattle with my male cousin. Ababa's friends from the neighborhood and Obo stayed with him. In our culture, especially in the villages, women, including wives, are not allowed to stay with their husbands. The women remained in the old roundhouse.

Within an hour, one of the elders came out to the field, "Your father wants to see you," he told me. I knew he had been in excruciating pain when I left him. "Why would he want to see me?" I wondered. I came in and sat next to him on the bed. I felt the weakness in his arm, as he put his arm around me, pulled me down to his chest, hugged, and kissed me. His body felt as hot as a burning fire. I also felt his ribs when I hugged him back. This was the last time we hugged each other. We both wept. Then I left the room. One of the elders put his hand on my shoulder. "You look just like your Ababa," he said. Soon after I left Ababa's bedside, I saw my mother and sisters crying in the roundhouse where they were waiting. I, too, began weeping. My sisters advised me to stay around the house instead of helping my cousin with the cattle.

I watched from a distance as the elders washed his body and put perfume on him. One of the elders brought in the white fabric my father used to sell. They wrapped his body in it. Two men brought in a large coffin made of wood from the old roundhouse. It was twice the size of the one my father had prepared for me when I was near death. My father purchased the coffin for himself before he was ill and had stored it in the old roundhouse where I was born. They covered it with a fabric and used it as a bench.

My father and our eldest brother shared the house that my other brother, the pastor, had built when Obo Deressa got married. This house had a rectangular shape and had two large bedrooms, separated by a wooden wall which was covered with a mud mixture, like a type of dark plaster. It had a window in each room. Ababa and I had slept in one room, while Obo Deresa and his wife slept in the other room.

After the men wrapped him, they laid him in the coffin. I couldn't take it anymore, as I watched the men nail the lid on the coffin. There were no funeral homes. His body was kept overnight in the house. I was thinking, "Couldn't Jesus raise my father from the dead as He raised Lazarus?" Then I remembered the comforting scripture passage, "*Be still, know I am your God*" (Psalms 46:10). Yes, God saved me from a deadly illness when I was just six years old. I should thank Him for allowing me to enjoy life with Ababa for three more years. My brother sent messengers to relatives to inform them of my father's death. Friends and relatives laid mats on the floor where the coffin was placed. I was overwhelmed with fear. "What will happen to me without my father?" I wondered. "Why did God allow my Ababa to die?"

I heard people chanting and crying loudly as they approached our house. Then, those relatives and friends inside the house joined them. They chanted as they wept. I didn't quite understand. I just cried. Meanwhile, several men went to dig the grave on the grounds of the church that our family attended. It was about five miles away from our house. In Ethiopian culture, a dead body is buried within twenty-four hours.

The next day, several men took turns carrying his body to the church graveyard. Hundreds of people walked with my family in the procession crying so loudly that it could be heard several miles away.

I remember when my family and relatives stood around the burial place. My mother and sisters tried to throw themselves in the grave. "Let me go in," each chanted. I didn't know what to make of it. I just sobbed uncontrollably. Next, my mother tried several times to throw herself in the grave chanting and crying, "Let me go in first." The men tried to hold her back.

I was puzzled at the sight because it was my first funeral. "I already lost my Ababa, and now my mother!" I thought.

After the pastor led the funeral prayer, the men laid the coffin in the grave. I watched as the men covered the coffin with a pile of dirt and my relatives and friends chanted and wept again. I just wept because I didn't know how to chant yet. It sounded like rhyming words. This was the only time female relatives expressed emotional pain.

Families and relatives mourned for about seven days. We sat on the floor and didn't look in the mirror during this period. Friends, neighbors, and church members provided all the food. As people from distant places approached our house chanting and crying, the family joined in weeping and chanting. There was no laughing or smiling during the mourning period. I recalled someone mentioning that a widow gave birth on the same day my father passed away. My male cousin and I, not knowing the tradition, started laughing. Then my mother reached out and pinched both of us. As was our culture's tradition, about the ninth day after my father died, everyone in our family and relatives shaved their heads as part of our mourning process.

The women dyed their traditional white clothes black to wear for at least one year. For a long time, I hoped that my Ababa would come back soon because I believed that Jesus would raise him from the dead. As I was going through deep sadness, the scripture came to my mind to cheer me up: "*I have loved thee with an everlasting love*" (Jer: 31:3).

23

Several months later, my other brother, Rev. Lamessa, whom I called "Obosha," heard about our father's death. He had been away for several years for pastoral training. The town was very far, and he walked by foot for several days to come home. He also started crying and chanting as he approached our house. The rest of our family joined him and wept. He was offered a chair to sit on as the mourning period was over.

Everyone was silent for a while and then family members and friends greeted him. I put my arms around him and didn't want him to leave. Everybody knew I loved him. We were all happy to see him again. This again brought back memories of my father's death. I felt the emptiness in my life without my father's hugs and companionship. However, I was so glad that my favorite brother, Obosha, decided to spend a few weeks with us before returning to his training. My two brothers, without the involvement of my mother or sisters, made decisions about my father's inheritance. I wished my mother and sisters were included.

Although our eldest brother had been physically challenged since his teen years, he took care of the whole family. According to the Ethiopian culture, the oldest son assumes responsibility as head of the household. However, I was puzzled why Obo never consulted with my mother and sought her advice about her children. In those days, it was uncommon for a widow to remarry. Therefore, my mother lived with Obo Deressa all her life, and so did all my sisters until they got married or moved away for school. My mother enjoyed raising her nine grandchildren from Obo, giving her a new purpose for her life.

CHAPTER THREE

NEW BEGINNING:
FROM A SHEPHERD TO A STUDENT
GRADES 1 – 8

When my brother's condition from his illness improved tremendously, he used two sturdy and solid sticks to walk around. The German Mission director asked him to be the first-grade teacher at their school. He was grateful to be asked to teach. I heard my mother and my sister-in-law, Soretti, asking, "Who would carry his books?" Why didn't my two sisters carry his books? I thought. They were already enrolled in the school. Again, I was reminded of the saying, "*One throws a small stone.*" I was the youngest and I was faster. My sisters had more chores to do and might not be there on time. I did not have any responsibilities, so it made sense that I would be the one to help him.

In 1953, at the age of nine, the year my father died, I enrolled in my brother's first-grade class at the German Hermansburg Mission School, which had opened two years earlier. There was only one class per grade level in the school. My two older sisters, Dessie and Terunesh, were already in the second grade. They were five and seven years older than I.

September 1953 was a new year for me. The school started a week after the Ethiopian New Year, called "Inkootatash" in Amharic and "Wagaa Haaraa" in Oromifa. It was always on September 11 (Western calendar), but it was on September 1 according to the Ethiopian calendar. The Ethiopians use the ancient Julian calendar, while Western countries changed to the Gregorian calendar in the late sixteenth century. Therefore, our calendar remains behind by seven to eight years.

On New Year's Day early in the morning while it was dark, adult men and women as well as children went to the river to wash themselves before the New Year began. Men and women went to separate areas but children could join either group. Those who couldn't go to the river took baths at home. Obo Deressa had a bath at home. What a great tradition this was. We washed ourselves from the past and started a new beginning. When we came home, my mother and Soretti prepared my favorite breakfast, injera, flat sour bread with home-processed spiced butter. Injera looks similar to a French crepe but is usually made of teff, a tiny grain that is a staple in Ethiopia. They brewed coffee from freshly roasted, ground coffee beans. Oh my! That was delicious! Then the young children went from door to door to collect money as it was our tradition at the new year, similar to Halloween in the United States. The boys chanted while the girls gave flowers. "I will get a lot of money because many people knew Obo because he is a teacher," I assured myself, as I picked flowers from our garden. My cousin and I went to our neighbors' houses. When we returned home, our families inquired, "How much money did you get?" "About $3.00 Ethiopian birr," (the Western equivalent of about $1.00) we replied. "That was a lot of money," our families commented. We both gave our money to our mothers to buy necessities for the family.

Monday, following our New Year, the school year began. As always, my brother Obo Deressa began the day with a prayer breakfast at our home. The neighbors came to our house, too. Thereafter, Monday through Friday, before we left for school and before families went to work on the farms, Obo led regular neighborhood prayer breakfasts at different homes. I enjoyed the variety of breakfasts served at each neighbor's house.

My first day of school was going to be exciting! I sighed as I walked about three yards behind Obo Deressa, carrying his books. In Ethiopian culture, children walk behind adults to show respect. Everyone in the villages walked barefoot, except those teachers who visited nearby cities.

Once the bell rang, my brother took attendance of all students as they lined up by grade level in front of the one-story schoolhouse. The first row was the first grade class. I was in the first line of four girls and about fifteen boys and young men. Behind me was my sisters' second grade class, four girls and about twelve boys. The last row consisted of eight third graders, seven young men and one young woman.

All students lined up like an army ready for routine exercise. We began by singing the Ethiopian national anthem and some spiritual songs. Devotion was led by one of the teachers. At the end of the assembly, each grade level marched to its designated classroom like soldiers. I led the first grade line to my brother's class.

Most students seemed to be grown-ups. I was puzzled as I looked around the classroom. Two of us girls were the same age, as was my cousin Bichaka, and two other boys. But some of the men appeared to be as old as my brother. Later on, I found out that these men were married and had left their children at home and come to have a glimpse of modern education. Because these young men were older than I, I had to address them with Obo (brother) or Ato (Mister) and their first names. The ages of the students in my grade ranged from nine to twenty-four.

Traditionally, the girls enrolled in school at an older age because they were discouraged from attending school. There was a saying in the villages. "Girls don't work in an office." For a girl to be educated was a big deal! This meant that they didn't need a career. Those who did start school frequently dropped out to raise a family.

The first school period was Bible study. Obo Deressa taught in my tribal language, Oromifa. It was the most widely spoken language in Ethiopia. It stood second among the many other African languages.

No one knew the Bible better than Obo Deressa did. He had read it three times from beginning to end while he was confined to his chair due to his illness for several years. He taught it from the heart. I enjoyed listening to him in school even though we had devotions twice a day at home. The Bible was a large part of my life.

After Bible study, we had half an hour recess. All the girls gathered like animals in a fenced-in area, while the boys freely ran around the school compound and played with their friends. Were male students considered wolves that we were being kept safe from? I questioned. I missed the freedom of running after the cattle, and racing against each other, and climbing the trees with my male cousin and neighborhood friends. "Your parents don't want you to be with the boys," the school director explained.

When the bell rang for the next session, everyone went back to their classes. My brother also taught the Ethiopian alphabet, called "Fidel," which consists of thirty-three letters. Each letter has seven variations, a total of two hundred and thirty-one symbols. The vowels are incorporated in the consonants. I believe that this alphabet is no longer used by my tribe. However, I continue to write my family using Fidel.

My brother had never attended formal school, but my siblings think that the German missionaries might have taught him. A poster on the wall had all the variations of Fidel. We recited after him, as he pointed to each symbol with a stick and said it aloud. Oh, that's easy, I felt, as I chanted each symbol. Once the students learned all the symbols, then learning to read and write was made simpler. Those who had money purchased the Fidel booklets for a nominal fee.

After another recess, a different teacher taught Amharic. It was the first official language in Ethiopia. It was a Semitic language, and some words were traced to Hebrew and Arabic, like "salaam" (peace) and "kebab" (circle). The national language was different from my tribal language. For example, a teacher was called "barsissaa" in Oromifaa, and "astamari" in Amharic. It used the same alphabet but with fewer variations. One could sound out the words in both languages without difficulty, but without understanding the meaning.

Then at six o'clock noon (12 noon) many of us went home for lunch. Students who walked long distances brought snacks and ate in the shade of a tree. In Ethiopia, we count the hours one through twelve, starting from the morning to evening. Therefore, there were twelve hours of daytime and twelve hours of nighttime. Neither my mother nor Soretti knew how to read and write, so reading a clock was impossible for them. Instead, they both watched the shadow from the roof of the house that fell on the ground to tell time. This was how they prepared lunch before we got home. Ethiopia straddles on the equator, therefore, when it was 6 o'clock at noon, one could not see his own shadow on the ground.

After two hours of lunch break, classes resumed at eight o'clock. The ringing of the bell echoed in the air, alerting the students and teachers of the afternoon session. All students arrived and waited in their designated lines, just like we did at the beginning of school each day.

An Ethiopian teacher came to my first grade class to teach mathematics. We all stood up until he told us to sit. In our culture, we stand up silently whenever a guest or teacher enters a classroom.

We got up and stood behind the long wooden desks until we were told to sit down. When a teacher asks questions, a student must stand and answer. If a student doesn't know the response, he or she has to stand up longer. The mathematics teacher had an elementary school education and understood some English. That meant he was highly qualified. He translated the mathematic problems from English to Oromifa for the students. Mathematics was my favorite subject, although I loved every subject so far.

After another recess, another punishing time-out for us girls behind the fence, the German Mission director came to teach the English alphabet. Now, this is when things became complicated. How were we ever going to learn three languages simultaneously? We also had social science, arts and crafts for girls, while the boys had physical education. Oh, how I wished I had physical education with the boys! I had loved the experience of running when I was a shepherd girl.

Finally, the school day ended at ten o'clock in the afternoon. While we were in school, my sisters worked on the farm and prepared dinner. As I was the youngest child, my mother did not allow me to have major chores, except helping my sisters, Ade Dessi, Ade Terunesh, and my sister-in-law when they asked.

It wasn't long before my classmates realized how strict Obo Deressa was. In Ethiopian culture, a teacher has the right to punish a student for any reason, including laughing. The younger students, including me, enjoyed laughing when something amused us. This angered my brother. "Malif koolfitaa kootuu," (What makes you laugh? Come, here) he called me to his desk. Then, he took a pencil and squeezed my ear between his finger and the pencil. It felt as if my ear was on fire. When the others laughed, "Atis kootuu," (You, too, come here) and "You deserve it, too," he told them. He punished everyone, including the older students who were as old as he.

There were three terms in a year. Each student paid three shillings, which was about fifty cents in U.S. currency. I was lucky that my brother paid for everything for me, including school supplies, while my two sisters paid for themselves.

My teachers and the director of the school were amazed at how quickly I progressed in school.

I enjoyed learning and it came naturally to me. I remembered the pages and visualized the text as I studied. I thanked God for giving me a photographic memory.

At the end of each term, comprehensive examinations were administered in every subject. I used to make up practice questions for my classmates. Our final grades were based solely on these test results. I remembered my first report card; the results were written both in English and Amharic. I earned one hundred percent in every subject. At the end of every term, a school-wide award assembly was held. The top three students from each grade level were selected and awarded for their outstanding academic achievement. I never understood why these assemblies or awards were given in the first place, because I enjoyed learning just for the sake of learning.

"Who was first in your class?" one of my relatives asked me when I came home. "I don't know," I replied.

"Who did Miss Rabin (Gifti Rabin), the school director call first?" another relative asked.

"She called me first," I responded. They all laughed.

Although I was nine years old, I didn't understand the importance of being first in my class. The joy was in the learning not the recognition.

At the end of the school year, students were required to take a test in every subject. This determined whether a student would be promoted to the next grade level or not. There was no exception for any student who might have had challenges in learning to read or write. The teachers had academic knowledge but did not understand the psychology of teaching and learning. I remembered some unfortunate students who were labeled "dumb," and repeated grades several times. Eventually, they dropped out of school. I recalled when one of the teachers slapped his daughter so many times because she didn't understand the concepts and skills being taught. She, too, dropped out of school to raise her ten younger siblings alongside her mother.

When I came home from school, I continued my hobbies. I completed school assignments, if there were any, and played with my niece. In the evening, I sat in the kitchen by the glowing fireplace that resembled a campsite and knitted in the radiating light. Though I could hardly see what I was doing, I managed to knit without a problem. I also watched my sisters prepare dinner. I wished I could cook like them someday.

The old rectangular house became the kitchen. All the women and children sat around the fireplace. They talked and laughed as they prepared dinner and they had a good time together. Obo Deressa sat separated from us, in the guest room, in the new rectangular house. This new house had four bedrooms and a large living room in the center. Each bedroom was separated by wooden walls that were covered with a mud mixture. Each room had a window. My favorite brother, Obosha (Reverend Lemessa), built this house, too. It had two entrances, one in the front, and one on the back, leading to the kitchen.

Obo Deressa stood at the door of the house that led to the kitchen and yelled, "You are not doing any work except laughing," he criticized, after listening to the giggling in the kitchen. Then my wise mother commented in a low voice, "We don't cook with our mouths." I thought that he felt lonely because there were no other men to talk to. He sat and knitted alone. The five ladies seem to enjoy laughter and conversations. However, when Obo's brother, Obosha, visited us, they enjoyed talking together. Traditionally, men never entered the kitchen for any reason. Occasionally, when a ball of yarn accidentally fell on the floor he asked for a candle for a better light in the room.

Before food was served, I brought water for Obo to wash his hands. Dinner was served about three o'clock in the evening. It was brought into the living room and was served on a large plate carved from wood, about twenty-four inches in diameter. The round thin bread was layered on the plate. Then, the spicy meat or bean sauce was poured in a bowl and placed in the center. Sometimes, the sauce was served directly on the bread. Family members sat around the large dinner plate.

My brother said table grace before and after dinner. Everyone took a bite size of the bread from his and her side and dipped it in the sauce. We ate with our fingers just as the people did in biblical times. Therefore, everyone washes his or her hands before and after eating. It is the duty of the youngest child in the family to offer water for hand washing. I was the youngest child. Obo led the evening devotion. Then one of us washed his feet. We also washed our feet before going to bed. We had walked barefoot all day long, so washing our feet was necessary.

After school, one of the missionary's wife asked me to play with her young children. I didn't get paid, but she gave me hand-me-down clothes, which I treasured. Until my father's death, my dresses had been specially made by a tailor, while Ababa and I waited. It had that special smell.

In additions to clothes, sometimes the missionary's wife rewarded me with a snack. My mother realized that the missionaries raised pigs and ate pork. In Ethiopian culture, pork is considered unclean. My parents used to tell us a tale that eating pig meat made one's teeth fall out. When I arrived home from a volunteer babysitting job, my mother warned me, "Don't touch anything, until you wash your hands with ashes." She offered me some ashes (homemade disinfectant) from the fireplace and some water. Ashes are considered a magic antibacterial cleanser. If I accidentally used a glass or coffee cup, she washed them with ashes too before anyone used them.

Finally, I had my first niece to babysit. Obo had his first child, a daughter. He named her Sarah. She was a beautiful girl. I was ten years old at the time. Obo told me that I was his oldest daughter. I felt like I had a little sister. I was sure he wished for a son, but knowing Obo, he was always grateful for whatever God gave him. According to the Ethiopian culture, if the firstborn were a son, he took care of the family, like Obo did. Furthermore, friends and villagers would call Obo "Abba" or "Hada" Deressa (father or mother of Deressa) as people addressed my father or mother.

When my niece was born, there was no maternity ward. A midwife assisted my sister-in-law during delivery. Similarly, experienced women from the neighborhood gathered around her to help with her delivery. These women served Soretti, my sister-in-law, as a support group for the next few months.

I didn't understand anything about childbirth. I watched Soretti during labor from a distance, hiding behind the wooden wall. I was determined to see what was going on.

She was agonizing in pain, but she couldn't express her emotions because it was against our culture. Why didn't my brother come and give her moral support during delivery? I thought. Later on, I found out that husbands didn't get involved during childbirth. It was a taboo. This was one of the many Ethiopian practices and customs. I hoped I didn't ever have to go through that kind of torture.

However, for several weeks, the neighborhood women had a wonderful time celebrating the birth of my niece. They prepared a special food, porridge made of roasted corn flour. They served it with flax and mustard sauce and sour milk.

That was a new experience for me. These women also helped my sister-in-law with bathing and feeding the baby. I enjoyed holding my niece in my arms whenever I had the chance.

During the rainy season, when school was out, I continued watching the cattle with my cousin. However, when school was in session, my brother hired a man to look after the cattle. There was no running water at home, so I went to the river to explore how my family washed clothes and made them look spotless. I was amazed how the villagers discovered all the natural resources that Mother Nature provided. I watched how my sisters and the women from the neighborhood boiled the seeds from a particular bush and used it to whiten the clothes. Amazingly, the clothes looked as white as clouds. The clothes were spread on the nearby bushes to dry while they continued to wash the remaining clothes. After they completed washing everything, they picked up the dried clothes. They brought home any wet clothes and hung them on the fence or on a rope in the kitchen, away from the fireplace to dry.

For the following school years, I continued excelling in school. Soon, some of the boys became jealous. They took my notebook and threw it in the outhouse. Why would anyone do that? Is it because I am the only girl who continuously excelled in the whole school? I wondered. On the other hand, I was humbled to hear positive comments from the adults. "*Wakayo mataa kenef*" (God blessed Aster with a good brain.)

I remember the time I had chicken pox and I had to be hospitalized. Luckily, at that time, the German Mission had built a hospital. The doctors felt that I should stay at the hospital so that my niece and nephew would not catch it.

When I returned to school after a week, to everyone's surprise, I was first in my grade. Those students who were jealous of me stopped throwing away my notebooks. They realized that it wasn't the notes that I took that made me excel in school, but what God had given me. In spite of all their jealousy, I continued sharing review questions with my classmates for the final examination.

I had never heard of teenage problems, and dating wasn't common in the villages. All children helped their parents at home and on the farm. There was no time to get into trouble. Once we learned how to write though, we started sharing love letters with each other. That was considered like a crime by school authorities. The boys initiated the letters and the girls responded by way of a trustworthy friend. I was one of the recipients. Unfortunately, a jealous student recovered the letter I had written and forwarded it to one of the teachers.

"Was this why you learned to read and write?" my brother scolded me when he found out that I, his famous sister of whom he was so proud, had written a love letter. I couldn't help it; I had feelings too, I thought to myself. For some reason, if I did anything wrong, the news seemed to travel faster than the speed of light, maybe because I was a sister of a highly respected brother. This embarrassed Obo, so I stopped with the letter writing.

Obo's reputation as a disciplinarian and spiritual person had reached the neighboring villages. There was no other elementary school within a hundred miles. At that time the German Mission hadn't built a boarding school for the girls, only for the boys.

Three families, who were our in-laws, requested of my brother that their daughters might stay at our house and attend school. Obo Deressa agreed, as he was always willing to help others. These families assisted my brother by providing food. I don't recall if they gave him some money, too. Our house became like a boarding school.

The girls and I were assigned chores. We took turns preparing breakfast, which was simpler than making dinner. Nevertheless, I was excited. Finally, I got to cook something! However, when it was my turn, my overprotective mother came alongside to assist me, making sure her youngest daughter learned the proper way to cook.

"I could cook by myself," I protested.

"You couldn't do it all alone," she insisted.

"Work would not kill her," Ade Terunesh, one of my sisters added. She was born before the two deceased siblings. My mother didn't pay attention to her comment. I enjoyed her companionship even though I insisted that I didn't need her help.

Obo Deressa became more concerned about us girls, including his adult wife.

When we went to the river to get water, he stood on the hill by our house which overlooked the valley where the water stream was located. He made sure we didn't stop and converse with each other. He hid himself behind the dense corn plants, out of sight, as a soldier waiting for the enemy, and caught us by surprise.

"What were you talking about?" he demanded, as we approached him. We sobbed as we walked on. We knew he was upset. Sometimes he hit us with his bamboo stick. There were times that he missed us and almost fell. We still retrieved the stick and placed it in his hand.

"Leave the children alone! One day, you are going to break their bones and you'll regret it," my mother warned him. He never listened to her.

Once a year my other brother Obosha (Reverend Lamessa) came home to visit. He had been assigned to a church in a small town after his ordination. It was about five days walking distance or three days by car. In the rainy season, sometimes it took him more than five days to come home because of the poor dirt roads and lack of bridges. Our whole family longed to see him, especially I. He brought us Western clothes and mine were especially beautiful. No other girls in the villages wore that kind of dress. Mine was the smallest and cutest, at least I thought so. Like the saying, "*Good things come in small packages.*"

When Obosha visited, his unusual laughter could be heard from a great distance, and the neighbors always knew he was at home. I communicated with him without fear, and he made me laugh often. I was known to be the happy girl in the village. I did everything for him: I washed his feet even though he wore shoes and offered him warm water to wash his hands and face and brush his teeth. In addition, I also knitted a sweater for him. Our whole family knew how much I adored my brother.

I was pleased when I heard my two brothers talking and laughing. "Maybe Obo needed an adult male to talk with," I concluded. Usually, he was surrounded by a dozen women. He was also blessed with three boys and six girls of his own. But he could not sit and have a conversation with his boys because of our culture.

I wished Obosha, could stay with us forever. But he had to go back where God called him to serve as a pastor. I began counting down the days he had with us, "Tuesday, Wednesday, Thursday, Friday, Saturday, Sunday, and Monday." The day of his departure arrived so fast. I wished I were on another planet where the days and weeks were longer. Relatives, friends, and neighbors gathered at our house to bid him farewell. When will I see him again? I was worried. The more I thought of Obosha the more I cried. For weeks afterward, I tried to immerse myself in my studies whenever I thought of him.

However, I was grateful to God that He provided me with two sets of fathers after my father's death. The eldest brother, Obo Deressa, had been my spiritual role model and continues to be so to this day. Yet my brother, Obosha, who was a pastor, became my physical provider. He brought me beautiful clothes and laughter when he visited us.

PREPARING FOR THE NATIONAL EXAMINATION

It is so true what people say, *"Time flies when you're having fun."* Before I knew it, I was at the end of the first phase of my education. It felt as if it were just yesterday that I started the first grade at the age of nine. In these past seven years, things couldn't be any better for me at school. I am grateful to God and Obo. Trimester after trimester and year after year, I excelled in my class. Those were exciting years.

When I started first grade, there had been about thirty students in my class. Now, seven years later, there were fewer than fifteen students, including two girls—and I was one of them. Many students had not been fortunate as I. It must have seemed as if the clock stopped running. "How could I help them?" I wondered. At the end of every term, my classmates and I reviewed every subject together. Even with these reviews, more students were left behind as a result of the rigorous end-of-the-year comprehensive examination. It reminded me of the athletes running a marathon where some remained behind as the race progressed. Only a few reached the finish line.

At this point, I had quite an enlightening experience. I don't recall what day of the week the incident occurred. Every grade level stood in line in front of the German Mission school for regular morning devotion. I was in the seventh row from the front of the school. The eighth graders stood right behind me. I bowed my head and closed my eyes as all the students did during the prayer. While the teacher was leading the prayer, suddenly Jesus stood before me. I was frightened. He then put his hands on my head and said, *"Aster, you'll be blessed."* I was stunned and speechless. He then disappeared from my sight before the prayer ended. What if my brother noticed a change on my facial expression? I was apprehensive. God had already blessed me with a caring family and the ability to learn and excel. He gave me back my life when I was ill. What else was He going to bless me with? I wondered. I was anxious to share this exciting experience with someone, but I couldn't.

In our culture sharing such a thing with your friends is considered bragging. What about telling my religious brother, Obo Deressa? He read the Bible from beginning to end three times. Isn't he the perfect person to share this with? But my inner voice warned me not to.

I had never yet conversed with him socially, except receiving commands from him. Nothing made me believe that he will listen to me now.

Finally, I followed my inner voice. It is not until fifty years later, that I am able to share this vision with you as I write this memoir.

At the end of the elementary school years, the eighth grade became more challenging. Every subject was taught in English, our third language. Amharic, the second language, was taught as a separate subject. Every so often, we came across unfamiliar words, which hindered our deeper understanding of what we were reading about. I turned to Bichaka, my cousin and shepherd companion, for help.

"What does that strange word mean?"

"I am not so sure," he responded.

Our only solution was searching in the English dictionary. Sometimes it was a dead end. The English explanation of the new word didn't make sense at all. At times, it frustrated me because the translation was also in English. However, I was determined to learn everything anyway, through memorization. Never had I imagined failing any grade. Learning was a natural drive for me.

There was much to prepare for. It was during the third term in the eighth grade that students took the Ethiopian Elementary School Leaving Examination to ensure students' competency to enter secondary school. Only those who scored above eighty percent were eligible to attend high school. Those who didn't pass would attend vocational education.

By the end of my eighth year, there were only about ten of us left. How many of us would go to high school? I pondered.

Additionally, I didn't know how I would ever pay to go to secondary school. I had never even heard of any high school within a two-hundred-mile radius. The cost must be substantial. The same God who saved me from the deadly illness, and guided me the last seven years, could provide all the resources, I assured myself.

We had already started reviewing what we had been taught in the last seven years as even more new concepts and skills were introduced. I was having fun preparing review questions and learning new things with my classmates.

Then one day during the first semester, I felt feverish. Oh, no! I think I am catching influenza, I told my mother. Influenza was very common during the rainy season. My body was aching all over. Then, my mother prepared a home remedy. She tore the soft part of a banana leaf, put warm ashes in it and patted it on my forehead. It felt so good. Next, every joint in my body began aching whenever I tried to turn or sit up. At seventeen years old, I felt like I had a body of an eighty-year-old woman. It felt as if all my joints were broken.

How could this happen to me? I was always so active. Didn't I chase the cattle when I was a shepherd? Hadn't I climbed the trees like a monkey? Now I couldn't even walk to school, which I loved so much. I was afraid. No one told me what it was. I waited patiently to get better. What went on in my mother's mind, when she discovered about my joints pain, I did not know. I was really worried. Didn't Obo have polio when he was in his teens, which left him with weak muscles for the rest of his life? Now, I had a similar illness that also affected my joints.

My mother decided to walk me to the German Mission hospital, which was a heartbeat away. In the villages, when a person was too sick to walk, he was carried on a bed or a mule was used to transport him. I managed to walk to the hospital with my mother's assistance.

The two female doctors who had treated my father and had told him, "Ato Bato, gareet, (good-bye) you'll soon die" still worked at the hospital. I was nervous that they might tell me the same thing. Maybe this time, they would not because the doctors were good friends with the elementary school principal, and I was her favorite student. Obo was also a good friend of the two doctors and the principal. The promise from Prophet Isaiah gave me peace of mind, "*Thou will keep him in perfect peace whose mind stayed on Thee*" (Isaiah 26:3). The two doctors examined me and gave me medicine, though I did not know for what, and for how long, and they sent me home.

"Giftee (Mistress) Rabin wanted you to stay with her," Obo informed me the following day. "How strange," I wondered. Why would she want a sick person to stay in her house with healthy and wealthy girls? Why couldn't I stay at our house? I was perplexed. I lived only five minutes walking distance from the school. Could it be that I would receive better medical attention because I would be closer to the hospital?

The director of grades one to eight at the German Mission school was a single woman who had a beautiful house with an extra bedroom. She converted it to an exclusive room for four girls as the school had not built dorm rooms for the girls yet.

Two of the borders were daughters of a very wealthy family who lived far away. They owned cars and several slaves who worked for them. The family even sent one male slave to stay with their two brothers, who were in a boys' boarding school nearby. He followed the two brothers everywhere and helped them with everything. He also helped the two sisters. Though the girls were two grades behind me, they already knew how to read and write and wore modern clothes and shoes that no other girls in the school had.

The third girl was the daughter of a community chief, whose parents were good friends of our family. She was the same age and grade as I. While her family did not own a car, they, too, were rich and had several slaves who lived in little huts around the chief's residence and worked for them. Her house was about thirty minutes walking distance from the school. She had an older brother who taught at the mission school. He was one of my third grade teachers. Both of us girls were the youngest in our families and started first grade together. The two of us shared a bunk bed, while the sisters shared the other one. We became good friends.

Late in the evenings, she and I studied for the Ethiopian Elementary School Leaving Examination. We had to review everything we had learned in eight years: Amharic, English, general science, world history, geography, and general mathematics. We had three teachers who developed study guides for us to use. They were experts in each of their respective fields because they had firsthand experience in each.

Now, that we had reviewed the materials and were prepared, we wondered where we were going to take this monstrous examination. The German Mission school was a privately owned institution. We were taught a nationally approved curriculum in order to be eligible to enter any secondary school in Ethiopia. But this private missionary school was the only elementary school within a two-hundred-mile radius.

I remembered that the last two graduating classes traveled about two to three days' driving distance to the next public school district to take the national examination. I had never traveled such a long distance. Although my sister had taken the assessment a year before me, I didn't pay attention when she told us about her experiences.

But it was going to be a long trip. One day the principal, the three male teachers, and the ten eighth graders got ready for the unknown long journey.

"Take good care of our students, especially the girls," Obo Deressa pleaded with the director and the male teachers.

She then assured him, "Obo Deressa, don't worry. Asta (that was how the missionaries called me) and her friend are in good hands," she promised. "Please pray for our safe trip and that our students would do well on the test," she requested. The other three teachers also promised my brother we would be safe as they had tremendous respect for him.

Our families prepared nonperishable food to eat on the way. Then our families and friends walked with us to the mission station. Everybody wept as we bid farewell to each other. I couldn't stop crying thinking that I would be away from my loving family for several days. This was the first time all of us students were going to be away from our parents for this long of a time. "Everything will be fine with your children," the director reassured our parents. Most of us were the youngest children in our families.

Unfortunately, it was the beginning of the rainy season. This made traveling very dangerous. There were no paved roads that led to the city where we were headed to take the examination. The winding dirt roads leading through the villages were muddy and slippery. The Land Rover's wheels spun and spun deep into the mud. Then the pastor who was driving yelled, "You, men, get out of the car and push." After several tries, the car was pushed out of the mud.

Kids in the villages chased the Land Rover screaming, "Faranji, Faranji, (foreigner, foreigner)" to the driver and the director of the school. That is how the villagers call white people. The young children followed and chased us as if we were hyenas until they couldn't run any longer and the vehicles were out of their sight. My classmates and I enjoyed the bumpy ride and beautiful scenery. I marveled at the many beautiful hills, valleys, and forests that Ethiopia has.

Suddenly, I felt sick to my stomach. "I feel like throwing up," I whispered to my girlfriend. We both giggled softly, making sure nobody heard us. No one understood about carsickness. How would we villagers know if we had never traveled in a car? In Ethiopia, nausea was associated with pregnancy. Please,

God take away this feeling from me, I pleaded. Thankfully, it eventually stopped.

I have never forgotten the moment we approached a shallow river without a bridge. My heart started pounding. How are we going to cross? My girlfriend and I began to worry. In the villages, women were not allowed to swim. There was a myth that girls might lose their virginity if they swam or rode a bicycle. However, the river didn't seem to frighten the male classmates and the director who all knew how to swim.

Then the driver ordered, "Everyone, get out of the car, except the ladies." Immediately, the men stepped out. He then told them, "Get behind the Land Rover and push while I drive." The principal, my girlfriend, and I prayed as the wheels spun up and down while the three of us were still in it. I couldn't help thinking, what if the car turned over with the three of us in it? After several attempts, the young men pushed the car out of the river and climbed back in. We were thankful everyone survived.

During the long ride, we asked each other several questions on the different subjects we were about to be tested, especially multiplication facts.

Then the director asked us which song we would like to sing. We learned many songs in school. We enjoyed singing familiar songs from memory in three languages, English, Oromifa (my tribal language), and Amharic, the national language. I chose my favorite song, "*He Leadeth, He Leadeth me, by His hand He leadeth me.*" Everyone sang along. This was a perfect song for our journey, I thought. It was also entertainment for the driver.

We forgot how far we were traveling because we were singing and having fun. We stopped on the way to eat the food we had brought with us. My favorite snack was, "chookoo." This was a typical nonperishable snack to be eaten on a long trip. It was made from roasted and ground wheat. Then it was made into a paste with "nitir kibe," butter cooked with onions, garlic, fenugreek, ginger, and cardamom. The paste then became solid. We cut a small amount with a knife and ate with water. Yummy! It is my favorite snack. We also enjoyed loaves of corn and "teff," a special grain grown only in Ethiopia.

The German Mission made arrangements to stop and spend the night at one of the mission institutions halfway through our travel. The director of our school slept in a room adjacent to ours to closely supervise us, keeping the promises she gave our parents.

Finally, after two days of travel, we reached Nedjo, the town where we were to take the national examination. We must be in another country, I thought. The town looked more modern than where we were raised. They had electricity and paved roads.

The roads were asphalt and less bumpy. The homes along the roads had tin roofs and looked as if they were covered with rocks. It was so different from thatched grass roofs in our village.

After we had eaten dinner at the mission school, we took showers and went to bed early.

Early in the morning, about six o'clock, the director knocked on our door, "Asta (most missionaries never seemed to pronounce the last sound of my name) and Mekadesh, Kaa amah (Wake up now)," she emphasized. She then instructed the male teachers to wake up the boys.

After breakfast, we walked to school where the tests were administered. We sat at long desks about three feet apart to prevent students from cheating on the examination. The scene looked like that of a courtroom. Then half a dozen men in suits walked in. Immediately we all stood up. Where were our director and teachers? I wondered. What are all these men doing? We are not criminals.

One of the men said, "Kooch baloo (sit down)" in the national language. Then another man from the group distributed the testing materials, while another one told us, "Don't open until everyone has one." I couldn't wait to start. The first test was general science, my favorite subject. It was administered in English. Once all of the students received their papers, we were instructed to begin.

I grinned throughout the testing time because I knew all the answers. Those men kept their eyes on us the whole hour. There were other students present, probably from that school.

"How was the examination (fatanaa)?" they asked us.

"Everything we reviewed was in it," some of us responded, while others kept quiet.

Before lunch, we took general mathematics, which included geometry and algebra, also in English. It was another of my favorite subjects. All students were required to recite multiplication facts one through twelve by third grade. The test contained several story problems, which involved addition, subtraction, multiplication, and division. We completed everything within one hour. If one finished early, he or she could review but not look around. We never dared to look in the direction of the officials administering the assessment. This was considered disrespectful.

Another challenging assessment was English grammar and composition. While I was taking the test, I thought to myself, "Why would anyone be assessed in a third language?" I was perplexed. English was an academic language, we seldom used it socially. Now that I had the foreign language behind me, what else could be worse? I wondered.

Amharic, our national tongue, was also a foreign language to us villagers. It was more strange than English because it was not an academic language. Still, we were tested in Amharic grammar and composition as well. Personally, I found out that it was easier to write in English than in the national language. English was used to teach all academic subjects from fourth grade on. However, those who lived in cities considered it their first language. I found it strange that we weren't tested in our tribal tongue.

Finally, we came to the last assessment, social studies, which included world geography and history. Although history was not one of my favorite subjects, I was determined to do well. After three days of assessment, we were relieved to finish. But each student couldn't help remembering part of the test that troubled him most.

"Do you remember the question about the cradle of civilization?" one student asked. "What about that science question on the three states of matter?" another student interrupted.

The following day, we were ready to return home. I was excited. Also, I was apprehensive about driving through that river and the muddy road we drove through when we came.

"Is there any other way to go back home?" I asked my girl-friend. "Why do you say that?"

"Do you remember the river we drove through and the muddy road the Land Rover's wheels spun and spun?"

"Oh, yes," she responded. "I'm afraid of it, too."

"That's no help," I told her.

We still had plenty of chooko left over. In addition, the boys purchased some *daboo* (western style bread rolls) from the *sookee* (small shop). Going back home seemed to be faster than coming here. Before we knew, we reached the river I was afraid of.

The missionary male driver yelled in his usual joking manner.

"Isin dargagoo koon, (you, young men), get ready to get out and push the car," he giggled. The students laughed too. Soon the driver ordered the students to get out. They all lined up behind the Land Rover.

"Push!" the driver yelled. The students were still laughing.

"Gifti" (Mistress) Rabin, the director of the school, screamed at the students, "Don't laugh, push harder!"

Finally, the car made to the other side of the river and the students got back in the Land Rover.

Suddenly, I remembered that my favorite brother, Obosha, traveled on the same road when he attended the seminary.

Isn't this the same muddy road he walked bare foot and the same river he crossed alone? I asked myself. And I'm riding in a car? Then, I realized why my mother was worried about his safety. Just the thought of it brought tears to my eyes.

"Why are you crying?" my friends asked me.

"I was just thinking how Obosha traveled this long distance on foot when he came home to visit us," I responded. Everyone comforted me because they knew how much I loved my brother. After few hours, the missionary driver saw from a distance the area where the wheels spun in the mud.

"You, young men are lucky," he assured the students. "The road is dry and you don't need to get out," he announced jokingly. Sometimes one never knew whether he was joking or telling the truth. Fortunately, this time the ladies stayed in the car while the men pushed. The road was not very wet. With just one push, the car was out of the mud.

"Hooray!" we all cheered.

On our trip, no one discussed what he or she would do if they passed the examination. A couple of boys from the previous two graduating classes passed the test. Some students attended vocational school at a nearby town, while others began raising a family. No student had ever attended college. The last two graduating classes were much older than us. My class was considered the youngest graduating class from eighth grade at the age of eighteen years old.

On the third day, we finally arrived at the German Mission. Each student carried his small luggage and walked home. All students lived within walking distance from the school.

First, Bichaka, walked with me to our house. My mother, sisters, and Soreti (sister-in-law) greeted us with kisses and hugs as if we had been away for months. In Ethiopian culture, daily kissing and hugging of family members was not common. This time, even Obo Deressa gave my cousin and me a hug. That's a rare treat! I thought. This was the first time I hugged him. I was always afraid to get close to him.

He even had a conversation with both of us. "How did the test go?" he asked.

My cousin and I could see a half smile and half frown on his face. He seldom smiled. His face always looked as if he had eaten a hundred lemons.

"It was easy and we knew all the answers," we responded.

Then, my cousin walked home. He lived a heartbeat away from our house.

A week after we returned from our trip, the eighth grade teachers celebrated the end of our elementary school years with a dinner. Their housekeeper prepared a delicious Ethiopian dish. It included injera, which is thin and flat sour bread, made of 'tef' (a very fine grain only grown in Ethiopia), which was served, with a spicy chicken stew. They served "tej", a homemade wine made of honey and hops. Those of us who didn't like "tej" were given a choice of "Fanta" (orange drink).

It was a wonderful celebration. The elementary school director, the three Ethiopian teachers, and our wonderful missionary driver (a pastor who taught us confirmation class) attended.

CHAPTER FIVE

THE UNESCAPABLE FEMALE CIRCUMCISION

As I was growing up, I observed there were things that I could avoid peacefully. I was not required to do house chores like my sisters. I didn't take turns at preparing dinner or working on the farm.

However, girls were required to pierce their ears between the ages of eight and ten to get ready for their wedding. I protested, "I don't want my ears pierced! Why would I force my future husband to spend all his money on expensive gold earrings?" I added. I watched when an experienced neighborhood woman or older sister performed the piercing of ears. It scared me to death.

First, they searched for sharp and sturdy thorns from a tree. Then, the areas of the ears to be pierced were pulled until they became thin and numb. Next, they quickly pierced with the thorn one at time and left them in each ear by breaking off the sharp ends. The girls themselves applied a little home-made butter periodically, until they were completely healed.

How come the ears weren't infected? I wondered. Somehow, I avoided this tradition. Amazingly, many years later, I chose to have my ears pierced along with my six-months-old daughter in the United States by her pediatrician. He said, "I will pierce yours first so that you can experience the pain your daughter will go through." Then he pierced hers. I told him that I refused to have it done back in my home country. He laughed.

Yet, there was a gruesome tradition that I couldn't avoid. Every young girl had to fulfill this obligation before she got married. While boys were circumcised at a younger age, girls faced it in their teens. I remembered my own fate. I had no idea about the procedure. I was young when my sisters were circumcised. No one in my family explained to me what to expect. My family set the date. I had no say in whether to have it done or not. I remembered refusing to have my ears pierced. My family did not seem to care, because I was the one who missed the gold earrings. But there was no way out of this. I didn't want to humiliate my parents. It was the most embarrassing experience for a family if the daughter was not circumcised.

I was about seventeen years old when my devastating day came. Prior to that day, relatives, friends, and acquaintances were invited to celebrate the occasion. If this were so big of an event, what would my wedding day look like? I was ecstatic. My heart began beating harder. There was no turning back. The celebration lasted about a week. My male teachers were also among the guests who were invited. What will my teachers think? I was mortified, as if they didn't know the ritual. At least

60

I am one step closer to womanhood. The guests would give me money for my bravery, I assured myself. I focused on the gifts of money rather than on the torture of the day. I calmed myself as that time approached.

The night before my big day, my sister kept reminding me. "Be strong. Keep your eyes closed. It will only take a short time." This time, I didn't pray that God would prevent this from happening to me. I was afraid that this would be another foolish prayer, similar to when I prayed that God would prevent me from going through my period, after learning about the woman in the Bible who bled for thirty-eight years and was healed by Jesus. I believed it was a curse on all women. However, I did pray that God would give me strength and peace of mind. That night, I couldn't sleep. The pounding of my heart kept me awake. It felt like someone was bouncing a ball against my chest. I thought my heart would soon be detached from inside of me.

Then, I heard the rooster crow. This was Mother Nature's way of telling the villagers that morning is approaching. This also meant that my time was approaching. There were no alarm clocks. This also reminded me of when Jesus told Peter, "I tell you, Peter, before the cock crows this day, You will deny three times that you know me" (Luke 22:34). The majority of people didn't know how to read or write. There were no clocks or watches. The rooster crowed every hour, beginning at 3:00 am (9:00 am Ethiopian time). It seemed as if he crowed every minute. Before the third crow, my mother warmed water and put it in a large basin. She advised me to take a bath before the lady who performed the circumcision and other women arrived. My mother brought me warm water in a large basin. My heart kept pounding and the water bounced off my chest as I bathed myself. I kept praying. I'll fulfill my family's obligation and make them proud of me.

Early in the morning before the sun rose, a married woman, who was a close friend of our family, arrived. She was asked to sit behind me on a stool. She was called "Jalla." She was an important person because she blindfolded me with both hands. If she touched my chest, my pounding heart would throw her off the stool, I thought. I couldn't help it. Two other women each held my legs apart, so that I didn't kick or move. I was shaking from fear. I am restrained like a bull to be slaughtered, I felt. It was offensive in our tradition for a girl to show any kind of discomfort during the procedure. Why should anyone have to suppress pain? I was at a complete loss. Tolerating pain has haunted me for the rest of my life.

Anytime a technician draws blood, I closed my eyes. One day a lab technician who was drawing blood asked me, "Why do you close your eyes?"

"This is my way of suppressing pain," I told him. He didn't get it. He just grinned.

With these three ladies in place, one behind me, and the other two on each side of me, the skilled and professional lady positioned herself on the provided stool. Then she took out a brand new razor blade out of little bag and cut off the most sensitive part of my private part as quickly as possible to mini-mize the pain. I felt a sharp sting. Immediately, she poured warm water over it. I felt a burning sensation. It was over. I expected the worst. When all was done, the ladies cheered, "L-L-L-L-L." This was a common cheer at a birth of a baby or wedding. I didn't give birth. It was less painful than I anticipated. I, too, was relieved. I prayed to God to give me courage and peace. He did!

I didn't move during the procedure. I didn't embarrass my family. For a while, I slept in my own blood bath from the procedure. My mother who cleaned me when I was a baby, made sure that her grown up daughter was clean and comfort-able. The love of a mother is beyond anyone's imagination.

Now, that everything was behind me, I wondered how much money people gave me for my bravery? I began to estimate. I don't remember how much money people gave me. For the next few days, I slept on my back with my legs wide open, to prevent the wound from sticking together. This also helped the healing process. The friend, who blindfolded me, sat behind me all day long. The next few days, she came and visited me to make sure I was healing properly. My experienced sisters also came along and gave me support. There was no anesthesia or painkillers. How did we endure the excruciating pain? I wondered. Recently, a friend in U.S. told me, "No one has ever received a medal for tolerating pain," she stressed when I refused to take a painkiller such as aspirin or Tylenol.

During the festivities, men were not allowed to visit me. I was glad because I was too self-conscious to face my male teachers. There were no female teachers except the director of the mission school. However, many women and girls came and congratulated me.

As I was writing this part of my memoir, I read a report online that more than 200 million girls and women worldwide have undergone female genital mutilation, a bloody ritual involving the removal of external genital in Africa and Middle Eastern countries. I am one of them. I'm grateful to World Health Organization, United Nations, and religious organizations for joining hands to completely eradicate this gruesome practice. I am especially grateful to those brave Ethiopian women for coming out in opposition to this practice. The article also states that more recently, the KMG (Kembatti Menti Gezzima) is focusing on "community conversations" where villagers gather every two weeks to discuss important social issues, including female genital mutilation, with the help from trained Ethiopian facilitators. This has prompted other nonprofits, government health workers, United Nations agencies, and religious organizations to join efforts to reduce the practice across Ethiopia.

I'm also grateful to know that both young men and women are involved in this effort. Young people are our leaders. In the article, a young man stated that "he will not marry a girl if she is cut." According to a recent article, it stated that the Ethiopian government banned genital mutilation ten years ago. However, there are still pockets of the country practicing it. It is the goal of World Health Organization, United Nations, and religious organizations to completely end it by 2025.

As for me, I was grateful that I fulfilled my family's wishes without causing any embarrassment to our eldest brother and the rest of the family.

CHAPTER SIX

HIGH SCHOOL YEARS

"God will take care of all my needs." (Phil 4:19)

One day, towards the beginning of August 1962, according to the Western calendar, I heard my brother calling in his usual serious voice. "Aster, kootuu (come here)," he said. I was sitting in the adjacent kitchen house, conversing with the ladies. I assumed he needed help with a ball of yarn, which sometimes fell off his lap while he was knitting in the dark. Occasionally he had fallen off his chair trying to pick it up. His polio illness during his teen years had left him with weak muscles.

When Obo Deressa called any of our family members, we had to be there as fast as the speed of light, or he would punish us with his solid stick. So, I walked to him as fast as I could. I looked at his semi-grinning face, making sure I didn't look directly into his eyes. That is considered disrespectful in our culture. I taught my children this when they were young. However, one day this practice had an adverse effect on one of my sons when they were attending school. My son and his classmates misbehaved in the cafeteria. The teacher called everyone and asked them what had occurred. While the rest of the students looked in their teacher's eyes, my son looked down out of respect. Unfortunately, the teacher suspected that my son was the instigator. When he came home from school, he protested, "I am not listening to you anymore!" However, during my teaching career, I had encountered many children from different countries who shared similar culture like mine. I understood and respected them when they didn't look in my eyes when we had conversations. I respected cultural diversity as well as cultural similarity. Whenever there was a teachable moment, I explained to my students that in America one need to make eye contact when speaking.

But it was not yarn that Obo Deressa wanted. Instead he informed me, "Giftee (Mistress) Rabin, the director of the elementary school informed me that she knows a lady from Germany who has promised to pay for your high school expenses. The director also told me that you'll attend the only Christian high school in Ethiopia, which is near Addis Ababa, the capital city of Ethiopia," he added. I still didn't officially know if I passed the eighth grade National Comprehensive Assessment, but I guess this news confirmed it.

I was so excited that I felt like jumping and dancing. Instead, I just stood there like a statue looking down. I couldn't show my emotions because it was against our tradition. I wanted to hug him but my brother had never been approachable. I wished "Obosha" my other brother was at home. I am not afraid to hug him, I thought. I can't wait until I see the director, to give her a big hug and thank her for what she has done for me. I was impatient. Obo is a man of great faith; he knew that God would help me to do my best as He has done in the last eight years.

"Right after Inkutatash, Ethiopian New Year," he continued, "you and I will fly in the missionary's four passenger airplane to Nekemt." This was the capital of the province of Wollega, where Obosha was working as a pastor. It was located between my home village and the high school.

Finally, I would see my favorite brother. I could share all my excitement and joy with him. I was thrilled and I was restless. Soon after Obo told me the good news, I went back to the kitchen laughing. Soretti, my sister-in-law, and my mother were surprised to see me so joyful especially after I went to Obo. Usually, I came back with a gloomy face.

"What happened?" they all asked me simultaneously.

"I am going away to attend high school," I told them laughing.

"Where and what was it?" they inquired.

"I don't know exactly where, but it is near Addis Ababa, and I will go to ninth grade," I responded. I heard my mother sniffling as her eyes were filled with tears. She knew that it was quite a distance from our house. This was going to be a very challenging separation. I was the youngest child in the family.

The elementary school director began preparing me for this unknown place. I remembered hearing from my godmother who visited her sister in Addis Ababa frequently that she took along heavy clothes such as sweaters as if she were going to Alaska. The capital of Ethiopia is cold compared to the village where I grew up. It is about two miles above sea level. I received beautiful hand-me-down clothes from the missionary family I babysat for and from the school director. They were overjoyed for me.

Sometime in the middle of August, both my brother and I walked to the place to board the plane. It was located on a flat hill surrounded by valleys. It was similar to a place helicopters use for emergency landing. It was the first time that we both flew on an airplane. I was terrified that I would be in that flying object in the sky. Everyone in the neighborhood came to the location to watch the oldest son and youngest daughter disappear into the perfect blue sky.

My mother, sister-in-law, sisters, and I were weeping uncontrollably as we bid farewell to everyone. Then we boarded the plane and we both sat in the back. The pilot advised us to buckle our seat belts. "Did the missionary pilot think that we would jump out?" I wondered. The people nearby were advised to move away to avoid injury caused by the turbulence as the plane took off. Gradually, the plane flew higher and higher, going between the eucalyptus trees like birds. My stomach was churning more and more. Progressively, the houses and giant trees looked like specks of dust as the plane climbed higher. I felt now I was closer to heaven. I was also sick to my stomach. I had a bag with me. I didn't know how Obo felt about flying. Even if he had motion sickness, he wouldn't tell me. I was confident that Obo trusted God that He would bring us safely to our destination. For a short period, there was no turbulence.

We were approaching Nekemte where we supposed to land. Again, as were descending, my stomach began churning.

Once we landed, Obosha (Reverend Lemessa) came to pick us up in a taxi. He didn't own a car. Car ownership is a status symbol. My brother was serving God and taxies and buses were readily available. He took us to his house, which was modern with extra bedrooms. His wife cooked the most delicious food for us. She grew up in the city and she was the best cook. She prepared chicken, beef, and vegetables in a variety of ways. Obosha also slaughtered a lamb, which was reserved for a special guest. This was Obo's first time to visit his brother. I was just his favorite sister. Obo Deressa and I had flown to the town by plane about two weeks early to spend time with Obosha.

I felt as if I was dreaming, traveling on another planet. I saw farmlands along the road. They used tractors to cultivate the land. It looked like a monster with hundreds of fingers, lifting up the dirt, and driven only by one person. I was used to when my father plowed with two oxen. I've never seen a farmland so green where crops were already growing. As we were nearing, I saw modern houses with two to three stories and tin roofs. There were markets and shops along the road where travelers buy souvenirs, and Ethiopian restaurants where we stopped to eat. I don't remember if we stopped to eat as most of us carried nonperishable food with us, such as spiced "daboo," similar to a loaf of bread but prepared on a circular clay pan. My favorite snack was roasted and ground wheat mixed with home processed spiced butter. One ate only a small piece and drank water. When we arrived in the city, I saw all kinds of cars on the streets. Drivers were honking, I didn't know for what. I preferred the mooing of the cows over the honking sound that irritated my ears.

But eventually a few of my classmates who took the National Examination also traveled to Nekemte, capital of Wollega. They had traveled on foot or by mule, which had taken them several days. Buses ran frequently between Nekemte and Addis Ababa. I traveled with my classmates to the German Mission in Addis Ababa where we were officially briefed on the results of the National Examination for the first time. Obo Deressa probably had known the results from the elementary school director before we departed from my home village, Aira.

Once we reached the German Hermansburg compound, the director and his wife greeted us and provided us a place to stay. I still had not learned how I did on the eighth-grade national comprehensive assessment. I remembered that tense moment after we ate dinner. We gathered in the living room of the director's residence. We were standing in the room and one of our former teachers announced each student's average results starting from the top. To my recollection, my cousin, another student, and I all scored above 90 percent, and everybody cheered and applauded. Then those who scored 80 and 70 percent were announced. Everyone cheered for them as well. I felt badly that those who scored high were not offered scholarships to the school I attended. Even though my cousin scored above ninety percent, he wasn't offered the scholarship.

It was all about who you know. God granted me this opportunity because I was the first and only girl from my village who ever passed the most rigorous examination, and because my brother was the most dedicated and respected man of faith who worked with the mission school and church.

I felt as if I were in a foreign country within my own country. As we were driving in a car, I saw cars everywhere instead of cows and other domestic animals. Also there were carriages pulled by horses. This was new to me. Students wore Western clothing and Western shoes. Even girls' hair was Western fashion. I was grateful for the hand-me-downs the German missionaries gave me. Also my brother and Obo purchased new clothes and shoes when we spent time in the city where Obosha lived. The high school that the director recommended was the most academically prestigious Christian high school in the country. It was the most expensive school because it included room, board, and tuition. Our class consisted of about twenty-five boys and five girls from around the country. Students came from thirteen provinces.

I loved the high school because of its Christian foundation. We prayed before breakfast, lunch, and dinner. In addition, we had evening devotions. I took part in leading the evening devotions even though I didn't speak fluent Amharic, the national language in which the devotion was delivered. We also had church services on Sundays in the school cafeteria and sang songs in Amharic and English. During my first year, I wept during the services because I was homesick. It reminded me of going to church with Obo, carrying his Bible and being with the rest of my family members. Soon, I became friends with a female student from another province. She was from a different tribe and spoke her tribal language, which was different from mine, and the national language. However, we spoke in broken Amharic. We were like-minded and took our education seriously. We started morning devotion together. We got up early in the morning before breakfast. We read scripture and prayed in a quiet place behind one of our faculty's residences. Monday through Thursday, following the evening devotion, we had study hours until 9 pm. Saturday was cleaning day. I didn't know about the boys, but the girls cleaned the glass windows in their bedrooms and washed the floor and waxed it. There was a common area which we all helped clean.

We had outstanding teachers from around the world; two were from the United States, one taught religion and the other chemistry, which was my favorite subject. Fifty years later, in 2015, when I visited Minneapolis, Minnesota, I spoke with my chemistry teacher by phone. It was an exciting event for both of us. To this date, I have the photographic memory of the periodical table in my head. A female faculty member from Norway taught religion. A Norwegian man taught biology and physics. Biology, chemistry, and physics were taught through all twelve grades. I enjoyed physics too. A professor from India taught us mathematics and physics. The family resided outside of the high school compound and the daughter was in our grade, younger than the rest of students in the class. Algebra, geometry, and applied mathematics were taught ninth through twelfth grade as well. We had the only Ethiopian teacher who taught Amharic grammar and literature while English was taught by an American lady. There were three terms per year with comprehensive exams given at the end of each in all subjects. A comprehensive examination was also given at the end of the school year.

God promised in the scriptures, "*God will provide all your needs*" (Phil 4:19). My room and board and tuition was paid for by a lady in Germany whom I'd never met, but heard about her through my elementary school director in my home village. I knew that Obo Deressa was a man of great faith and knew that God would provide me with everything I needed. I was also grateful to God that He blessed me with the ability to learn and do my best.

I participated in three clubs: drama, Good Samaritan, and the literacy campaign. Once I took part in a production of *Romeo & Juliet*. However, my two favorite clubs were Good Samaritan and the literacy campaign. As a member of Good Samaritan club, we went into the nearby village to share the gospel. For this, I went with a student who was more experienced. In the literacy campaign, once or twice a week after school, we walked to the nearby marketplace to teach men and women how to read. At that time, Ethiopia had a high illiteracy rate and education was not mandatory. Every week, we saw the progress the men and women made. One could observe the excitement on their faces as they tried to read. I enjoyed helping them. Could this be my calling? I wondered.

In Ethiopia, Easter is a religious holiday just like in the biblical times. In big cities, Christians fasted for forty days just as Jesus did. At our Christian high school, the cafeteria didn't serve meat on Fridays. Instead, we ate shiroo, spiced split pea stew with injera, the national sour flatbread. They served also rice (ruuz). I had never seen rice before and I didn't like it.

Good Friday was a somber day for me, which was the day Jesus was crucified. We had church services, remembering every step Jesus took until His burial. The time of day was the same as biblical times. I became emotional when we sang, *"Were you there when they crucified my Lord..."* Even to this date, my eyes tear up when I hear that song.

Easter Sunday at the Ethiopian Evangelical College high school, in Debre Zeit, the city where I attended high school, was a memorable and exciting day. Debre Zeit means Mount Olive. I thought I was on Mount Olive where Jesus ascended to heaven. I still remember to this day when the girls woke up early in the morning at 11 o'clock Ethiopian time, walked into the boys' dormitory singing, *"Christ is risen today, hallelujah!"* and waking up the students. Girls were forbidden to go into the boys' dormitory. However, the head of the girls' dorm gave some of us permission to go and sing. And we were not interested in boys in the first place. A few of us were good friends with the girls' dorm head; therefore, she trusted us.

"Weren't the women the first to proclaim to the disciples that Christ was risen?" I thought. We walked to a nearby mountain that overlooked an amazing lake for a sunrise service. After that we came back to the school to eat breakfast.

Those students who came from Addis Ababa or those who came from rich families were picked up by car to go home for Easter vacation. When these students returned to school, they brought us delicious Ethiopian food, which I missed. Many of us came from far away and couldn't afford to go home until the end of the school year.

The city where the high school was located was a beautiful resort area. Near the school was Emperor Haile Selassie's weekend residence. On a Friday afternoon, we could see his motorcades from behind our school's cement wall. People were cheering and falling on the ground. We were prohibited from going outside of the school compound, but we could observe all of this because the school was situated on a hill.

Close to the emperor's weekend mansion, there was an air force base. Once in a while, the air force would hold a fundraising event. Students were asked to help. I enjoyed volunteering and soliciting money and sometimes my friend and I raised the most money. I was not afraid to ask people to donate. My philosophy was, *"No, is better than not asking at all."* To this day, I never stop asking when I solicit things for school or my church.

I have never forgotten March of 1965 when I heard from my brother Obo Deressa and the elementary school director the news informing me that I would go to Germany. I had no idea why I was going. In addition, I heard that one of my elementary school roommates would go to Germany as well. She was two grade levels behind me. I was in eleventh grade and she was in ninth. I was excited to go to another continent but did not know the reasons behind it.

"What happened to the plans God provided when I was given everything I needed to attend the most academically prestigious high school in my country?" I was perplexed. I was in my junior year, was doing great academically, and was looking forward to my senior year. My brother probably felt that meeting my future husband in Germany was prestigious. The pastor I was supposed to meet was an Ethiopian and highly educated and respected in my country as well as in Germany, where he received his advanced theology education. He was my brother Obosha's classmate when they were in the seminary in Ethiopia. I did not comprehend why this was happening now, before I finished the high school. I was perplexed.

CHAPTER SEVEN

An Unsuccessful Arranged Marriage

My girlfriend and I were scheduled to depart for Germany in March of 1965, just before the end of the school year. I was only in my last term in eleventh grade. The timing seemed strange, but I returned to my home village to bid a farewell to my relatives before embarking on this new journey. My mother worried when I left for another city within the country and I came home only once a year. Now, I was being shipped to another country, another continent.

I heard only through a grapevine that I would meet the highly respected pastor.

He and my brother Obosha were ordained together before I was enrolled in elementary school. He had traveled around the world sharing the gospel. He was highly educated and was respected in the Ethiopian Evangelical Church community. It sounded prestigious to our family to marry such a man. I was sure that Obo Deressa, who had raised me and had been my spiritual role model, was thrilled that his youngest sister would one day marry such an accomplished pastor. This pastor was about fifteen years older than I. I had met him a few times when I was in elementary school and he had made a presentation to the student body. Later, he traveled to Germany to advance his education.

Interestingly, his youngest sister was one of the girls my brother Obo Deressa provided room and board for while she attended elementary school. Maybe her brother was looking for a home grown, disciplined, and highly qualified girl.

Once my girlfriend and I arrived in Germany, we stayed with the German Mission director. Later, we stayed with different German families so that we could practice the German language. My girlfriend, too, was supposed to meet someone who was already in Germany to study. In the afternoon, the missionary director's wife taught us German grammar. Then she invited the two men to meet us for coffee at her house. I didn't know that the missionaries were in the matchmaking business. My girlfriend's boyfriend was one of my elementary school's most qualified teachers. When I saw the pastor, I did not look in his eyes because I respected him, as I did my brothers and other older men.

There was a big culture shock in Germany. First and foremost, everyone was white and spoke German. Secondly, in Ethiopia, we ate spicy food and used our fingers. Now we used forks and knives. Germans use the left hand for the fork, and the knife is held in the right hand. After cutting the food with the right hand, one should not switch back and forth between the two hands as I was to learn to do in the U.S. One put food in the mouth with the left hand. Both hands remain on the table until they finished eating. One time, I put one hand on my lap and the housewife commented, "What are you hiding under the table?" I was embarrassed.

The weather was completely different; I was cold. As winter approached, the missionaries provided us with woolen overcoats, gloves, and boots. We had to cover our heads, ears, and mouths. One morning I woke up thinking the clouds had come down. I couldn't wait to go outside and touch it for myself. My host family advised me that I should put on gloves. It reminded me of cotton when it was fluffed before spinning. So I put on my gloves and boots and ran outside. It looked like cotton, but it was freezing. Now, how would I describe this to Obo Deressa, Obosha, and the rest of the family in the village? This was what I wrote home describing what snow looked like:

"*The ground was covered with white stuff. It looked like fluffed cotton but I can pick it up with hands and make a snowball. Also it looked like sugar but it melted when I held it, and so on....*"
I loved when snow covered the evergreen branches. Mother Nature decorated so beautifully for Christmas.

Although my girlfriend was younger than I, she knew her friend well. She had also lived in big cities before so she was not as timid as I was. The missionary director's wife tried to be the best mediator possible between the Ethiopian pastor and me. Over a few weeks and months, I was able to talk with him as a friend. A heart-to-heart connection wasn't there, yet. This reminded me of the negotiations in the villages between the elders representing Obo Deressa and the elders representing his future wife's family. My two older sisters had met their future husbands secretly and approved of them before sending the elders to my brother to discuss the dowry obligation and to plan the wedding date. Shouldn't I have the same courtesy to decide about my future husband? I guessed that Obo Deressa was excited about the future of his youngest sister and the idea of me going to another country. I believed he always wished the best for me. He walked by faith all his life and always thanked God.

Late in the summer of 1965, the pastor and his colleague traveled to our villages, to visit our families. The pastor was lucky; I didn't need gold earrings because I refused to pierce my ears. My girlfriend and I continued to learn German almost every afternoon and learned to cook German cuisine. The mission's plan was to send us to home economics school in a variety of different cities. During the language sessions, she taught us the love song in German. In English: *"If I were a little bird, and had two little wings, I'd fly to you. But as it can't be but as it can't be, I always stay here."* This made me homesick for my family.

About two weeks after the men's return, the German Mission, along with my host family, planned an engagement ceremony for the pastor and me at the host family's house. I recall vividly it was Christmastime. An engagement ceremony is very important in our culture. The missionary pastor led the ceremony and there were witnesses. We exchanged engagement rings. I was locked in without the existence of love between us.

I asked God to give me peace of mind. However, as time went on, my heart became more distant from the pastor. There was nothing that I could do. Where would I go? I remembered the scripture, *"Be still, and know that I am God"* (Psalm 46:10a).

The missionaries had planned trainings that would make me the most qualified pastor's wife. The first year in Celle, Germany, at the German Hermansburg missions headquarter, we concentrated on learning the German language in the afternoons. In the mornings, we helped our host families with housekeeping and cooking the German way. It sounded like hands-on home economics because we helped the host family with preparing dinner and ate with them. My host family was elderly and had a girl in high school. The wife and husband didn't speak English or our tribal language. Wow! I used sign languages until I learned a few German words. The family was very kind but they had more compassion for the pastor. I became resentful.

I recall spending a couple of months with an executive's family. They had two young girls. His wife graduated from an accredited home economics school, and she was an accomplished housewife. Both husband and wife were middle-aged. They were a lot of fun to be around. The kids were good at teaching me German. They made me laugh; it was a joy to be around them. It reminded me of being with my nieces and nephews as I grew up. This German family even took me along with them when they went to Denmark on a two-week vacation. I enjoyed Denmark tremendously and the company of such generous people.

The Ethiopian pastor and I were engaged for a couple of months. The missionary sent both of us on a mission trip to Leipzig, East Germany. I was uncomfortable traveling with someone I had known for less than a year but went along with the plan. We spent about two weeks visiting different churches in East Germany. They were great people but they didn't have the freedom to talk to strangers like those in West Germany did. Luckily, when we visited the churches, they were more open and talkative. I was amazed when we visited the place where Martin Luther defiantly nailed a copy of his ninety-five Theses to the door of the Wittenberg Castle church on October 31, 1517. We also visited the church at which he preached. This was a great learning experience. However, sharing these experiences did nothing to improve our love relationship.

In 1966, one year after I arrived in Germany, the German Mission enrolled me in a state-certified home economics school in Kassel, West Germany. As always, room, board, and tuition were paid. It was an all-girls school, and the students came from different cities in Germany. There was a student from South Africa. It seemed that they had finished high school and weren't planning to attend higher education. This was a vocational school. I was blessed to be the oldest in the school because the head of the boarding school provided me the only private bedroom. It was located at the end of the large bedroom where the rest of the girls slept on bunk beds. I got along with all the students and they taught me to communicate better in German. Every time I went to my bedroom, I had to pass through a room which smelled of cigarette smoke and drinking. As soon as the boarding school leader entered, the girls hid the drinks under the bed. Sometimes they came to my bedroom to offer me cigarettes and drinks. They begged me to sip just a little liqueur and a take a puff of a cigarette. I'm so grateful that God gave me such strong willpower to resist the temptations. Obo Deressa's upbringing helped me to withstand all adversities. When I was doing my morning and evening devotions, the girls came to my bedroom and asked me whether I was reading a newspaper. Luckily, I met a student who wanted to go to church with me on Sundays and we did. What a joy!

A dozen subjects were offered in German, now my fourth language. The courses included: cooking, sewing, baking, nutrition, gardening, and more. I was overjoyed about finally learning how to cook and bake. In order to do well in more than a dozen subjects, I had to study more. Sometimes I was teased for putting too much effort on my education. When I did not understand a word, I looked in the German-English dictionary, or in a German-German dictionary. That didn't bother me at all because I always wanted to do my best and God did the rest. Tests were administered periodically and my schoolmates wanted to copy my answers. When I covered the test with my hands, they pushed away my hands. I found it humorous and embarrassing that they would copy my answers. I was new and didn't even know the German language well. I ultimately gave in and let them copy my answers. On most of my written tests, I received "sehr gut" (very good); Sometimes I got "ausgezeichnet" (excellent).

I also remember that the home economic students visited Berlin, East Germany.

At that time, it was a communist country and separated from West Germany by a concrete wall. There was only one gate through which visitors could enter each side of the country, called Check Point Charlie. It was guarded by German, British, and Russian soldiers when going from West to East Germany. I was the only student who went through the gate because I was the only foreigner. I had to show my passport to each soldier. The farther I went from the West German soldier, to the British, and finally to the Russian soldier, I was apprehensive. I was the only Black person. He appeared to be very serious and looked like a giant. I couldn't wait to join my classmates on the other side of the wall.

For the final examination at the home economics school, we were asked to prepare a main course with a side dish or dessert. I chose a main dish and side dish. For meat, I prepared "sauerbraten" according to the proper recipe and marinated the meat overnight. For vegetable side dishes, I selected cauliflower, carrots, and green beans. Early in the morning, I roasted the sour meat according to the recipe. Also I made a dark sauce from the drippings by adding flour and seasoning it with salt and pepper. Next, I steamed the vegetables until they were tender. I made white sauce with flour and milk and added salt and pepper to taste. I put the whole cauliflower head on a flat medium-sized serving plate and arranged the steamed carrots and green beans alternately around the cauliflower. Then I poured the white sauce on the cauliflower and sprinkled it with chopped parsley. The sauerbraten took about three hours. I sliced the "sauerbraten" into a quarter of an inch-thick slices and lay them on a round platter, decorated with radishes cut into the shape of roses and garnished with parsley stalks around the meat. The food was tasted by state officials from the home economics department during lunch. I received a score of "ausgezeichnet," which means excellent for presentation and taste. Finally, I could cook. This was something I had wanted to do since I was very young.

During the 1967-1968 academic years, I was enrolled at Gemeinde Helfrin Seminar in Bad Salzuflen, West Germany. Also, room, board, and tuition were paid for. This was a seminar for women who would assist the pastor in their service to the congregation. These women came from diverse backgrounds and their ages varied. My roommate was already engaged to a pastor of a congregation, and she was close to my age. We had our devotions before eating breakfast in a common area. There were devotions following breakfast and before classes resumed. I was excited to be part of this religious community. There were women pastors and probably one male pastor who was one of the female pastor's spouses. There were four professors in all, as I recall.

Although I spoke German better at this point, home economics and Bible studies terminologies were like heaven and earth. Yet, I was fortunate to have read the scriptures in our tribal language. When the pastors referenced Hebrew words, I already knew the meaning. The Ethiopian language is a semi-hematic language. In addition, being nurtured with God's words around Obo Deressa gave me a great advantage. Learning the Bible in depth gave me a better understanding of the scripture when it was first written and translated into various languages. In addition, we were taught music and spiritual songs and how to conduct a choir. I cherished spiritual songs because they reminded me of heavenly angels singing.

Sometime during the year, the seminary sent a group of us to Holland to visit a unique church. "I was already a foreign student, why would they choose me," I wondered? The church was located on a small peninsula and the pastor of that church gave us a tour. There were about six of us students. I also saw windmills for the first time that generated electricity.

I had no doubt that all the training I received at this seminary would make me a great asset to any congregation. Likewise, I would be the most qualified housewife for the Ethiopian pastor. Unfortunately, my heart was moving further and further from him. Coincidently, for Christmas 1967, one of the women at the seminary invited me to spend Christmas with her family in Munich, the capital of Bavaria. The family paid for the train fare and it was an amazing trip. It was a first class compartment and we slept whenever we were tired. The people in Munich spoke German, of course, and they were very friendly and used polite words similar to the southern hospitality in the United States. My friend was the youngest in the family and had two older siblings, a boy and a girl. I was amazed at the musical talents of each family member: my friend played guitar, her brother played trumpet, her sister played the flute, and her parents played piano.

On Christmas Eve after church service, the family served an elegant dinner.

Before eating all kinds of incredible homemade Christmas desserts, the family members performed a home concert. It reminded me of the angels singing the night Jesus was born. I enjoyed singing with the family in German as well as in my tribal language. The German Mission in Ethiopia translated some of songs to Oromo language when I was in the elementary school. I was homesick for my family particularly because Christmas was my favorite Christian holiday. However, I enjoyed spending my favorite holiday with this family. At no time did they bring up about the Ethiopian pastor I was engaged to, and I am grateful they didn't. During the day, the family gave me a tour of Munich and its historic sites. After the New Year, we returned to the seminary together.

After many months of counseling with a senior female pastor, who taught at the seminary where I attended, I was at a turning point. She took me for walks, trying to convince me to marry him, but I could not see myself as his future wife. My heart was hardened. Although I was worried what Obo Deressa would say and how disappointed he would be, I just could not go forward with it. Our engagement was dissolved in 1968 just like a marriage. Instead of continuing the practical training of the seminary, the German Mission returned me to Ethiopia in April of 1968. If I didn't get married to the man they arranged for me, I didn't need to stay in Germany. I was concerned that Obo Deressa would be disappointed with me, but I remembered a verse in Psalms, *"Be still and know that I'm God"* (Psalms 46:10a). I departed for Addis Ababa, Ethiopia, my first stop.

CHAPTER EIGHT

ONE DOOR CLOSES
ANOTHER OPENS

If I knew what kind of obstacles awaited me, I might despair. But God has perfectly planned every path I might take. That is why the scripture advises us to *"Walk by Faith, Not by Sight"* (2 Corinthians 5:7). Before my travel back to my home village, I stayed at the German Mission compound in the guesthouse in Addis Ababa, Ethiopia. At that time, my brother Obosha, Reverend Lamessa, was a pastor at a nearby church. I spent a day or two with the family. Obosha had never discussed with me about my broken engagement. Still, I had no idea what I would do next, only God knew.

I was concerned about what the future would bring after I turned down a marriage proposal from the most educated and respected pastor I knew. Another scripture verse came to my mind, *"Thou will keep him in perfect peace, whose mind stays on thee" (Isaiah 26:3)*. I was comforted by this. To this day, this plaque is hanging on my bedroom wall, reminding me of God's constant presence.

God was working through the mission, through the pastor of a large Evangelical church in Addis Ababa, and probably through my elementary director and my brother. God had lined up my spiritual advocates and attorneys, whom I would never be able to pay back. Even though I had no say in making decisions, I just had faith that everything would be okay. I had two dilemmas. First, what can I do as a single woman after refusing to marry a pastor? Second, how was I to use my training in Germany that I was taught to help the church women, youth, and children. No one would accept me in a village as a pastor's assistant. No woman has ever done it and no pastor had the training to work with any woman who was trained abroad. Maybe, I would be considered overqualified.

The pastor of the Evangelical church Mekane Yesus in Addis Abeba and his wife received their education in the U.S. To the best of my knowledge, the pastor received his Master of Divinity at Luther Seminary in Minneapolis, Minnesota. I didn't know exactly in which field his wife had her higher education. Before I returned to the village, someone contacted this pastor to inquire if he could use my expertise at his church. He agreed, and I was thrilled, and I went for an interview. He then presented me to the church elders for approval and they approved my hiring unanimously. I thanked God for how He had planned my destiny. I am forever grateful to the pastor of that church and the elders.

The members of the congregation spoke many languages, then the national language Amharic, my tribal language Oromo, another tribal language Tigrigna, and English. However, the majority of the people in the city spoke the national language, Amharic. I had never been a city girl. My high school had been my introduction to a city environment. This church had an elementary school, first through sixth grades. The director of the school was from my tribe and I had known him in the past.

When I was in the seminary in Germany, I was trained to teach the Bible and music. The church also needed a church secretary. One of the assignments was typing in the Ethiopian language of Amharic. Wow! I had never even used an English typewriter, which was only twenty-six letters. The Ethiopian typewriter had to accommodate two hundred and ten letters. That meant one had to hit a key two to three times just for one character. I remembered reading in my devotional book, "*If God allows you to walk on a rough road, He will provide you with proper shoes.*" I was determined to do my best. Then I thought of great comfort from the scripture: "*I can do all things through Christ who gives strength*" (Phil. 4:13). One of my nephews made me a plaque of this scripture and it is hanging on the wall in my family room today. I was grateful to be given this opportunity. The church pastor and his wife were very understanding. Both of them spoke three languages: their tribal language, which was different from mine, Amharic, and fluent English. I was grateful to be offered 100.00 Ethiopian birr a month. My room was paid for, and I ate lunch at the pastor's house, and there were no transportation expenses.

The church was far away from the German mission where I was staying. It took two buses to get there. The buses were so crowded, we couldn't breathe. That wasn't the worst problem, however. Thieves would target someone in these crowded buses. I have never forgotten the day I took a bus to visit my brother. I had a less expensive wristwatch on, the only one I ever owned. After I stepped off the bus, a lady said to me, "someone took your watch." *Why didn't she alert me?*" I thought. I was horrified. My brother met me at the bus stop and we walked to his house. When I shared the incident with him and his wife, they told me it was common, and therefore, bus riders put everything in their purses and held them tight. I had no idea.

I am grateful to God and extend my heartfelt gratitude to the pastor and others who helped in solving my transportation issue by providing me with a place to stay, so that I didn't spend so much time on the road. An arrangement was made that I stay at the church hostel with a lady who was an employee of the Ethiopian Evangelical Church Mekane Yesus Headquarters. The hostel was only a few yards from the church. I was about to begin my next destiny.

Before I started my new assignment, the pastor and the church elders let me go and visit my family in my village. I was overwhelmed with gratitude to have a job I was trained for in Germany and to see my family after three long years. However, I was apprehensive what my brother Obo would say about my decision to break up with the Ethiopian pastor to whom I was engaged. I trusted that God would work on my behalf with my brother.

I traveled to the village on the missionary four-passenger airplane from Nekemte, where I had first landed on my route to the high school with Obo Deressa. He was as excited to see me and I was to see him. Everybody was excited to see me back, especially my mother. Every day, a relative or a friend would come to visit me and my mother, and Soretti would make freshly roasted and ground coffee served with injera (sour flatbread) spread with spiced butter. That was my favorite food with coffee. I also visited elderly family friends who lived half an hour or more walking distance. Everywhere I visited, my friends made coffee and offered me something to eat. I didn't gain any weight because my brother, the Reverend Lamessa, was also visiting and we walked everywhere. It was great. I have never forgotten as we were passing through a dense forest, I saw monkeys on a tree. I stopped to take a picture. It jumped from one branch to another because it thought I was about to shoot it. I left it alone. Finally, after about two weeks, I returned to Addis Ababa.

The former church secretary gave me an orientation on my assignment in the church office. I would also assist the church school director with necessary office work. The most exciting job I was offered was to teach the Bible and music to the students in grades one through grades six. That was what I was trained for. However, it was mostly in Amharic, the national language. Rightfully, I was teased that my accent sounded like Ferenji (foreigner). They were right because I didn't grow up in a city and I seldom used it as a social language. I truly enjoyed teaching the kids the Bible and music. I taught the songs in Oromifa, Amharic, and English. Sometimes, we sang for the congregation. When I was not in the classroom, I practiced on the typewriter to perfect my typing speed. I was grateful for the opportunity to learn something new.

As the Christmas season approached, I began teaching the students Christmas songs I learned while attending the German Mission school. These songs were common in the church. The Christmas holiday meant so much to me for various reasons. First and foremost, it is the birth of our Lord Jesus Christ. Second, when I was in elementary school I took part in a nativity play and I portrayed Mary. This was my first Christmas at the church where I was working. In addition, I was familiar with many of the Christmas songs I sang at the high school in Amharic and English. Next, we selected biblical verses associated with the birth of Christ and let the student memorize the verses. During this holiday, I was able to utilize my experiences growing up and my more advanced training I learned in Germany, such as directing a choir and teaching the Bible.

The Christmas program that the students presented to the congregation went very well, and the church members enjoyed it. I spent the Christmas holiday of 1968 doing what I was called to do: serving the congregation through a teaching ministry to the students. I was overwhelmed with joy and gratitude.

Trust in God's Timing

The church I was assigned to was located a stone's throw away from the Ethiopian Evangelical Church Mekane Yesus headquarters. The pastor of the church and his wife received their education in Minnesota. As a result of this connection, many visitors from other countries worshiped at our church. In January of 1969, a group of students led by their professor from St. Olaf College in Minnesota worshiped with us. This was part of a program called Interim Abroad. The whole group was very pleased with the church service and program.

Upon their return to the United States, the history professor who led the St. Olaf College students decided to offer a scholarship to one of the church members for a year to study playing organ at the college. The college is known for its music department and had an internationally known traveling choir. St. Olaf College was academically well known and very expensive compared to other Lutheran and state colleges.

Next, an unimaginable thing happened to me. The congregation suggested two church members as candidates for a scholarship to study at St. Olaf: both were church employees, the male church school director and me. I was dumbfounded, "Why me?" I questioned. "Didn't I come back from Germany less than a year ago?" The more I resisted the idea of going to the United States, the more I was encouraged by the pastor and the church president. I was hard on myself thinking, "What would people say? I didn't like to stay in my country?" God had already decided my destiny. What if the German Mission sent me back to my country because I dissolved my engagement less than a year earlier? I asked God for His forgiveness; I had doubted His gift, instead of receiving it with gratitude. The guilt of the past three years crept up on me, telling me that I did not deserve it. Then, I realized that God saw my future, and it didn't matter what I had done in the past. God placed these church leaders in my life to cheer me on. The male church director applied for the scholarship: however, the church elders decided to award me the scholarship. I did not even play any instruments. I had only played a recorder when I was in Germany. Why the church leaders trusted me with this scholarship, only God knew. I only knew how to lead a choir. I was overwhelmed with joy. However, I truly felt badly for the male director who had been at the church longer than I had. When I visited my country in 1994, he jokingly mentioned that I took the scholarship away from him. His family invited me to an elegant dinner to show their support of me.

Immediately I called Obosha, who was a pastor at a sister church in the suburb of the capital city. "I am going to America to study organ," I announced. There was silence. I was sure he was in disbelief as I had been. Then he asked, "When and who is paying for you?" "Sometime in August, a group of students and their professor visited our church and offered a scholarship to any church member. The director of the school and I were both candidates. The church awarded it to me," I told him. "Waqao isanif hakenuu, atis Waqao si haebisu (God reward them and God blesses you)," he responded. I wept for joy and also sadness that I was again going to be separated from my family.

The Ethiopian Evangelical Church Mekane Yesus, the church I was working at, was big and well known in the capital. Therefore, many people who moved from my home village to the city came to this church to worship with us on Sundays. I met a few former elementary and high school classmates who were all male as well as my former elementary school teachers.

One of the teachers and I became friends. He knew Obo very well when he was my teacher at the German mission in Aira. At this time, he worked in Addis Ababa and worshiped at our church frequently. I had never lived in a big city and there were no girls from our village in the city, so he helped me get acquainted to the city environment and things girls living in the city should be aware of. He knew that Obo was strict and a man of great faith. I had great respect for him because he was my elementary school teacher. He knew my sisters who attended school and especially my brother, Reverend Lamessa (Obosha).

Over time, our friendship grew to a different level. As my departure for the United States neared, through the encouragement of friends, we planned our engagement. We agreed to get engaged before I left for the U.S. The pastor of the church, the school director, my cousin, and other friends were at the engagement ceremony.

Again, I returned to my family in the village to bid them farewell. Obo was so happy and thanked God for all He had done for me. It was overwhelming for my mother because I was going farther and farther from home. My mother, Soretti, and my sister Dessie prepared my favorite foods for the short time I spent with them. I was grateful for their loving care all these years. I told them that the scholarship would be for a year. God willing, we would see each other again, soon. Also, friends and neighbors stopped by our house to say goodbye. Obo read the scripture from Psalms, *"I lift my eyes to the hills- where does my help come from? My help comes from the Lord, the Maker of heaven and earth.... The Lord Watches over you.... The Lord will keep you from all harm.... He will watch over your life; the Lord will watch over your coming and going both now and forever* (Psalms 121: 1-8). This was an emotional and comforting farewell.

CHAPTER NINE

A TURNING POINT IN MY LIFE: MY JOURNEY TO AMERICA
1969-1970

God has known me since I was in my mother's womb (Psalms 139). Each path He has predestined for me within a purpose in my journey. I could not have asked Him to grant me or to show me His purpose in my life because I couldn't see one step ahead of me. If I knew the disappointments I would encounter along the way, I would have asked Him for an alternative. He would tell me, "My child you're still young in your faith. Let me guide you the way that I prepared for you before you were born." Then, I would tell God, "Thank you for giving me my brother Obo Deressa who guided me in the Word and took me along with him while I was still young in my faith."

The turning point in my life began in the summer of 1969 when I was offered a scholarship to go to the United States to attend college. This was the most unpredictable opportunity. God's timing was perfect. I returned to my country, Ethiopia, from Germany in 1968. Being forced to return home because of my broken engagement could have been considered an embarrassment to me and my family, but God turned it into a blessing instead.

In the middle of August 1969, again I departed my country for what seemed to be another new chapter in my life. This time I was going to America, a country I had no knowledge of except from books. To my recollection, my plane ticket was paid for by Saint Olaf College students and their professor, who extended the scholarship to one member of our church. I also extended my heartfelt gratitude for their generosity.

My sponsors in America had already arranged every detail of my trip, all the way from Africa to my final destination in the U.S. I was flying in this giant airplane, Pan Am 65 on August 21, 1969, from Paris, France. During the nine-hour flight, I marveled at God's wonderful creation. As I looked out through the window from my seat, and saw the glorious blue sky, I made a local call to my heavenly father for a safe flight. Then I looked down to see the amazing blue reflection from the sky, I thought I lost my mind. I came to my senses when at that moment, the pilot announced that it was the Atlantic Ocean. My previous geography lessons had finally become a reality. After few hours of flight, again the pilot made an announcement that we were in a different time zone, indicating the sunrise.

While marveling at God's creation and the knowledge God gave the pilots to maneuver this giant flying object, I landed in Chicago, Illinois, in the evening. I was grateful for the safe flight. I was met by one of the students who had visited our church in Addis Ababa in January of 1969. To my recollection, he came with family members to pick me up in a big bluish car. Unfortunately, I couldn't tell you what kind of a car it was. It was different from the cars I had seen in Germany or in Addis Ababa.

In Ethiopia there was a perception that America was so rich, and that money grew on trees. We also believed that there were no poor people in America. Apparently these visiting college students and their professor heard this through the grapevine when they visited Ethiopia. The student and his family wanted me to see reality with my own eyes to disprove this false notion. Right from the airport, before they took me to their suburban home, they drove me through downtown Chicago to see the truth for myself. I could hardly open my eyes due to jetlag but I saw people sleeping on the side of the streets dressed in ragged clothes. Some were begging; I don't know whether it was for money or something else. Honestly, I could not believe my eyes that something like this also existed in the United States. In Ethiopia, there were many poor people, and they sat along the roads at churches and begged for money.

As we were driving to their residence, they explained to me why they wanted me to see the reality in America. "We are about to take you to an affluent neighborhood," the student explained. He continued by saying, "The college you are about to attend is a high-class college and students come from rich families or are on scholarship grants. Probably the families you will meet also live in nice neighborhoods," he added. I was absorbing everything. Once we arrived at the student's family residence, he introduced me to his parents. His mother showed me the bedroom where I would stay for the next couple of days until we drove to the college in Northfield, Minnesota. I was so tired. The family told me that I could sleep as long as I wanted and would talk with me in the morning. I was grateful for their hospitality and for making me feel at home.

The following morning when I woke up and was ready, I went to the kitchen to greet them and thanked them for picking me up from the airport. I also thanked them for welcoming me in their home. The mother asked me whether I preferred coffee or tea with my breakfast and I told the mom that I preferred coffee if they had it. I enjoyed my first delicious breakfast served with scrambled eggs and toasted slices of bread. After breakfast the family showed me around their home, which was located in an upscale neighborhood on a hill. The best part was that we could communicate in English. Although I had had two American professors in high school, I had difficulty in understanding them because of their rolling tongue expression. The family showed me around the suburbs and part of downtown Chicago. I couldn't see the sky due to the overwhelmingly tall buildings and skyscrapers. I couldn't imagine how one lived in such an area all of their lives.

After the third day in Chicago, we departed by car for St. Olaf College in Northfield, Minnesota. It was about 402 miles and took about five and half hours. The road was great and driving was faster than I anticipated. However, since I sat in the back, I soon felt nauseated. I mentioned that I had motion sickness. Then, they asked me to sit in front. I appreciated their compassionate attitude. On the highway, I saw a sign that said, "Do not pass" but he kept driving anyway. I thought he was going to crash into oncoming vehicles. Luckily, it didn't happen. Later on I asked politely what "do not pass" meant. I was told that a driver shouldn't pass another car when there was a solid line between the two driving lanes. I was relieved.

We arrived in Northfield, a small town without high buildings like I had seen in Chicago. I thought, finally I could see the sky. The college was situated on a hill and the structure was amazing. If I recall correctly, I met with the rest of the students and the professor who led them. After a brief introduction, they gave me a short tour of the campus, emphasizing the famous music department and the college chapel, which was close to my heart. I was also introduced to the sister of the pastor I had worked with in Addis Ababa who was enrolled in college already. What a small world! She also had attended the same high school I attended in Ethiopia and was ahead of me by two grades. She was a nursing student.

I realized that all students entering college take college entrance examinations and have completed high school. Foreign students are required to take the Test of English as a Foreign Language (TOEFL) designed to measure the English proficiency of non-English speaking people. I did not even complete eleventh grade and yet I didn't need to take the required tests. Amazingly, the professor who sponsored me waived all requirements for me. Above all, I thanked God who was in control of my life. I couldn't thank the admission's office enough for believing in me. God's plan was beyond my comprehension. I went to the girls' dormitory and met with the lady in charge. Room, board, tuition, and all college supplies were paid for as part of the scholarship.

Because men were not allowed to go into the girls' rooms the professor turned our tour over to the woman in charge of the first floor waiting room, and there I was introduced to my junior advisor. She was a music major and was in her third year. My sponsor requested of the junior advisor to guide me until I got acquainted with the campus environment. She was a cheerful individual and was delighted to assist me. She also knew a few international students that she thought I might like to meet. There were students from all over the world and there was an International Students Club. At the ISC I met another female student from Taiwan and we remained friends through graduate school and beyond. I was reunited also with a female student I met in Bonn, Germany. This group got together frequently and sometimes sponsored international food for the faculty and student body.

When I registered for approved courses, I remember my junior advisor suggesting that I avoid registering for a particular music class. She told me that it would be difficult for me because it was for music majors only and she was one of them. However, I insisted. I registered to study playing the organ, but I ended up only practicing once a week. I guessed

I should have practiced more. I still got a B grade, for which I was grateful. I also registered for introduction to psychology, American history, religion, and algebra.

St. Olaf is a Lutheran college and we had worship services on Sundays in a beautiful college chapel. Sometimes the amazing college choir sang. I continued with my daily morning and evening devotions as I had been doing since I was a young girl. It had been my guide and strength every day. Now that I was in a strange country, this Christian environment still comforted me.

During one of the semester breaks, my college advisor took me to one of the Lutheran churches in Oshkosh, Wisconsin, to give a speech. I assumed he had already established a relationship with the congregation.

"I want you to give a speech," he told me. "What am I supposed to say?" I asked him.

Then he handed me a typed speech to deliver to the congregation. It was an amazing speech which included my background, where I was going to college, and why I came to this country as well as what I would be doing when I returned to my country. All I had to do was to read and memorize the script. God's gift of photographic memory came in handy and I delivered the speech. It went well. To my recollection, afterwards, we met with small group of church leaders. I thanked my advisor for all he had done for me and for inviting me to speak. I had never been afraid to be in front of a large audience beginning from elementary school. If I ever felt fearful about speaking in front of a big audience, I reminded myself, "If Peter, Jesus' disciple, spoke in front of thousands of people the day they received the Holy Spirit, I could do it too."

In addition to room, board, and tuition, the college even paid for my school supplies and gave me some spending money. I remembered signing up as a student assistant in the college library as part of a work-study program. I can't recall if the money was used toward school supplies or for personal spending money. For a while, I had difficulty understanding what the professors were saying because of the rolling tongue pronunciation of some sounds. Back in Ethiopia, English was an academic language and basically was spoken with a British accent. Since it was difficult to understand everything my teachers were saying, I decided to read the chapters before the lecture. The professor eventually learned that I already knew the material being taught and was able answer discussion questions easily because I already read ahead of each lesson. In Ethiopia and even in Germany, the tests primarily contained short answer or essay questions, with few multiple choices. Nevertheless, at this college all tests questions were multiple choice. That didn't go well for me because all the choices were similar and confusing. I was disappointed to receive an "F" grade in introductory psychology because of all the multiple choices.

I was overjoyed when I met a female student who lived on the same floor as I. When she saw me, she was excited and asked me, "Where are you from?" "I am from Ethiopia," I replied. I saw her eyes filled with tears and then she followed with another question, "Did you know a girl from Addis Ababa named Imnet?" We both became emotional. As I was confirming that I knew her, her eyes welled up with tears of joy. She told me that the girl was an exchange student for two years and she stayed at her house. I told her that she was my high school classmate and roommate for three years. During those three years, we had morning devotions together. We both hugged each other and wept. Following our conversations, she called her parents and related the news. The parents were overjoyed and gave me a round-trip airline ticket to Nebraska to meet them during Christmas. I was overjoyed by this surprise. I thanked the family for their generosity. I was grateful to spend my first Christmas in America with such a wonderful and devoted Christian family.

During the fall season, I experienced God's wonderful creation when leaves changed from green to an amazing psychedelic brownish, yellow, and red colors. I knew this was to be followed by bitter cold weather I had never experienced. When I lived in Germany, there was snow, but not compared to the cold in Minnesota.

"Why did you choose here?" some students asked me. I told them that the kindest and most wonderful people of this state chose me and I was grateful for their generosity. Sometimes the temperature reached twenty to thirty degrees below freezing point. Sometimes, the wind chill factor was fifty degrees below freezing point. Luckily, the buildings where I took classes were close to each other.

I was thankful to everyone who helped me purchase the necessary clothes I would need, like boots, mittens, a hat, and a scarf to cover my neck and mouth. I had a brown warm coat and all the accessories. Thinking about the warmest and most kind-hearted people in the college community helped me forget about the bitter cold.

During the summer of 1970, I was introduced to a former missionary family in Ethiopia who lived in Minneapolis. They had three young boys and I enjoyed being around them and the whole family. They had many memorabilia from Ethiopia which reminded me of my country, and the family's warm welcome made me feel at home. They informed me that there was an international gathering once a month which was sponsored by a dedicated and loving Christian couple. This was held in a remote suburb of Minneapolis. I understood that the pastor I had worked with in Addis Ababa had visited this family when he was studying at Luther Seminary in Minneapolis many years back.

Also, this summer, I attended an event at the International Student Fellowship in Eden Prairie, a remote suburb of Minneapolis. It was established by a devoted Christian couple (Mother and Father Gregson as all students called them) to provide free food and housing during various vacations and summer to foreign students who were studying at nearby colleges and the University of Minnesota. The enormous house was situated on about seventy-five acres of land and was previously owned by a wealthy family. It had an upper and lower deck with multiple bedrooms: king and queen bedrooms, other mid-size bedrooms, two large kitchens (upstairs and downstairs), and a heated indoor pool. Once a month on Sunday afternoons there was an event where Christians from various churches were invited to hear inspirational speakers. During the summer I was a manager and host for foreign students. I welcomed them and cooked or helped them cook food provided by friends of the International Students Fellowship Center. There were students from different countries and diverse religious backgrounds. Sometimes I found myself sharing my Christian faith with Muslims and Hindu students. The dialogues we had were an eye-opener for me and I was grateful for having this opportunity.

CHAPTER TEN

A GLIMPSE OF MY PROFESSION
1970-1971

"Growing up I had no dream because God was in charge."

An amazing thing happened towards the end of my first year in college. My advisor informed me that they wanted to extend my scholarship for another year. I was in disbelief. I wasn't sure if I was happy or disappointed. I was disappointed because I was homesick every Sunday for my family, and for the teacher I was engaged to prior to coming to the United States. On the other hand, I was happy that I could continue to play the organ. Was I to become a professional musician, playing the organ, or something else? There was never a dull moment in my journey.

Growing up I had no dream or vision of what my ultimate profession would be. There were no Ethiopian women in the village who had a profession except getting married and having children. At some point, I wished to get married and at have at least a dozen children. One of the courses I registered for during my second year at the college gave me a hint as to what my future career might be. In addition to registering for my organ lessons and general classes, my college advisor helped me register for classes in child development and psychology.

Back when I was in elementary school, there were no Ethiopian women who had a profession that I looked up to. I thought of being like the German female director at the German Mission school. But to dream of becoming an educator was wishful thinking then. In our culture, there was no such thing as, "I want to be a teacher, a nurse, a doctor, or anything else." It happened only by chance or when opportunity knocked at the door.

The second year at the college was less challenging than the first year. I was accustomed to the college environment and was able to understand when the professors were lecturing by reading the materials before the class. However, the class that changed me forever and gave me a glance at my future profession was when I was immersed in the child development and psychology course. In addition to the class, there was a daycare center where I applied what I learned in theory. The more I visited the daycare, the more it became obvious that this might be my calling. I continued doing well in my other classes; however, it became evident that my passion was being with children. My college advisor realized that as well. What would be the solution?

Unfortunately, the college didn't offer elementary education at that time. That was a dilemma. At that point I trusted in God that He would use His power to fulfill His plan for me as He had always done in the past. I believed when God is in charge nothing is impossible for Him. I recalled the scripture verse in Romans. "And we know that in all things God works for the good of those who love Him" (Romans 8:28). I also believed that He would guide my advisor and others to carry out His will. I continued to work smart and hard in all the courses I registered for. I kept walking by faith.

For the 1970 Christmas holiday, a female student on the same floor invited me to go with her to Atlanta, Georgia. I always checked with my college advisor and my friend from Ethiopia to make sure it was safe. The student's family paid for a round-trip airfare ticket for me. I was grateful that the student asked me to go with her and for her family to pay for the airplane ticket.

When I was in my country, we learned about every country in the world. Regarding America, we learned about every state and capital. But I didn't remember paying any special attention to the weather in each state. When we boarded the airline in Minneapolis, Minnesota, it was cold, and I had proper clothing on. After almost three hours, we landed in Atlanta. When I got out of the plane, I thought I was in a boiler room. I was drenched with sweat and miserable. I wished I could shed some of my clothes. That was misguided thinking. Instead, I thanked God and the family who invited me and gave me the opportunity to see another part of the United States of America.

This family lived outside of Atlanta and, unlike the family I had visited in Nebraska, this family was reserved. The reason might have been that the family in Nebraska had had an exchange student from another country, but this family lacked this experience. For the first time I saw how television could control family time. I noticed the couple argued frequently when commercials interrupted their favorite television shows. However, I enjoyed spending time with the family and was grateful for their hospitality to experience another part of this great nation.

When we returned to Minnesota, I thought I was in the North Pole. The college is located on the hill; as a result, the temperature is colder than the surrounding areas. I constantly reminded myself to think about the generous people who supported me to attend this prestigious college. That thought warmed my heart.

I kept doing my best in all of my courses. Although English was an academic language in my country of Ethiopia, as a foreign student, I put extra effort to do my best. That meant I had to give one hundred fifty percent more effort than my American counterparts. In my country, during that time, education was not mandatory. Coming to another country was a privilege and an opportunity.

I was sure that my college advisor was puzzled about how he could support my new ambition to work with young children. Being an experienced professor in the Midwest, he knew other Lutheran colleges that offered educational training in my desired field. He informed me of Augsburg College in Minneapolis, which was known for its education department, primarily elementary education. He seemed to know all the key players at the college. He arranged for both of us to meet with their college's registrar.

I don't recall all of the exact details of this meeting, but I remember how the registrar made me feel welcome from our first meeting. I was confident that my advisor and the registrar had prior discussion about my educational goal. It seemed that the meeting had a positive outcome. If I remember correctly, the registrar, my advisor, and I visited the admission office. Like the saying goes, "One never has a second chance for a first impression." I was impressed by how friendly everyone was. The registrar also showed us various important locations such as the female students' dorm, the library, the chapel, and the cafeteria, and also introduced us to key people on campus. I truly appreciated the registrar's hospitality to make the transition from St. Olaf College to Augsburg College so smooth. I was grateful to my college advisor for his tireless effort to find an institution where my dream finally could become a reality. It was this same registrar who had welcomed me with open arms who later hosted my graduation party for me and my friends at her house. I was eternally grateful to her. Three years later she visited me and spent a week at my house in Miami, Florida. We had a great time together.

In the summer before entering my dream profession, I applied to work at the Billy Graham Association Headquarters in Minneapolis, and I was accepted. I heard about Billy Graham when I was in Ethiopia and, to my recollection, he had held one of his crusades in Ethiopia. At the beginning, I was a receptionist answering phone calls and typing labels on envelopes to individuals. The association received thousands of letters from around the country and the world requesting prayers and donating money to the organization. Later on, my responsibility was to sort those envelopes.

I was amazed at the Christian environment in that organization. There was devotion before starting the day, and at lunch as well. They served a free lunch for the workers. Every employee was so friendly and did their work with enthusiasm. It looked as if this environment was designed for this ministry. I was grateful for this experience.

CHAPTER ELEVEN

A New Year—A New Kind of Profession Planned by God
1971 – 1973
(Augsburg College)

I started U.S. education with a one-year scholarship to Saint Olaf College to study organ. The scholarship was extended another year, during which I discovered my passion for working with children in my child development course. Then, another two-year scholarship was given to me to study elementary education at a sister college, Augsburg College, in Minneapolis, Minnesota. I will be forever grateful to Dr. Olson at Saint Olaf College and Ms. Mildred Joel, a registrar at Augsburg College, whom God put in my path to support and guide me throughout my educational journey. They arranged free room, board, and tuition for me. I had no idea who paid for me or where the money came from. It was one of those miracles that God provided for His children as He promised in the scripture: "*And my God will meet all your needs according to the riches of his glory in Christ Jesus"* (Philippians 4:19). I also received assistance for school supplies. Now that I had all the general courses behind me at Saint Olaf, I registered for courses that were required for elementary education. Just like my two years at Saint Olaf, I continued to read the materials before the professors lectured. I registered for the maximum load possible and I did my uttermost in every subject. In addition, I had three semesters of junior field experiences in elementary school to determine if teaching was to be my future profession and to prepare me for student teaching in my senior year. I received satisfactory grades all three semesters.

I was assigned to a wonderful student junior counselor who shadowed me and gave me necessary assistance. During my junior year, 1971-1972, I lived in an all-girls dormitory. However, during my senior year I was moved to a coed dorm where my student counselor lived. It felt odd since I'd never lived in a coed dorm.

While I enjoyed school and the extracurricular clubs I joined, just like at my last college, I was not looking forward to the winter season. I was thinking of the two bitter cold winters I had spent at Saint Olaf College. Strangely, however, the temperature in the city seemed less cold. I guess it was because of the many buildings and more human interaction. Whatever the reason, I was glad for the nicer weather.

I spent Christmas vacation with an American family who were missionaries in Ethiopia. There was no greater gift than celebrating with a family who spent their lives serving God.

Once again I was made to feel at home. Their three boys reminded me of my nieces and nephews in Obo Deressa's family.

Towards the second half of the semester, I was asked to be a member of the Women's Honorary Society and also the Timia Students' Honorary Society. Later on I found out that the membership in these societies was based on academic performance. I was not aware that one could belong to an elite group for just doing her best. I was amazed. I was immersed in my education and completed every assignment with great enthusiasm, knowing that I wanted to practice this profession for the rest of my life.

The following academic year, 1972-73, the professors in elementary education concentrated on lecturing on teaching methods in all subjects including physical education and music as well as lecturing on how young children learn. Once we completed all the courses needed, the elementary education professor identified a local elementary school for student teaching for the last semester prior to graduation. Our whole class prepared practice lesson plans in every subject for the professor to review.

I was assigned to Hennepin County Public Elementary School in downtown Minneapolis. I was assigned to teach first grade. It was an interesting coincidence, seeing as I taught first grade during the last seven years of my professional teaching career. Driving through the neighborhood with my college advisor for the first time gave me chills. I noticed that some of the buildings were of a high standard compared to where I used to live. I had no clue why the professor chose me for this school. Maybe she believed that I could handle these kids better than my classmates. I had never lived in this kind of neighborhood. Once again, I had to take public transportation. I was fortunate that the bus stop was just a few yards from the school. I was determined to do my best all the way to the finish line. I was reminded of some words of encouragement from my daily devotion: *"If God allows you to walk through rough road, He will provide you with proper shoes."* I realized that what mattered most was not the environment, but my love for children. In addition, I purchased professional clothing and shoes for my student teaching assignment.

After my lesson plans were reviewed and approved, I was ready to embark on my student teaching assignment: first grade. For about two weeks, I only shadowed the classroom teacher. During my classroom observation, I spotted a blonde boy with curly hair who seemed to come to school every day in dirty shirts. His name was Mark. Sometimes he was overlooked by the classroom teacher even though he sat in the first row. When I asked the teacher privately what the problem might have been, she told me it had to do with his family.

Finally, it was time for me to begin my student teaching. Everything went smoothly and I really enjoyed teaching the young children. One day, in middle of my presentation, Mark raised his hand. I asked him if he had a question and he responded,

"Yes. If you love children so much, why don't you have your own kids?"

"I will have one day when I get married. For now, you are my kids," I answered.

Everybody laughed. The teacher heard the laughter and thought the kids were misbehaving. I was touched by his observation. He gave me a hug during dismissal. To this date and throughout my teaching carrier, parents frequently commented, "You love your job and the kids: You come in the morning with a smile and dismiss the kids with a smile."

The classroom teacher left the kids under my control for the last four weeks of my student teaching. In the middle of one assignment, the college supervisor stopped at the school to check on how I was managing thus far. Classroom management is one of the most important aspects of teaching. I rewarded good behavior by giving students positive comments such as, "*I like the way Mark entered the classroom and sat…completed his/her work quietly etc.*" Or I put a star next to a student's name whenever I saw positive behavior. At the end of the day, I gave those students stickers. I avoided raising my voice. I thanked God and was grateful to my college professor and my classroom supervisor for their trust in me and for guiding me through my God-planned profession.

Upon my return from student teaching, the registrar of the college informed me that I was nominated for *Who's Who Among Students in American Universities and Colleges for 1972-73*. I was in shock and asked my student advisor, "What did I do wrong now?" She told me that this award is a national recognition for students of outstanding merit and accomplishment.

I was overjoyed and we hugged each other. Then she added, "Every college and university around the United States submits a student and you were selected from Augsburg College." I had not enough words to express my gratitude to God and the people He put in my path. Then we completed the application before the deadline. I also ordered a hard copy of the 1972-73 publication of all students in the U.S., the certificate in a plaque form, and a necklace.

It was amazing that I was at the finishing line of my preparation for my chosen profession. I was earning a Bachelor of Arts degree in elementary education, with a minor in German. Because of my background in the German language during my studies in Germany, I was exempt from taking all the required courses except for the advanced courses.

As the day of graduation was approaching, our class was rehearsing with the professor in charge of the ceremony. Students were given invitations for their family and friends. I was amazed at the preparations; it reminded me of a wedding ceremony. I, too, was given invitation cards to attend a luncheon given in honor of the graduating class. I didn't have any immediate family in the United States, but thanks be to God He provided me with an American family, the Reverend and Mrs. Flachman, former missionaries to Ethiopia with whom I had stayed frequently.

The registrar of Augsburg College, with whom I bonded the first time when I came to the college with my college advisor from Saint Olaf College, planned a graduation party for me at her residence. I was overwhelmed by her compassion and the love she had shown me. The list of guests included the American family, a few college professors I was close to, and my advisor from St. Olaf College. It was the most memorable time of my life, thanks to God and the generosity of those who were involved. We were invited to the registrar's residence after the commencement and had an unforgettable celebration.

I was proud to earn my Bachelor of Arts Degree at twenty-nine years old even though my classmates were probably only twenty-one or twenty-two. It is not the age that matters, but the finish line.

CHAPTER TWELVE

GRADUATE SCHOOL: BLESSINGS BEYOND EXPECTATION
1973-1974
(UNIVERSITY OF MINNESOTA)

It was summer of 1973, right after I received my degree in my dream teaching profession. Out of nowhere, I was told that I had been offered a scholarship to attend graduate school at the University of Minnesota. To the best of my knowledge, I don't recall discussing with anyone what my next plan was. In May, God finally helped me reach my teaching profession; He was in charge. I thought that I would probably return to Ethiopia. No one had mentioned this possibility to me.

Now, my room, board, tuition, and supplies were being paid for by the American Lutheran Church Women for me to continue my education career in educational administration. I recall extending my heartfelt gratitude to the organization. I registered for two courses for the summer session. I also continued working at Saint Mary's Hospital a few hours a week as a nurse assistant which I started in my senior year at Augsburg College. My former junior advisor, who also graduated from Augsburg, and my Chinese friend from Saint Olaf College rented the second floor of a family residence for the academic year 1973-74. My graduate advisor's office and most of my major courses were at the Saint Paul campus. I took buses that picked me up right behind where I lived and dropped me off right in front of the building where my advisor's office was. Some of the graduate courses I took were offered at the Minneapolis campus, which was within walking distance. Como Avenue connected both the so-called twin cities, Minneapolis and St. Paul.

The community where we lived was called Dinky Town, known for its large population of university students. I loved this area because of its friendly atmosphere. According to my graduate advisor's recommendation, I registered for two graduate courses during Summer Session I and earned an A in both courses. I registered for two more graduate courses in Summer Session II, and I received an A and B grades. I found that the materials became less challenging or maybe that the courses were within my profession, and I enjoyed them.

During the fall semester, I registered for four courses, earning good grades in each: Introduction to Guidance and Counseling (A), Elementary School Principal (B), Elementary School Curriculum (A), and Social Psychology of Education (A). Most of the students in my Elementary School Principal class were already experienced in school administration and were older than I. I hadn't even started teaching at this point. One day during class discussion one of the students made a remark. "How come you know so much about school administration? How long have you been a principal?"

"I have never been in a classroom except during my junior year field experience and senior year student teaching," I answered.

Again, another student asked me. "How did you know about school administration?"

"I read a lot of materials on the subject and hope to apply those skills when I get the opportunity," I told the discussion group.

Later on, I discovered that many of graduate students in educational administration courses were attending to renew their leadership certificates. They were veteran teachers. Finally, I felt like the youngest student compared to my college classmates.

I met many students in my classes. There were few students in graduate school, unlike the large number of students in undergraduate classes. A female graduate student and I, who shared an advisor, became friends. To my recollection, she was in a few of my classes. Because she was from Israel and I was from Ethiopia, we shared similar customs such as not eating pork. When our advisor realized that we both were away from our families, he invited us to Thanksgiving dinner. We met his whole family and had an amazing dinner. I recalled my friend and I brought the family a bouquet of flowers. We extended our gratitude for their generous hospitality. I'd never experienced such professor-student relationships before.

I continued taking required graduate courses per my advisor's recommendation.

One of the courses was about community school where we applied the skills we acquired in social psychology. The university made arrangements with the nearby junior high school for one of my female classmates and I to observe a variety of classes. For the whole semester, we concentrated on observing the environment in which the students learned best: cooperative versus competitive. We researched to support our findings. The students were the same in their academic performances. With the assistance of the classroom instructor, these students were equally divided into two groups: cooperative and competitive.

We were amazed that our classroom observations were in correlation with research findings. The students in the competitive environment, a heterogeneous group made up of various academic levels, excelled in what they were instructed because the average students looked to those who excelled and wanted to perform the same. On the other hand, the cooperative group, made up of children with similar academic levels didn't make any improvement because the group members had one common goal, to do their best. I reflected on my student teaching experience in the previous year, I noticed that they were a diverse group, which was why they did so well. My colleague and I received an A grade. I heard through other individuals that our project was published in the *Social Psychology Journal*. Later in my profession, when I taught first and second grade classes for over seventeen years, most of the students assigned to my class were a homogeneous group, all advanced students. Although it was easy to teach these students, I had to offer them more challenging activities to stimulate their minds. A few years later, I had a diverse group of students and I grouped the advanced students with those who needed help on a project. I found that peer assistance was beneficial for both types of students.

I continued to take more graduate courses during winter, spring, and the first part of the summer of 1974. I also wrote a research paper on elementary school teachers' training and qualifications in Ethiopia, worth nine graduate credits. I completed the required graduate courses in Educational Administration. I earned my Master of Arts degree on August 24, 1974, just one year and two months after I received my teaching degree. The graduate degree gave me an in-depth understanding I used throughout my teaching career.

I will always be grateful to God for all His blessings and owe my heartfelt gratitude to the American Lutheran Church Women and all those who were responsible for my educational journey.

CHAPTER THIRTEEN

How I Met My Husband

A defining moment in my marital relationship was about to happen. I had never dated any man in my life until 1965 when I became engaged to a pastor and teacher from Ethiopia whom I met while studying in Germany. After three years we had drifted apart, and sadly we decided to end our engagement.

Now, however, my life was about to change. I met a dynamic inspirational speaker at the International Student Fellowship Monthly Christian event during the summer of 1970. A devout Christian lady who sponsored the event, invited a doctoral student named Dominic as a guest speaker whom she had known for several years. She gave an extensive introduction to his background and current status. At that time, he was a doctoral student at the University of Minnesota. He had received his Bachelor of Arts and Master of Arts degrees in Wisconsin. She also stated that he fled his country, Southern Sudan, because many of his countrymen and immediate families were persecuted for their Christian beliefs by the northern Sudanese.

Dominic had converted to Christianity long before he came to America. Then she said, "Please welcome our special guest speaker, Dominic Mohamed!" Everyone welcomed him with great enthusiasm and applause.

When he stood up to speak, I was taken by surprise that he spoke so eloquently and with such compassion for his people in Southern Sudan. He mentioned that two hundred of his family members were killed during a wedding celebration. I could see the emotion on the faces of the event attendees, including me. Many were students and the rest of the attendees were American families who came to hear him speak. After the event, refreshments were served and during that time the host introduced him to us individually. When I introduced myself to him, I saw the excitement in his eyes. For the next couple of months, we saw each other at the monthly Christian event.

While working towards my Master's degree in Minnesota after leaving Ethiopia, I tried to secure a scholarship for my fiancé to schools in the U.S. I mailed several applications to colleges and universities. None of the responses I received were promising. When I was still in my country, people recommended that we get engaged because then the American people would be more sympathetic to us. I found out that wasn't the truth. I continued wearing the engagement ring, and people often asked me if I was married. A few months later, I shared with my fiancé that my efforts to bring him to America weren't successful. No colleges had sent him an acceptance letter. That wasn't the only news I shared with him. I also told him that

I met a very special man from Sudan. At first, he was upset with me, and rightfully so. Later on, he apologized for being so upset and appreciated my honesty in telling him about meeting another man.

Meanwhile, Dominic and I became good friends over a period of time. Neither of us talked about marriage. He had responsibilities representing his country in the U.S. and Canada. There was a good chance that he would be summoned by his government for a special post. One time I got to accompany both concerned community leaders and Dominic to the United Nations in New York to let the world know how his countrymen were being oppressed and murdered. It was a successful rally as he was a dynamic speaker.

In 1973 when my brother Obosha traveled to Pasadena, California, for training, he stopped in Minneapolis to visit me along the way. By that time my friendship with Dominic had grown. I didn't know for sure, but I think the Lutheran Church let Dominic live in the house adjacent to the church. It had upstairs and downstairs bedrooms, a kitchen, dining and living room. When I told him about my brother's upcoming visit, he offered him a place to stay at his house. I was grateful that the two would be able to get acquainted. I couldn't host him because the place where my former college mates and I were renting was close to where my brother was going to stay, but was only for women. I cooked dinner for the three of us at Dominic's place. My brother never questioned me about what had happened with my previous engagement, which was a relief.

He was open-minded to different countries and cultures and both had a great time together. I thank God that my brother was able to meet my future husband and share this news with our relatives back home.

When I received my Bachelor of Arts degree from Augsburg College in Minneapolis, Minnesota, in 1973, Dominic earned his doctoral degree, a Doctor of Philosophy (PhD) in Educational Policy from the University of Minnesota. Immediately after receiving his degree, he was recruited, because of his background and extraordinary qualifications, to teach at the newly established Florida International University, in Miami, Florida. The university was in its third year and growing quickly. He was selected from among thirty candidates across the country.

I earned my Master of Arts degree in Educational Administration in 1974, a year after I received my Bachelor of Arts degree. My goal was to go back to Ethiopia to share and give back all that I had learned. Unfortunately, there was a change of government and political unrest in my country. As a result, the people I worked with at the church in 1968-69 had left the country. I was in a great dilemma. To remain in the United States of America I needed to renew my visa status. My friend Dominic, who was in Miami in his second year of teaching at Florida International University and was familiar with the educational system in Miami-Dade County Public Schools, suggested that I move to Miami and stay with mutual friends of ours while working on a student visa to attend Vocational Cosmetology at Miami-Dade Public Schools. At Florida International University, he taught adult students from various professions and industries, teaching methodologies and practices. He thought that Vocational Cosmetology would be beneficial for me. "God's hands are still leading me, I just trust in Him," I was confident.

With the help of the foreign students' office at Miami-Dade Public School, I secured a student visa and my passport was renewed for another year. To my amazement, the instructors in the cosmetology department were Dominic's students at the university.

Some of the students questioned me, "What are you doing here if you already have a degree in teaching?"

"Maybe I can add to my teaching degree to teach adults," I replied.

Another classmate asked, "What difference does it make if you already have a teaching certificate?" The majority of these students were taking vocational cosmetology as an alternative to attending college.

"My certificate qualifies me only to teach elementary school children," I informed them.

I stayed with a Peruvian family with a son who was eight years old. They provided me room, board, and a car to drop off the son at his school. Then, I drove to the school board building administration where the vocational education department was located. I took several classes: from learning the chemistry of our hair, and face, and how to take care of them to how to style hair and manicure. Before we worked on customers, the instructors modeled how to work on dummies with fake hair. Then we practiced on each other. Finally, we worked on customers under the supervision of the instructors. After a year of training, we took state testing both on theory and practical aspects to earn the State of Florida Occupational License Certificate in 1975. Only those who passed in both areas received the State of Florida Certificate. I renewed my certificate annually to keep it active for several years by attending professional development seminars. However, I benefited from knowing how to take care of my own hair and of my family members. I had never put my training into practice.

At this point my student visa expired and Dominic and I had to make decision about getting married. He had over a month-long vacation from the university during their summer break. Over the years, we both had made many friends, and our hearts and close friends were still in Minneapolis. We decided to have our wedding where our love journey started. Our friends in Minneapolis organized everything so that our wedding took place within Florida International University's summer vacation. One of our friends sewed matching African shirts (dashikis) for all men in the wedding party, matching African dresses for the women, and I made my own African design beautiful wedding dress. We also made outfits for the pastor and his wife who had been missionaries to Ethiopia.

They arranged for our wedding service and reception at their church on August 15, 1975. It was a memorable wedding. Five years after we had met our wedding became a reality. *No engagement this time.* There were about seven nationalities in attendance because we had met at the International Student Fellowship Christian event and we knew many students from across the world. God had never forsaken me even when I had made mistakes in the past and I thanked God for making our wedding day a reality. We also extended our heartfelt gratitude to all our Minnesotan friends for taking such heartwarming roles in our wedding.

Yes! God took part in guiding me to get it right this time. Every misfortune that occurred in my life's journey had a purpose in God's plan. I'm grateful for this.

CHAPTER FOURTEEN

EXPERIENCES AND SURPRISES IN MIAMI

After our wedding day, we spent a week visiting with friends in Minnesota. A couple, who had known Dominic for several years before he and I met, often held parties at their residence. They also met each other at the International Student Fellowship.

I remember our mutual friends loaned us their camper to save us money on hotels for a honeymoon trip. We stopped at various rest places or national parks and barbecued or heated our food. We drove straight from Minneapolis through the East Coast states to Miami, Florida. This allowed us to transport all of our belongings and gifts. Many of our friends gave us household items for our apartment as wedding gifts. I noticed there were no gift cards. At the time, I had no idea about a bridal gift registry. Even if we had known this custom, it was impolite in our culture to suggest what gifts guests might give the bride and the groom.

After a few days of driving and sightseeing, we arrived in Miami. We settled in my husband's one-bedroom apartment while we looked for a two-bedroom apartment close to Florida International University, which was then in its fourth year. Unlike Minneapolis, Minnesota, we had some roadblocks when we looked for apartments. After we identified the location of an apartment and its availability, we made an appointment to meet the apartment manager. When we arrived within minutes, the manager notified us that it was already rented. In those days, Miami was primarily for the rich and retirees. Neither were we. I remembered my husband commenting under his breath, "They're rednecks." For a long period, I looked for red marks on people's necks, especially on older men. He had studied in the United States for many years and was familiar with local terminology and slang.

As we were driving along a busy highway, I noticed a strange advertisement in a small shop. "Body Shop!" By that time my heart was pounding. I turned to my husband Dominic and asked, "Do people in this country sell human body parts?" He started chuckling.

Dominic was still laughing when I asked him, "Why are you giggling?"

"It's car parts." He taught auto mechanic teachers and was familiar with the term.

When we drove into another neighborhood, every other street ended with a "Dr." I decided not to ask my husband again. I knew that "Dr." meant medical doctor in my country.

I thought to myself that this country has one doctor for every other block, while in my country there was one doctor for every seventy thousand people. The same was true in my husband's country. Eventually, I discovered on my own that "Dr." stood for "drive," another name for street.

After a few days of searching, we found our dream apartment on the second floor of a newly built apartment complex. It had a master bedroom, a guest room, a beautiful kitchen with a counter, and a living room. The manager was so pleased when he found out that we're from Africa and my husband was a professor at the nearby university. We had a great rapport with the manager. He was helpful to us the whole time we lived there until we moved.

My husband made sure to utilize my training as a teacher. He had connections with the Miami-Dade County Public School (M-DCPS). He trained school administrators on educational policy. When one of the school administrators suggested that I take a part-time position as an instructor to high school dropouts, which was federally funded, I learned it was not so simple. I had only a temporary certificate to teach in the State of Florida because I was foreign-born. I was unaware that this regulation existed in the state of Minnesota. I was perplexed that Florida's Department of Education required me to declare my intention to become a United States citizen. After that, I was provided a green card and was able to teach. I was grateful for this opportunity. However, since I didn't hold a State of Florida Teaching Certificate, I was a teacher assistant with a

Master of Arts Degree in Educational Administration for the rest of the year. In April of 1976, I took maternity leave because I was expecting our first child.

My husband's friends at the university planned a baby shower for us. When he saw a display of a stork as a center-piece, "What does a stork, an ugly bird, have to do with my unborn child?" he questioned. His colleagues laughed uncontrollably. One of the faculty members explained to him about the American tradition.

In those days an ultrasound to find out an unborn child's gender was not a common practice. Besides, it was against our culture to determine God's gift before birth. Even a baby shower was new to us. We received beautiful supplies for our unborn child.

As a bonus, there were a few experienced moms and dads to give us advice. One of the faculty members told my husband and me, "Get your suitcase ready two weeks before the due date."

"Where would my wife go with my unborn child?" Dominic naively asked. "When she begins having contractions close to each other, you drive her to the delivery room," confirmed the male faculty member.

The doctor estimated the birthdate of our first child to be July 4, 1976, which was a bicentennial year for the U.S. I was excited when I heard that every child who was born on this date would receive a two-hundred-dollars saving bond. We waited anxiously. I vividly remember when my unborn baby kicked me constantly during choir practice in my sixth month of pregnancy. He must have loved the melody of "Hallelujah Chorus." To our surprise, the child couldn't wait until July 4. Instead our firstborn son arrived on June 29 at about 12:30 p.m. after twenty-eight hours of labor. He weighed 8 pounds and 11 ounces and was 21 inches long. I refused to take any kind of medication because of the possible side effects to the unborn baby. I breastfed until I was pregnant with my next baby.

Now that we knew that our firstborn was a son, we debated whether his name should be Ethiopian or Dinka (the Southern Sudanese tribe of my husband's origin). We couldn't agree. Therefore, he had two nationalities names: Eba (Blessed-Ethiopian) and Dut (Gift-Dinka). Therefore, we combined the two names and our firstborn son was named Ebadut (blessed gift). Culturally men gave names. However, we were educated parents, and therefore, I had my fair share of participation.

While in the hospital I had a private room for up to five days because I had no help at home at all. With the help of God and friends from church I managed to take care of the baby and myself. My husband felt awkward in helping me with the baby as many African men do. I thanked God for the university insurance for providing such excellent medical coverage.

When our son was about three months old, the manager of the apartment complex kindly informed us that children and pets were not allowed. He allowed us to stay thus far because we were young parents and he wanted to help. He told us that we could stay until we found another place. One of my husband's colleagues was a realtor and started to search for us in a more affluent neighborhood to raise our child. We, too, did our homework by asking friends for neighborhood suggestions. One Sunday a member of the church and I were babysitting during church service.

"Where do you live?" she asked me.

"We're living in a new beautiful apartment by the university where my husband works. But, now, the manager has informed us, that 'no kids, no pets,' are allowed."

"My neighbor just moved to another state, and their house is for sale. It is a corner house. They haven't put up a 'for sale' sign yet," she told me. She stressed to come and see it that day. I promised that I would share this idea with my husband when he got out of church. She also got a chance to talk with my husband about the house. He told her that he would make an appointment with a realtor that afternoon and we would let him know. I got the address from my church member. I was pleading with God that He would guide the realtor and us to a safe neighborhood in which we can raise our children.

When we met with the realtor, we gave the address where our church member recommended so that he could show us that location, too. The realtor was amazed that it was the same house my friend told me about that he had planned to show us. We were stunned! God had planned it long ago. To make sure that this was the best house and location, my husband invited his colleague to come and inspect it. He was amazed, too. It was a five-minute drive to the university. There are no houses in front of our house. It was an undeveloped parcel planned for a community park. My husband had been thinking for a while about having a family and a house. He had saved money to make a down payment on the house. Everything went well as planned and we were ready to move in on October 3, 1976. Through our church friend, half of the neighbors already knew about us.

It was a community of about five thousand residents, and they were our age. Most of the wives were stay-at-home moms, planning to stay home to raise their children until the kids entered school. Five of the housewives on the same block were teachers and were on maternity leave like me. My husband and I were surprised to find out that there was an elementary school built a year before we moved in behind what seemed to look like a jungle. It has not been developed yet.

My church friend, who was my neighbor, invited all the ladies in the neighborhood to meet another neighbor on the other side of her and I for coffee while the men were at work. There were about ten mothers at the welcome coffee. I was amazed to find out that most of the mothers were professionals and teachers who were on maternity leave. The mothers brought their kids. My son was the youngest, only three months old. The mothers and the kids had a great time. I thank God for bringing my church friend and me together and for her hospitality. It reminded me of the comradery in the villages where I grew up. There were probably no other African families that we knew when we moved to the Kendale Lakes community. However, several years later I found out that two other African families lived in the community.

It was our first time to own a house. Because it was a corner lot, we had plenty of grass to cut. My church friend and neighbor showed my husband how to take care of our yard: to cut the grass, edge, and trim the shrubs. It had a beautiful landscape. After a little practice, my husband became a professional in taking care of our yard.

One day, a middle-aged white male was driving by and stopped by when he saw my husband taking care of our yard.

"You're doing such an excellent job with the yard. How much do you charge for a lot like this?" the man asked.

My husband stopped the lawnmower. "Sir, I'll charge you by the hour and it would be $100.00 an hour," my husband replied.

The man could not believe his ears and asked again. "Could you repeat it?"

My husband replied, "Yes, it's $100.00 an hour because I earned a doctorate for the job." Then the man drove away now more bewildered than ever. The man thought that my husband was a yard man.

After two months, we knew at least twenty neighbors or more. In the afternoon, before the husbands came home from work, moms were strolling around the blocks with their kids, getting acquainted with more neighbors.

Three of us teachers who enjoyed cooking organized progressive dinners for the holidays for about twenty-five families with the consent of all the neighborhood moms. It included three parts: appetizer, main dish, and dessert. It was agreed that my

Italian neighbor would prepare the appetizers; I was responsible for the main dish. And my neighbor who moved in at the same time as I did, would be in charge of dessert. She was a home economics teacher. All three homes were on the same block. First, we walked to the house that hosted appetizers and took a little rest, and then we all walked to our house around the corner to experience a spicy Ethiopian dish and sour flatbread. I made some sweet and sour chicken, too. They loved it. They probably had never eaten at an African family's home. The last course, a delicious dessert, was one house away from us. This tradition went on for several years. What an amazing experience and fellowship. The husbands appreciated the idea, too.

We also started a tradition for when one of the neighbors moved away. We organized a farewell party. We prepared a photo album of all the neighbors and presented it to the family who was moving at the going away party. As I am writing this story, many of the original residents have retired and moved away.

My church in Kendall also started progressive dinners at church member's homes. I hosted the main dish part two times. Because many of the members lived far apart, the church rented a school bus to accommodate everyone. It was always a joyous event.

In December of 1976 on Christmas Sunday, we asked the dynamic pastor I met on Easter weekend of 1975, to baptize our first son. The pastor stated that he normally didn't baptize, however, he would gladly do it for us. We asked the friendly family who embraced me and invited me to an Easter dinner to be our son's godparents. They accepted with enthusiasm.

I love to bake and make finger foods. We invited all church families and neighbors to this most memorable day for us. From that date onward my son's godparents became like my American parents and my three kids' grandparents because we didn't have family members in U.S. then. We trained our children to call older people grandma and grandpa, especially our American family. Every holiday we took turns hosting dinner for the whole family.

One day when my son was four years old, he asked, "Why do we call them grandpa and grandma?" "They're white and we're Black," my son challenged. (The godparents are of Scandinavian descent.)

"They're mom's and dad's American parents, and you call them grandpa and grandma," my husband stressed. My husband didn't know where his parents were during the terrible civil war. I couldn't afford bringing my mom and brothers to U.S.A. due to its financial burden.

When our son was one year old, the administrator where I worked as an assistant teacher asked my husband if I could teach remedial language arts and mathematics classes to high school dropouts, to help them to acquire skills they needed to be employable. Their ages ranged between eighteen and thirty-five. There were about twelve to fifteen students and the classes were based on individualized instruction. Although I only taught them for three hours every morning, it was the most rewarding and defining moment of my teaching profession. These students improved three to four grade levels in both subjects, language arts and mathematics. The best part of this federally funded program was that these students were paid for attending school. I stressed to them that they should seize this opportunity to advance their career and never miss a day.

One morning in the middle of February, when I came to my classroom, there were no students present. After waiting for half an hour, I contacted the counselor and the administrator's office stating that my students were all absent. Then the counselor asked me to come down to the principal's office.

"Why am I being called to the office?" I questioned.

"Let's call some of the older students," the counselor suggested. The administration and the counselor already knew why students didn't show up. I was called to the principal's office so that they could set up the classroom room for a special surprise.

Half an hour later, the female counselor walked me to my classroom and opened the door. Wow! I was stunned and dumbfounded. The students had organized a baby shower for my second child. I've never seen such extravagant decorations and food. I was overwhelmed with emotions and gratitude. They even purchased an African dress for me to wear. I was embarrassed and felt badly that I had been strict with them. To show my gratitude, I prepared Ethiopian food and brought them for lunch in appreciation of their generosity. The students, the staff, and the administration enjoyed this. This was the most memorable and rewarding experience of my early teaching profession.

I had two obstetricians who were partners: one was conservative and the other was liberal. The latter one delivered my first son. He even asked a nurse who attended my church to take pictures during delivery.

It seemed that childbirth became easier with each child. The total time of my labor for my second child was only five hours. As with the first child, I didn't want to know whether our unborn child was a boy or a girl. As with my first time, I refused to take any kind of pain medication. My first priority was the safety of our unborn child. But unlike the liberal and nice doctor who delivered our first son, his conservative partner refused to let us take pictures. He stated that taking pictures of childbirth wasn't for public consumption. We were disappointed, but there was nothing we could do. Our second son was born on April 9, 1978, at 1:20 pm. He weighed 8 pounds and 6 ounces and was also 21 inches long. It seemed that was a standard length. My husband and I were excited to have two boys. In our culture, it was believed that boys took care of their parents when they grew up. I was disappointed because I was not part of naming my second son. My husband had already a name in his mind that would remind him of the struggle and war in his country of Southern Sudan. Therefore, he named him "Tac," which meant a son born during war.

I was fortunate that I still had basic clothing from my oldest son who was twenty-one months at the time my second son was born. Still, my neighbors organized a baby shower after he was born at one of the neighbor's houses. Now my second son has his new clothes. Also, my friends from church gave me even more clothes for him. The same pastor baptized our second son during the summer of 1978 and we requested another dear family to be his godparents. We had a reception at our home and invited church families, friends, and neighbors.

I thank God always for providing us with such caring neighbors and church families. Most of the moms stayed home to raise their children, and therefore, I had constant moral support every step of the way. This reminded me of the customs in my village. Sometimes we had coffee together to uplift each other. Most of the mothers didn't have their families with them either.

CHAPTER FIFTEEN

MOTHERHOOD AND THE EVOLUTION OF COMMUNITY INVOLVEMENT

Motherhood is a full-time job. Growing up, I helped my sister-in-law with watching my nieces and nephews. But I did not have full responsibility. Every member of the village supported the well-being of children, ensuring every child grew up to be a responsible community member.

Like the African proverb, "*It takes the whole village to raise a child*," I was surprised to see this was taking place in America, too. In my neighborhood, Kendale Lakes, the residents cared and informed each other about the kids' behavior. I thank God for the opportunity to live in this neighborhood. Most of us knew each other as well as where we each lived. The amazing part of this neighborhood friendship is that we trusted each other to the point that we left our house keys with each other when we went out of town.

I have never forgotten the day the neighbors took care of our yard: cutting grass, edging, and trimming the bushes. At this time our oldest son was hospitalized for several weeks, and our second son was just a few months old. One morning, I heard a lawn mower, an edger, and more. When I looked through the window, the neighbors brought their tools to take care of our yard in my husband's absence. I was overwhelmed with emotions when I saw husbands and wives working together on our yard. I saw a neighbor's wife who had never worked on her own yard, sweeping our sidewalks. I came out to thank them with tears rolling down my cheeks. I had never seen such caring and compassionate neighbors. They all came from diverse professions and religious beliefs. God provided all our needs when we least expected it.

I started a family late in life. However, I am grateful for the opportunities I received before starting a family. My husband and I agreed to have at least three children. Before I came to the United States, I wished to have a dozen. At the time, I didn't understand the financial obligation associated with raising children and educating them in an industrialized country. In both my husband's and my country, having many children is a blessing. In the villages, children helped their parents on the farm. Both of my two brothers had nine children each. Thankfully, nowadays, children start school at an earlier age. I am grateful they raised me first and then their own children. Their children were educated both in our country and abroad.

I had not returned to teach between my two pregnancies since they were only twenty-one months apart. Now I was expecting my third child, and because of my age, the conservative obstetrician insisted that I go through a procedure to determine if my unborn child would be healthy or not. However, his partner disagreed with him by saying that the procedure in itself might cause serious issues. My husband and I were one hundred percent confident that we would accept God's gift, whatever the outcome might be. Therefore, we declined the procedure. I personally had faith in God and I was willing to take the risk to receive His gift. I have never forgotten what my respectable obstetrician told me. "Pray that I will be on call when your child is being delivered." I was touched by his comments. We did not want to know whether our unborn child would be a boy or a girl. We already had two boys, but if it were God's will, he could bless us with a girl.

I was relieved that, indeed, my favorite doctor was on call when my third child was born. Wow!

Having a third child was as easy as having one, two, three. As soon as I felt the labor pain, my husband drove me to the hospital, directly to the labor room. The same nurse who delivered our two boys was still there and she exclaimed, "The third time!" Immediately she hooked me to the heart monitor. "Think pink, think pink!" the nurse chanted. I had no idea what they were referring to. I had never heard of that terminology. Within less than an hour after arriving at the delivery room, I gave birth to a beautiful baby girl on April 2, 1980, at 12:30 pm, delivered by a wonderful doctor. She was 8 pounds and also 21 inches long. Then I realized what they meant by "*Think pink.*" My husband was quick to name our daughter,

"Adhar" in Dinka, which means "continuity." He overheard visitors saying how beautiful our daughter was and he watched over her as long as I was in the hospital.

I was grateful and thanked God that our neighbors and our American parents took care of our boys while I was at the hospital. I spent five days at the hospital and my husband went home to check on the boys and spend the night with them and bring them food. They were glad to see him. As soon as I arrived home, I made sure that they held their baby sister. I saw the smiles on their faces as they put their tiny hands around her.

While I was living in Ethiopia, I watched my sister-in-law breastfeed her children, and I enjoyed watching her. In the third world country, breastfeeding was the only option. There was no such thing as formula. However, when I shared with my relatives in Ethiopia, they laughed and told me that things have changed since I was young there. I marveled at their reaction. Unfortunately, with progress there is always displeasure with the most admirable custom. I read that breast milk is nutritious. As for me, it was the best choice I made and most natural way to feed my baby. My pediatrician always commented. "Breastfeeding is natural in your country, therefore, you don't need my advice. You could feed twins if you needed to, and you know how to do it best." All my three children slept through the night after I breastfed them. My oldest son did not taste any baby food such as applesauce until he was nine months old. He was so big and healthy just from the breast milk. I was very selective about what I ate so that my babies received the healthiest milk possible.

Growing up, children slept with their parents for protection and due to lack of space. In our case we had a split house plan: the master bedroom was on one side and the other two bedrooms were on the other side of the house. However, my husband and I decided to build an additional master bedroom on the side with the two bedrooms, so that we all would be on the same side of our house. We even made a door from our master bedroom to one of the children's bedroom where our daughter slept, once she was a few years old. The boys shared the other bedroom.

Every night, before bedtime, I read to my children, which I had missed growing up. My parents were illiterate and no one in our family understood the value of reading for enjoyment except to gain knowledge about specific subjects. In addition, I prayed with the three children together as my eldest brother had modeled for us when I was growing up. My brother had been a model of my faith throughout my life, until he passed to heaven at the age of 86 in 2008. I also taught my children at early ages to pray for others. Now, I am praying with my granddaughter before bedtime.

In 1981, in the evening, the president of our homeowner's association invited all the residents who lived within a mile radius to organize a neighborhood crime watch. The neighborhood crime watch coordinator explained the different roles we needed to fill to make a successful neighborhood crime watch. I remembered distinctively the role of block captain: he/she needed to 1) have the names and phone numbers of each resident (cell phones didn't exist), 2) know the addresses of each resident within the designated boundary, and 3) inform residents when he/she received news of any criminal incidents in the neighborhood through a phone chain, until everyone was alerted. There was more information but these were the duties what I remembered. An alert signal was a phone call followed by turning on lights.

The neighbors were debating who would be the best candidate for neighborhood block captain. Suddenly, my husband whispered under his breath, "Aster would be great." I could not believe my ears. Everyone agreed to his suggestions. Next, I started collecting $2.00 from each resident to purchase and post crime watch signs at every major corner of the neighborhood. Likewise, we received crime watch stickers to be placed on our windows to deter possible thieves. I called all residents within the neighborhood crime watch boundary to determine the number of window stickers needed. I had also a co-captain to assist me on the other side of the neighborhood. Once we collected all needed items, the president of our association called the meeting to distribute the window stickers. I was amazed how cooperative the neighbors were. Soon county officials also posted crime watch signs.

Now that my oldest son was four years old, my husband and I decided to enroll him in our church preschool for half a day. This would give him a head start before entering kindergarten when he turned five. In the beginning, he did not want to go to preschool because he did not want to leave his mom and his siblings behind. With him at school, I would be able to spend time with our two younger children who were almost two years apart. After more than a week, he assimilated to the school environment and even made a few new friends.

Every afternoon, moms walked around the block with their children. There was so much camaraderie between the mothers. We discussed how we could beautify the empty parcel across from our neighborhood homes, and how to get involved when the neighborhood park was in the process of being built. My involvement in this neighborhood just kept growing.

Meanwhile our second son soon turned four years old and was eager to attend the church preschool his brother had attended the previous year. Now his older brother was ready for kindergarten. We were grateful that the community public elementary school was located on the other side of the vacant parcel. It was built in 1975, a year before we moved to our neighborhood. We had not noticed that the school was within walking distance until now.

Soon we had a steady routine. Students in kindergarten and first grade were dismissed at 2 pm. This was convenient because I was able to pick up my second son from church preschool, which was about five miles away. Then, I gave him lunch and breastfed my daughter before I picked up my oldest son from kindergarten. Soon, my daughter felt she was left behind and wanted to attend preschool like her brothers. At the age of three, she was enrolled in the church preschool. At that time, I had a son in kindergarten and two in preschool. It was a busy time.

In the meantime, it became evident that the surrounding residents needed to become more involved with the development of the vacant parcel in front of the surrounding homes. Every homeowner was a member of the association. However, there was a need to elect a board of directors. The homeowners' association elected me as one of the board members. The residents were convinced that I would do a good job based on my experience as block captain. By nature, I was a shy person, but with my husband's encouragement and support, I was able to participate in the evening board meetings once a month. I prepared dinner and I gave the children their baths, I read to them, and I held evening prayer, and then I put them to bed before I left for the meeting that was down the street from our house.

One of the concerns by county officials and the residents who lived across from the park was where the main entrance to the park would be put. My husband and I preferred not to have the entry in front of our house. So did everyone else who lived in the corner houses adjacent to the park. We didn't have major streets close to our house. After weighing the pros and cons of each entrance, it was agreed that the entry to the park would be in front of our house. This would not conflict with the traffic that enters the school compound. The distance around the park (perimeter) was about a mile.

When the park was completed, with input from the residents, it was amazing. It had a children's playground with a sandbox, monkey bars, swings, and many more appropriate play structures for school age children. Our neighborhood children enjoyed it tremendously. There were benches along-side the playground for parents to sit and watch their children. The landscape of the park was attractive with fabricated hills and plenty of trees native to Miami. In addition, the county paved walkways with exercise stations at different locations around the park. In the center of the park, tennis, racquetball, and basketball courts were built. Plenty of parking spaces were included. Although the park was designated as a neighborhood park, its beauty attracted other outside neighborhood residents.

I have never forgotten one afternoon when I saw young people from the surrounding neighborhood racing their cars down the hill in front of our house. I was by myself with the kids, but there were many of the moms across from the park. My husband was at the university.

"Cars are racing down the hill across from our house," I told my husband on the phone. I was petrified.

"Call the police immediately!" he stressed. I gathered my children with me and went to the back room, away from the front of the house and called 911.

"I'm alone with three kids and soon the cars will run into our house," I expressed to them. Immediately several police cars appeared. Those who were racing their cars drove different directions and terrorized the whole neighborhood. I was confident the police officers pursued them.

The car-racing incident led me to another neighborhood project. There was nothing which prevented cars from entering the park from any direction. After discussing with the residents, it was essential to build a fence around the park. This required county approval and residents' signatures from the surrounding occupants. With the assistance of some volunteers, I collected over 800 signatures and submitted them to the county and a fence was built.

I was notified by the president of our association that barbecue grills would be installed in the neighborhood park. The barbecue grills could be hazardous to the children. Unfortunately, the visitors might leave a fire which would endanger the children as they walked to and from school. The major local newspaper interviewed me and I expressed the concerns of the residents as it related to the safety of the children walking to and from school. This information was published, and the residents' wishes were honored and permanent barbecue grills were denied.

After a few years, we needed lights along the walking trail for safety. With the help of another resident, we collected signatures emphasizing why lights along the walking trails were essential. Some residents who lived across the park disagreed. However, the majority ruled. Soon lights were installed. They were beautiful and served the community as a deterrent. I thank God and am grateful to be part of the decision-making for my neighborhood. I'd never imagined that I could contribute in such a way because I am shy by nature.

My husband was always proud of my involvement and accomplishments. He volunteered to me for the very first time and since then, it has been a domino effect. Somehow, the rumor traveled that I could organize an activity in the community. In

1983, the president of the school's PTA (Parent and Teachers Association, Inc. which is an independent parents' and teachers' organization to this day) asked me to be on their board. "The board wants you to be in charge of the end of the year teachers' luncheon," she said. "You're a good organizer and we'll help you," she added.

What had I gotten myself into? I thought. With board members' assistance, I managed organizing the teachers' luncheons for a couple of years. For our monthly board meeting, the officers and chairpersons took turns making refreshments. One month I tried to bake sour cream coffee cake with walnuts. Like always, I enjoy experimenting with different ingredients. I substituted walnuts with chocolate chips. That coffee cake has become everyone's all-time favorite everywhere to this date.

In the same year, my son's kindergarten teacher and I implemented the first African American Soul Food Luncheon at our school and I was a co-chair (1983-1998). In Ethiopia, we ate completely different food than people eat in the U.S., and I enjoyed cooking for this luncheon, too. However, I had to confess, I had no idea about soul food. My son's teacher is from the U.S. and she is an expert in this type of food. Both of us created a menu that included main dishes, side dishes, desserts, soft drinks, and paper goods and requested teachers to sign up for whatever they would like to bring. We set up in the teachers' lunchroom. The staff ate at their designated lunch break. The food was delicious. We had plenty of food, enough for everyone, and even some leftovers to take home. I was grateful to all the teachers who supported this initiative. I learned about other cultures by getting involved.

The Kendale Lakes community is part of a larger community called the Kendall Federation of Homeowner Associations, Inc. (KFHA). Our association was entitled to four delegates to the federation based on our population of five thousand residents. In 1983, I was one of the four delegates selected to the Kendall Federation of Homeowner Associations Inc. I am still on the board today and currently serve as vice president of membership. Over the years, I have served as internal vice president, member of transportation, education (school boundaries and Operation Turnaround) and police and fire committee, zoning committee, and member of Political Action Committee where we interview political candidates running for public office. History was not my favorite subject. However, the hands-on participation gave me great awareness into politics when choosing the right candidate for a political office.

In those days, the six graders who were qualified served as safety patrol in the school vicinity as well as at an intersection very close to the elementary school. The four-way intersection became busy and dangerous for these young students. Being on a school's PTA board, member of the Homeowner Association board, and a delegate to the Kendall Federation of Homeowner Associations, Inc., gave me influence to request the county commissioner install a traffic light at the intersection where safety patrols stood. Others and I attended county commissioners' meeting and submitted an official letter requesting the installation of a traffic light. Then they sent engineers to conduct a feasibility study. Within a few weeks, I received a letter from our district commissioner confirming that the traffic light would be installed. It was also advertised through a local newsletter to alert the community about the new installation. I am grateful that the commissioners honored our request instead of putting the lives of our safety patrols in jeopardy.

Soon my two boys were enrolled in elementary school, and my daughter continued to attend our church preschool. I carpooled with two other moms whose kids were the same age as my daughter.

Once or twice a week, I volunteered in my sons' classes with whatever the teachers needed. In addition, I was a room mother serving as a liaison between my sons' teachers and parents. One time I demonstrated how to make pizza from scratch using measurement tools and following directions. The children learned how to make pizza that we baked in the school kitchen and ate it. Although making bread was a long process, I also demonstrated the process of making challah (Jewish bread). From the same dough, the students made croissants and ate them, as well. What a great way of learning than eating their own project. Whenever I demonstrated these projects, my son's teacher invited her colleagues of the same grade level to attend. I'm still making challah bread frequently from scratch for my family, and sharing it with friends, too.

When my daughter started attending the church preschool, the board asked me to serve as their secretary. I was honored and delighted to serve on my children's preschool board. I served on South Miami Lutheran Church Preschool board as secretary from 1982 to 1984.

After we moved to Kendale Lakes in 1976, the community grew, and as a result, an Evangelical Lutheran church was built about a mile from my house. My husband and I decided to transfer from South Miami Lutheran Church (where I met my American family in 1975) to Lord of Life Lutheran Church in 1984 where I am still a member. The community grew and the congregation included many young families with children. Many of the children were the same age as ours. The best part was that there were Sunday school classes for every age group, including an adult class.

There is nothing more exciting and humbling than being asked to serve in a leadership role in the house of worship. In 1985, the church council appointed me to serve on the church council overseeing their Christian education. I was in charge of Sunday and Vacation Bible School (1985-1988) and I was a member of the preschool board at its inception. As the demographics of the community changed, there was a need to launch a Christian-based daycare center as an outreach to the neighboring community. Over the past thirty years, I have been honored to serve as member at large, vice president, and president of Lord of Life Lutheran Preschool several terms. The congregation also elected me to the church council as vice president (2004-2005) and president (2005-2006). It has given me great joy and is a humbling experience to serve God by being a reader and communion assist once a month from 1985 to the present and Liturgy Assistant from 2000 to the present. I am grateful to the members who supported me and give God the glory for His everlasting blessings.

I relished being a full-time mom during the day. During the evening, the Miami-Dade County Public Schools (M-DCPS) offered adult education programs. After discussing this with my husband and making sure which evening he would be at home, I registered for a class in floral design at a nearby high school adult education program in 1984. Once a week I learned how to work with fresh and silk flowers, from everyday arrangements to wedding arrangements. I donated my service to my church by making flower arrangements for our sanctuary. During that same year, I began holding flower arrangement shows for friends and neighbors at my house to showcase my seasonal and everyday arrangements. I designed several Christmas arrangements, as well. I was constantly creating new designs. I created my own photo album of my work so that people could order arrangements.

I was humbled to be asked to make all of the fresh flower arrangements for one of the school parent's family member's wedding, including the bridal bouquets, boutonnieres, and church and wedding reception area decorations. My spare bedroom, bathroom, and refrigerator were full of fresh flowers. I tremendously enjoyed making these arrangements and the wedding host loved them, too. There were challenges to working on such a large project. Fresh flowers must be refrigerated and kept fresh. Luckily, I had a spare bedroom and bathroom in which to store them. Following the wedding, the same parent asked me to make silk flower arrangements for her boss's office, only giving me a description of the office and its color scheme. I enjoyed using colors I never dreamt of mixing together. Silk flowers were easier to work with as they did not require any maintenance like fresh flowers do. I became quite knowledgeable about all types of flowers and their names.

When my second son was in first grade, his first grade teacher's family asked me to design silk flower arrangements for the bride and bridal party for their child's wedding. It was less challenging than my first wedding, as these arrangements did not require refrigeration. It turned out to be gorgeous. The bride's family loved the arrangements.

At that time, I also held a certificate in advanced cake decorating. For my son's teacher wedding day, the bride's family requested that I make a birthday cake for the bride's uncle in the shape of an airplane, because he was a pilot. No matter how perplexing the project might be, I accepted the task. I made the cake that resembled a jumbo jet with two layers and wings. I was amazed how beautifully it came out. I transported it very carefully to the wedding reception, which was quite a distance. The bride's and the groom's families were as surprised as I was. My greatest joy was making birthday cakes (any character) and cupcakes for my children. I loved to hear my children proudly tell their friends, "My mom made it!"

I continued my hobby as a self-employed floral designer for three years. I invited friends and neighbors over for coffee to place orders for special occasions. The most popular were Christmas arrangements, followed by Valentine's Day and Easter. I also made molded chocolate roses, hearts, and Easter bunnies. Sometimes customers mistook chocolate flowers for actual flowers.

During that same time, I stayed home taking care of my children, and I enjoyed listening to their every word. For example, my husband told my sons to stay away while he was painting a room because of their allergies.

Then one son refuted by saying, "Paint it black!"

"Son, all paints smell the same," my husband responded.

"How can I be allergic to myself?" he protested.

These kinds of intriguing statements from my children prompted me to investigate the gifted education program at Florida International University in 1984. I wanted to understand my own children, as well as being able to identify other gifted students when I resumed my teaching career. I completed all of the requirements and became certified to teach gifted education to students in grades 1 through 12. This endorsement was added to my Florida Teacher Certification.

I didn't know whether my qualification as a gifted teacher or my involvement in the school community prompted my oldest son's gifted teacher to ask me to be the Odyssey of Mind competition team coach (1987-1989). Each school selected seven members and one alternate to compete in the region, which was Miami Dade County Public Schools. The contest problem the students were asked to solve dealt with the best way to rescue a stranded animal, "Omar to the Rescue." The students built the vehicle used in the rescue mission. The gifted teacher and I provided the materials and facilitated the process at our house. The students practiced several months in advance of the event. On competition day, we were spectators, while the students performed under strict rules and allotted time. They were also tested in spontaneous oral questions. Our school team placed second and proceeded to the state-level competition, which was held in another city in Florida. To my recollection, they earned second place in the state competition, as well. We were proud of our students. I was humbled and honored to serve as site liaison for the regional competition. When my second son competed, I was a teacher coach and a board member.

It was ironic that later on my son became an auto mechanic instructor by attending vocational education before completing high school and through hands-on experiences. At that time, high schools solely focused on academics and going to college, and therefore only limited career and vocational opportunities were available. He attended Robert Morgan Technical school where he studied auto mechanics. He owned his own auto mechanic shop for five years in Miami, Florida, from 2005 to 2010. Then he taught auto mechanics at one of the largest high school in California from 2010 to 2016. In 2015-2016, under his leadership his class invented a solar energy car charging station and won a national award. As a result, they were invited to the White House in April of 2016, and met President Obama and the Energy Secretary. As I write this memoir, he is creating online educational tools for electronics. I am very proud of him.

I had been actively involved in my children's school since 1983. I had started as our PTA board secretary and the teachers' end-of-year luncheon chair. For six years, I co-chaired cultural arts day, the most educational and entertaining activity of the year. We invited over fifty vendors to come and highlight their businesses and talents with all students, kindergarten through six grade, for the entire school day. My co-chair and I began preparing for this day six months to a year ahead. It required a lot of organization on our part, making sure it was age appropriate. My co-chair and I were certified teachers and that helped, too. In addition, we formed subcommittees to oversee certain activities of the day, such as food for the vendors, classroom assignments, and so on. We also provided teachers and vendors with feedback for future cultural arts days.

In 1987, the school community elected me as first vice president of my children's elementary school PTA board, overseeing several committees. During the fall of that year, I applied for a substitute teaching position at the school, and I was welcomed wholeheartedly. Often, substitute teachers are at a disadvantage because students consider it a free play day. The rumor traveled fast when I was the substitute teacher for their classes. "You better behave because she knows our parents and she'll tell them if we misbehave," students warned each other. Peer influence is powerful. Everyone completed their work without any disruption, thanks to my students' backing. The teachers were pleased, too.

The following academic years, 1988-1989 and 1989-1990, I was elected president of our PTA, while I continued substitute teaching. I had three vice presidents under me and each was responsible for various subcommittees. I am grateful for everyone's dedication and cooperation. I worked with the nicest and most committed group of people I had ever met.

My involvement in Miami-Dade County Public Schools and the community at large grew exponentially. At the district level, the area superintendent for our schools sent me a letter of appointment to serve on the site selection committee of a new school which was being built to relieve the overcrowded schools. I humbly accepted the appointment. The committee met during the day when my kids were in school. Once or twice, I drove to the district office, which was about twenty-five miles away from our house. This appointment in 1988 apparently led me to represent the schools in our area on the District Advisory Committee from 1988 to 1994. This committee met monthly, and each representative brought concerns or recommendations that were conveyed to the superintendent of schools. This was an important job because Miami-Dade County Public Schools is the fourth largest school system in the country.

My involvement in the community created a domino effect. A community newspaper writer, whom I had known since I moved to my community, invited me to get involved in Miami-Dade Police Citizens Advisory Committee in 1986. The meetings were held on the last Wednesday of every month. I do not recall what month I first attended the meeting, however, that evening it changed my perception about police officers forever. The major of the department gave us members an overview of the crime statistics in our community. He asked the members to be the ears and eyes for the department. A year after I became a member, the major asked me to ride with one of the officers on an eight-hour daytime shift to observe their services to the community. After shadowing the police officer for the whole day, I was overwhelmed with emotions. I was amazed at how the officer deescalated domestic violence incidents and conducted himself in a professional manner in all situations. The following day, I wrote a letter of commendation to the director of the police department and sent a copy to the major. I served as past vice chair and chairperson and have been a member of this organization to this date. Sharing my knowledge and information from the police department with the community at large, school, and church community gave me great joy and fulfillment.

In 1988, a dynamic and influential educator and administrator invited me to an event at a local chapter of the American Business Women's Association. We both belonged to the Kendall Federation of Homeowner Associations and the Police Citizen Advisory Committee. At first, I did not understand why she would invite me to a business group. Soon I discovered that the majority of members are educators and others from diverse business backgrounds. One annual event immediately stole my heart. A committee gave scholarships to young women who had a desire to enter college and needed financial assistance. The scholarship was awarded through an application process. My colleague immediately requested that I should be on that committee. I was honored to serve on this meaningful committee because my whole education career had depended on scholarships.

The mission of the American Businesswomen's Association is powerful and inspiring. It is responsible for bringing together businesswomen of diverse backgrounds and providing them opportunities to help themselves and others to grow personally and professionally through leadership, education, networking support, and national recognition. I was elected vice president, president, co-chaired Woman of the Year Award, Boss/Business Associate committees, and membership chairperson. I was honored to be selected to the national Top Ten American Businesswomen Nominee from the local chapter and named Businesswoman of the Year from our local chapter. It was during the time, from 1988 to 1998, that I acquired my public speaking skills because of all the public speaking I was required to do in front of all of these large groups of people, including public officials and business professionals. This helped me grow both personally and professionally.

The year 1988 was an exciting year for our family. First, my oldest son, Ebadut graduated from sixth grade and entered middle school (often junior high school). The following academic year, I joined my son's junior high school Parents Teachers and Students Association (PTSA) and became their program chairperson. The middle school was located less than two miles from our house. According to the Miami-Dade County public schools, school buses would be provided if our residence was two miles or more from the school. To my recollection, while the school was working on determining where the bus stop would be, I drove my son to school. Our other two children were still attending elementary school.

The second thrilling news I received was that I was selected by the school community as the elementary school's exemplary school volunteer of the year. This award was based on the total number of hours I volunteered at the school and my participation in the community. I was humbled to receive this honor. I was nominated again in 1989. I enjoyed giving my children's school all the help they deserve.

Finally, yet importantly, in October 1988, I became a United States citizen after waiting for five years. By this time, I had already completed my undergraduate and graduate studies in the United States. The Immigration and Naturalization Service gave me a handbook to study for the citizenship oral and written questionnaire. They were the easiest questions I had never been asked in my lifetime. The Immigration and Naturalization officer asked me questions such as, "What holiday was celebrated on July fourth?" Right after I was sworn in with thousands of immigrants at Miami-Dade County Auditorium, I immediately went and registered to vote as a democrat. (We did not have voting privileges in my country of Ethiopia at this time.) This gave me an opportunity to sign legal documents that required citizenship. I don't recall if I voted for a president that year, however, I made sure I voted for local and state officials. I recalled volunteering for our Florida state representative and knocking on hundreds of doors of residents in my community. This representative appointed me to serve on West Kendall transportation and West Kendall School Construction Oversight committees.

I was grateful to him and thank God for giving me the courage to serve our community. I was familiar with the candidates who were running at that time. What a great honor to vote and to know that my vote counts. To the best of my knowledge, I have never missed an opportunity to vote in any election since then. This is an honor and privilege. I never had the chance to vote in my country.

PHOTO SECTION

*My mother (Hortu)
is weaving a basket
in her late 80s, which
she did when she
was a young girl.*

*The Reverend Lamessa
(Obosha), my second oldest
brother, was away for pastoral
training most of his life. He
supported himself by working
as a nurse, cook, carpenter, etc.*

I am with my nephew Reverend, Dr. Dinku, my second brother Reverend Lamessa's son, at his dedication in Minnesota in 2018.

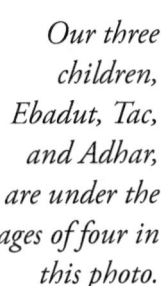

Our three children, Ebadut, Tac, and Adhar, are under the ages of four in this photo.

Receiving the volunteer of the year award from Miami Dade County Public Schools, the fourth largest school system in the United States, at their annual volunteer's luncheon. I am with my regional school board member and school board chairperson.

Photo with Obo's children and grandchildren.

Grateful to be the 2000 Teacher of the Year finalist recipient and featured with my district school board, Mr. Holmes Braddock, and region superintendent, Dr. Koonce.

I am at Miami Dade Auditorium after I was sworn as United States citizen in 1988.

I am receiving a plaque from incoming president, Dr. Lisa Plano, and our church pastor, Rev. Eliezer Ortiz, for my service as church council president, 2005-2006.

My third older sister, Ade Terunesh, visited me in the United States in 2001.

I am holding my three-and-a-half-year-old granddaughter and few-month-old grandson.

The beginning and first official political invitation to Senator Bill Nelson's campaign.

I am visiting our eldest sister, Ade Galitu, and her husband and three daughters in 1994.

Our international wedding consisted of friends from seven nationalities hosted by Rev. Flachman and his wife at their church.

186

I am visiting my second older sister, Ade Dessi, and her two daughters of four children in 1994.

Our brother, Obosha, Reverend Lamessa, is visiting his two sisters, Ade Terunesh and me.

187

I was one of the selected volunteers invited to meet President Obama at Miami International Airport in 2012.

My husband, Dominic, is with his seven-foot and seven inches tall cousin. Both are from Southern Sudan.

My children and I are visiting their godparents in Ocala, Florida, where they retired.

I am visiting my mom's burial place who passed away at the age of ninety-two, six months before I visited my birthplace.

Two of my children and I, visiting my first and former employer and his wife at their retirement residence. He was my greatest supporter in good and bad times.

The first telephone building was built in my birthplace two months before my visit in 1994. I had just called my children in the USA.

Obo, our eldest brother (sitting), is visiting our sister Ade Terunesh and her husband (back), and surrounded by her five children. She was a pharmacist and nurse. She was my source of information when I lived abroad and while writing my story.

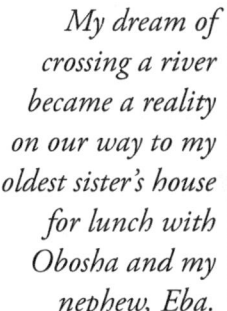

My dream of crossing a river became a reality on our way to my oldest sister's house for lunch with Obosha and my nephew, Eba.

191

My granddaughter is reading to her pet at the age of four and later to her baby brother. She later became an avid reader and writer.

I am holding Dominic, my first grandson, who is a few days old.

Our Christmas dinner with the whole family: Standing in the back, left to right, my ex-husband's wife, me, my oldest son, my second son, Taj, my grandchildren's mom. Front, my granddaughter, Johanah, my ex-husband, Dominic, my grandson, Dominic, and my daughter, Adhar. (2010)

An emotional farewell to a dear friend, neighbor, prayer partner for twenty-five years, to my left: Fred and Donna Hedges, my ex-husband, and another mutual neighbor, Dr. Jose and his wife, Pilar Rovira, far right.

Unforgettable experience: I am holding the local newspaper and about to climb to the top of the Great Wall of China during our 100 USA delegation to the Republic of China in 2001.

I was at my second older brother Rev. Lamessa's house for dinner. He is with his wife, left, two sons, three girls of his nine children, and granddaughter in 1994.

For the duration of my two weeks at my birthplace, I sat between my two older brothers: left my second brother, Rev. Lamessa and to my left our oldest brother, Obo Deressa.

A dinner is always followed up by scripture reading and prayers. Here, three of Obo's nine children are reading scripture.

Manut, Dominic's very tall cousin, with our children.

CHAPTER SIXTEEN

FROM SHEPHERDING CATTLE TO A CLASSROOM TEACHER

GOD'S PLAN: MY BROTHER'S FAITH
1989-2006

Who would have ever thought that a cattle shepherd in a remote village in Aira, Ethiopia, would become an educator in the world's most industrialized country. What a journey! I firmly believe that God planned for my life before I was conceived! I believe with my whole heart that God created me unique and for a unique purpose as it is written in the scripture: *"Before I formed you in the womb, I knew you, before you were born I set you apart"* (Jeremiah 1: 5a). It has been a winding road but God has been always by my side as He promised. *"I will be with you until the end of the world"* (Math. 28:18). I am grateful and thank God especially for Obo, our eldest brother, a man with great faith, and other people He put in my pathway in order to fulfill His plan.

Growing up I had no dream because I believed that God was in charge of my future. There was no female Ethiopian teacher in my village that I could look up to. His plan for me became clear during summer of 1989. With the help of the administration and the office staff of my children's school, I embarked on what seemed to be my mission for a lifetime. The school system was already familiar with my work ethic through volunteerism and my previous substitute teaching. Now I was moving into a full-time teaching position. After compiling my credentials, I submitted them to the human resource services office and set up an interview. When I arrived at the district office, the interviewer came out to the waiting room to get me. I was in shock when I noticed that he was a mutual acquaintance of my husband's and mine. The interview went very well and I was officially hired as a new full-time teacher.

When I went to my country years later to visit, my eldest brother who raised us after my father's death, commented to me. "You found favor from God," I remembered a devotional text he read to us from Psalms when I was a young girl. "*The lord bestows favor and honor. No good things does he withhold from those who walk with Him*" (Psalms 84:11).

In August of 1989, I attended an orientation for new teachers hosted by Miami-Dade Public Schools (M-DCPS) and the United Teachers of Dade organization. The M-DCPS made several presentations as it related to Florida State Education laws and district policies addressing the responsibilities of teachers to the students and their relationship to parents. After the presentation on the rights of teachers in the teaching profession, the union representative approached me to sign up to be member of the bargaining unit. I was confident that my principal would be on my side and God would not allow bad things to happen to me in my professional career, but I signed up, anyway. As long as my principal was an administrator, he treated me with the utmost respect. Several times a year, I invited him to our community town hall meetings that dealt with school issues, and he always attended.

During his tenure at school, we both were appointed to serve on two regional principal of the year selection committees (1991 and 1992). He represented the school principals, and the regional superintendent appointed me to represent my community. I also held my position as PTA president for two years because of the support of my school administration and the school community at large.

My principal assigned me to a fourth grade class located in one of the portables, which were semi-permanent classrooms to handle the overflow of students from the main buildings.

The grade level chair was highly qualified and respected by her peers in the school community as well as teachers in the fourth grade level. I remember when my second son was in her class. She was knowledgeable and organized. I was amazed at her teaching ingenuity as well as her sense of humor. She used hands-on techniques when teaching science to her students, making learning fun and long lasting.

Several years later, one of her former students, now an AT&T specialist, came to my house in response to a request for technical support.

"While driving around the park, I noticed the school I attended in fourth grade," he said. "I have never forgotten how my teacher taught us about the transmission of electricity with wires and batteries," he added. Right then, I knew whom he was talking about and when I mentioned her name, he was so excited.

I loved it when I could make exciting learning connections with my students. On November 9, 1989, during our morning class, the Berlin Wall came down. As my students and I watched on television, history was made. I pointed to one of the gates that led to East Germany called Checkpoint Charlie.

"I walked through that gate when I visited East Germany," I told them.

They asked, "Were you five years old?" they questioned. I laughed.

"I was the only young girl from Ethiopia in my group, and was studying in West Germany," I replied.

"You still look like a young girl," they assured me. It was the greatest teachable moment for my students and me. I shared my experiences with the students that at the time the communist regime was oppressive and there was no freedom of speech like there is in America. There was a tall brick wall between the two countries. Now that the wall was down, people could travel freely between East and West Germany.

The administration assigned four new teachers and me to this amazing fourth grade teacher. I had a positive and rewarding experience in my first year of my teaching profession thanks to my principal and my fourth grade mentor. Like the saying goes, "*You never get a second chance for a first impression.*" Therefore, I received my first picture-perfect impression of teaching and leadership from a colleague.

As a current and former volunteer leader, I encouraged and welcomed parents to get involved in their children's learning in my classroom. Although the administration had volunteer orientation for those parents who would like to assist their children's teachers, I reminded my volunteers to keep each child's classwork and behavior confidential. If they do not follow the guidelines, they may forfeit their volunteer privileges. Right from the beginning, I established positive relationships with the families. Sometimes, I had about four volunteers helping in my fourth grade class. It was unusual to get so many volunteers in upper grades. I was lucky and grateful for all their help.

Twenty-eight years later, my grandkids and I were at the neighborhood park playground and a woman approached me. "I was your room mom when my son was in your fourth grade class," she stated. Immediately I recognized her and visualized her son. He was so shy that he did not answer when I took attendance. I reminded her about the perfect report he completed as part of a class project on the state of Florida which was worthy of publication. I was so proud of him and his classmates soon began to recognize his accomplishment.

"What did he study?" I asked her.

"He is an attorney in a nearby county," she answered. "He is doing great! He had enjoyed being in your class, thanks to you."

My eyes filled with tears of joy. This was my first year teaching young children. As a teacher, I didn't know how the students and parents were touched by my attitude towards teaching. I remember every morning during my devotion, I asked God to make me an instrument of His love and peace. He did!

I was elated and humbled when I received an email from another former fourth grade student about ten years later. "I miss you and will always remember you. I will never forget when you helped my mom and me. My mom was going through a divorce, and you helped her." I was in shock because I did not recall counseling both mom and daughter. I thanked God for giving me a photographic memory. I visualized the student as if it were yesterday, including where she sat. Immediately I responded to her stating how proud I was that she was attending college in Texas.

In January of 2018, I received a message through social media from another of my former fourth grade students. I was thrilled that he would be visiting our community from out of the country and would like to stop by to visit me. He now had a boy the same age as when he was in my class. I asked him if he had my address.

"Are you still at the same corner house?" he asked. "Yes," I confirmed.

It had been twenty-nine years since I last saw him. Sure enough father and son knocked at my door. What a great joy to see both of them with hugs and kisses.

The summer after my first year of teaching was a nightmare. My principal assigned me to the third grade level, which was in the main school building. In my first year of teaching, all fourth grade classes were housed in the portables because there was no space in the main building. Therefore, I packed all my teaching materials in my van and took them home.

The next day, at about midnight, we heard a big explosion. We looked through our bedroom window and the van was gone with everything in it! I was devastated. Immediately my husband and my oldest son, fourteen, jumped into the spare car and chased them through the neighborhood until they lost sight of the van driven by the thieves. They left their marks behind by dropping my belongings, including a coffee peculator which we used for our meetings, on the streets. I was concerned for my husband and son's safety. I am grateful they came home safely. (Nowadays the police warn us citizens not to be the officers. Instead, we are to be only the ears and eyes of the department. Even the Homeland Security model warns: *See Something, Say Something.* Criminals carry handguns.)

When my husband and son returned from pursuing the thieves, we reported the incident to the police officers. After receiving the description of the van and the direction the thieves drove, they promptly left in search of the thieves and the van. Luckily, they left traces of my materials thrown on the streets, changing directions as to try to throw off the officers as they drove frantically through the neighborhood. I was proud of our police officers and thankful for their service.

Four hours later, they located the van completely disman-tled, front seats full of blood, twenty-five miles away from our house, in the opposite direction from which they had stolen and driven away. The police officers concluded that the thieves were amateur because they used their hands to break in and remove all electronics. The van was towed and we contacted our insurance agent. When we saw the condition of the van, my heart was overwhelmed with grief. But I gave God thanks because a car can be replaced, but human beings cannot. The insurance agent concluded that the vehicle was a total loss, and therefore, needed to be replaced.

We lived in a safe and upscale neighborhood. "Why me and why now?" I thought. My neighbors and friends asked me if I failed any student recently. No teacher wants to fail a student but instead would prefer to assist him and turn him around. I suspected it was a specific student who was disruptive and never took his education seriously. He enrolled in the school late in the year. After consulting with my grade level chairperson, I referred the student to the school counselor and then the administration. Ultimately the administration decided to retain him. To my recollection, he didn't return to school the following academic year. Unfortunately, we never found out who had stolen our van.

As my second year began, I was assigned to a third grade class with a veteran teacher. I knew most of the teachers assigned to this grade level because of my previous involvement in our PTA. To my recollection, there were four teachers, including me.

The school was built during the time when the open classroom concept was popular. Sliding doors divided the classes; therefore, a teacher could hear his/her colleague teaching right next door. Luckily, in those days, the children were well-mannered. Teachers could supervise two classes simultaneously in case of an emergency, with the approval of the administration, of course. The library was located in the middle of the building on the second floor bordered by classrooms. Similarly, the cafeteria was situated in the center of the first floor and was also surrounded by classrooms. Over the years the parent organization raised funds and helped the school build sound-proof dividers around the media center and cafeteria and each classroom to help with the noise levels.

A teacher's assistant was assigned to help us with making copies and collating various lessons for the students. Although we were required to teach the same curriculum, each teacher was allowed to use her or his own style to deliver each subject in a meaningful and creative way. Each teacher taught all subjects with the exception of music, art, and physical education, which were taught by specialized teachers. Science and mathematics remained my favorite subjects throughout my teaching profession. I recalled one lesson where I cooked hot dogs using solar energy. We covered paper plates with aluminum foil, placed a few hot dogs on each plate, and placed them in a sunny location. Wow! My students and I were excited as the aroma of the hot dogs traveled through the air. We could not wait to eat them. Our only misfortune was the uninvited guests, ants, who invaded some of the hot dogs. The ant-free hot dogs were delicious and tasted just like barbecued hot dogs.

Our teacher's assistant requested the administration to enroll one of her sons in my class. Later, her other son was also enrolled in my class. I was not sure whether our science experiment inspired her sons, but one of her sons was later employed with NASA.

Many years later their mom, my former teacher's assistant, and her husband joined the police Citizens Advisory Committee. I still see both parents periodically. It is heartwarming to meet former students' parents with whom I had established positive rapport in our community. When parents and students meet me after so many years, the first question usually is, "Are you still at the same house?"

"Yes, I am. Please come and visit me," I assure them. My students and their parents always knew where I lived.

In 2016, my neighborhood elementary school where I taught, where my children attended, and now where my grandkids are attending, called me. They conveyed to me that one of my former third grade student's mom visited the school to inquire whether I still lived in the community and left her phone number to contact her. As soon as the receptionist told me the mother's name, I could visualize her son, the color of his jacket, where he sat, and his beaming face. Immediately I called the mother. She was excited to hear from me. Their house is a few blocks from my house. She informed me that her son had earned three master's degrees and a Ph.D. in computer science engineering and works in another state. He is married and has a boy. At the time I called, my former student and his wife were out of the country. However, when they returned, I visited them. It was a pleasure to see him. After twenty-six years he now stands over six feet tall with a beautiful wife and baby boy. I had pictures taken with them. What an exciting experience!

It seems everywhere I go in my community, I run into my former students (now young men and women) and their parents. One day I visited Hobby Lobby for the first time since it was constructed. It was within walking distance from home. I had to go to the shop because the items that my friend's ninety-five-year-old father wished for his birthday were available only in that store. When I asked a lady who worked there for assistance, she addressed me by my name and continued by saying, "You were my third grade teacher! I only remember my favorite teachers' names, and you are one of them," she added.

I thanked her and asked for her last name to refresh my memory. We hugged each other. She was very helpful in locating what I needed. Whenever I had to recall my students' names, I asked for their last names. Then, my photographic memories of them when they were in my class appeared. Later on, I called my friend and thanked her for referring me to Hobby Lobby.

In December of 1990, a year after my God-planned profession, I faced the worst fear in my life. My three children finally expressed their feelings that there was only peace at home when their father was gone from our home on a business trip. I agreed with them, it concerned me tremendously. Something had to be done.

CHAPTER SEVENTEEN

FACING MY FEARS

God promises, *"Because he loves me, I'll rescue him. I'll protect him, for he acknowledges my name. He will call upon me, and I'll answer him. I will be with him in trouble; I will deliver him and honor him"* (Psalms 91:14-15 NIV).

My husband was an intelligent and hardworking man and had been the single breadwinner for the family. I am grateful to him and God for bringing us together in a foreign country. He encouraged me to get out of my shyness after our marriage and get involved in the community, especially in our children's education. He participated in our church activities and our children's Christian upbringing.

He was one of the first professors at Florida International University in Miami, Florida. He taught vocational education and policies to professionals during the week, and then also on weekends to accommodate his students who worked during the week. His colleagues respected him. He served as department dean in the College of Education. I recall him telling his friends that he would rather be with his students in the classroom than be an administrator.

He served on the board of trustees of colleges and universities in the southeastern district of the United States on accreditation. During the summer, many families accompanied their spouses during the accreditation conferences in various states and stayed in five-star hotels. Our family accompanied my husband as well.

During the year, he attended meetings in different states. On one of his trips, he purchased me my first miniskirt. It was beautiful. People at school and church were surprised. What better answer to give than, "My husband bought it for me?" He always bought the best clothes for his family and high-quality goods for the house. Finally, when we thought our children, who were ten, twelve, and fourteen years old, could be a little more independent, I started my career as an educator.

A year after I started my God-planned profession, however, I faced the worst dilemma in my life. My kids expressed that the house environment was much more peaceful when their dad was away on a business trip for a few days. I agreed with them, because I too felt the tension when he was home. He had an alcohol problem.

During the drug awareness month, teachers discussed with their students about alcohol and drug abuse and its consequences. I signed up for a support group in my community and took my children along. But my husband refused to attend any program. The problem escalated. We noticed that his health was affected as well. His doctor warned him, too.

In 1987, I reached out to our pastor for advice and support. He told me that it is an illness that affects not only the individual but also the whole family. He shared with me that unless the person admits that he has a problem, no one can help him. The pastor visited our family to discuss the issue. Then my husband stopped attending the church. I felt stress from his behavior for over ten years. I stayed strong and did not share any negative feelings about their dad with my children until they expressed it. I was embarrassed to share my husband's problem with my friends even when they shared that their family members had alcohol abuse problems.

Divorce had never been in my vocabulary. It was not common in our culture then and it was discouraged. In addition, I took the Christian wedding vow, at our wedding, "… *in sickness, and health, to love and cherish; from this day forward until death do us part.*" I was confused, "if alcoholism is an illness, why doesn't the individual seek help?" I reached out to my spiritual advisor, Obo, our eldest brother. He promised me that he would pray for God's guidance for my life. After we finally divorced, he assured me that it was the best decision I had ever made.

In December of 1990, just before winter vacation ended and school resumed, there was a chaotic episode between the three children and their dad. They were ready to go to bed. I was helpless. We ran to my neighbor's house, the third house from ours, and called the police. Thankfully, they came quickly. We met the officers in front of our house. One of the officers recognized me probably from the Citizens' Advisory Committee. My oldest son was the last to exit the house. My husband was still in the house. The two officers began to interrogate the children. They were 14, 12, and 10 years old and told the officers what had occurred. The officers also asked me for more information. Then, one of the officers asked the children,

"What do you want?"

"We want our mom to divorce him," one of the children responded.

I was overwhelmed with grief. I never expected to hear this from the children.

Then, I realized how much trauma they had undergone all these years. I tried to suppress negative feelings towards their dad because I did not want to hurt their feelings. I felt they probably blamed me for my silence. I attended community meetings just to get away from the chaos and stress, but I didn't realize how much negativity the children had experienced. When the officers asked the children to go inside and sleep, they refused because they were afraid of their dad. I was too. Then the officer entered our house and explained to my husband that the children were afraid to sleep in the house. Therefore, they needed to gather their clothes and belongings for school for the next day and sleep elsewhere. While my husband and the police officers were talking outside, the kids and I gathered our belongings and left for our neighbor's house with heavy hearts. My neighbor had been aware of the problem with my husband and the children and had tried to help in the past. They are devoted Christians and have great faith. They had two children, a girl two years older than my oldest son and a son the same age as my middle son. They all went to the same middle school except my daughter who was graduating from fifth grade June 1991.

The next day, I contacted our school's principal and arranged an emergency meeting with him. He knew of our family's situation previously because my oldest son started misbehaving in first grade and beyond. I requested a leave of absence to take care of the situation and our unknown future. My principal approved of it.

The following days, when my husband was at work, I went to our house and collected more necessary items for the children and myself. My neighbor was Godsent and she allowed us to stay with her as long as it took me to resolve the situation. God prepared the family long before this incident by giving me a community of friends to support and love us.

My next stop was the district police department. I met with the major of the police department. I'd known him for the past five years and had a good rapport with him. He was very sympathetic to my issue. He summoned a female police officer to discuss my predicament. Meanwhile, my heart was pounding for fear of the unknown. The major and the officer suggested that they would serve him an injunction. "What does that mean?" I asked.

"The court will serve him papers to move out his belongings within two weeks and he cannot come to the house," they assured me. Now, I felt regretful for him because he was responsible for the purchase of the house. I had to choose between the well-being of my three children and my husband, the person I tried to help stop drinking for years as the alcohol affected his health and his family. We loved him.

"What do I need to do?" I asked.

"You need to go to court and pay $140.00 to serve your husband the injunction document."

"Sometimes husbands close joint bank accounts. Therefore, withdraw one thousand dollars, and deposit in your own account for rainy days," they advised me.

Now I felt as if I were stealing money. I was apprehensive. They assured me that it is common to do so. In my heart, I was calling on God and I trust in His guidance and peace through this ordeal.

I left the police department and headed to the courthouse about twenty miles away. I sobbed from the time I left my house to speak to the principal until I arrived at the courthouse. The clerk there assumed that I had been physically abused. My eyes were red, and tears were still rolling down my cheeks. I felt like the sky was falling on me. I told them my situation with the three school-age children and that we were staying with a neighbor. They told me that it cost $140.00 and would take more than two weeks to serve him the injunction. I was sobbing uncontrollably.

Then she said, "If you know someone in law enforcement, they can expedite it quicker, but you still need to pay the fee."

I told her that I was on their citizen's advisory committee. Then, she suggested that I contact them. My heart turned from anxiety to peace within minutes. I didn't know what the outcome would be, but I trusted in God that He would take care of my children and me. I thanked Him for His presence thus far. I did not recall if the court clerk gave me the paperwork after I paid, but I went directly to the police station. They were happy to help me and started the process immediately. It was a tough situation to go through. Within a few days, they served him the injunction, ordering him to move out of the house within two weeks. Meanwhile, I resumed working and still kept close attention to the children. Close friends advised me to secure an attorney for the next step.

Originally, I had refused to add a legal family option to my health insurance during the open enrollment. But then, I remember, I changed my mind. I recalled when the insurance agent made a sarcastic remark. "Are you anticipating something soon?" I never dreamed that I would ever use a lawyer this way. One never knows what the future brings. It's better to have it now than be sorry later. I also remember reading that *God helps those who help themselves*. I did not realize that it would happen so soon. A friend whom I met at the American Businesswomen's Association recommended an attorney who specialized in marital proceedings. I thanked God for His guidance and for preparing all the people who assisted me through these calamities. I am grateful and indebted to them, especially my principal who gave me time off every time I needed to attend court hearings.

My fears increased day by day. I had never walked this path before. I had faith in God that he knew everything that was coming my way. The scripture verse in Hebrews gave me comfort and hope. *"Never will I leave you; never will I forsake you. So we say with confidence, "The Lord is my helper; I will not be afraid."* (Hebrews 13:5-6). Therefore, I trusted in God that He would take care of my children and me.

My attorney notified me by mail that my husband, his attorney, my attorney, and I were summoned to appear before a district judge. As soon as we arrived at the judge's office, my lawyer went in to report our presence. When he came back, he seemed to be concerned.

"Your husband brought in three witnesses, and you do not have any," he stressed. I realized that the three were his colleagues who worked with him during the day. One of them was his student and the others were neighbors.

"Yes, you're right. My husband brought witnesses who work with him during the day in his profession. He is a great professor, a good dad and a husband. However, only God, my children, and I were witnesses at night," I said with confidence.

"God is not going to come down and be a witness for you right now and the children are not here and not allowed in the court room," he vehemently contradicted my statement.

As soon as both parties were called and entered the judge's chamber and seated, the female judge said, "Ma'am, I know you from somewhere,"

"This is out of order, your honor," my husband's attorney said.

"I am the judge and I have the right to ask the young lady," the judge silenced him. When I mentioned the name of the most influential community organization I belonged to, the judge agreed that it was from there that she knew me. I was confident that the Holy Spirit prompted her to ask me. Suddenly my heart filled with peace and my fear subsided. During the meeting, our attorneys went back and forth with the judge. My husband and I spoke only when the judge asked us to clarify certain issues. Otherwise, the meeting went smoothly, considering it was my first experience in court.

The process seemed to go faster than I expected. I called my eldest brother to let him know and to pray for me. I recalled my attorney had to set another court hearing date at the county level. That courthouse was about twenty-five miles away. I drove my car to the train station and then took the Metrorail to the courthouse. I was grateful to my friends; they had taught me the most convenient way to travel to downtown for the first time.

My attorney met with me to advise me what to expect next. It was during my divorce process that I learned to answer a question with "yes" or "no," without explaining it. That is helpful even to this day. To my best knowledge, we met three to four times before the final dissolution of our marriage. When we were discussing our finances, my husband complained to the judge that I took money out of the joint account. The judge didn't make any comment. This was my second year teaching and I hadn't invested in my retirement. I was in charge of our family financial transactions. I had never been a treasurer in my life. During our marriage, we decided all expenses together.

Throughout the divorce proceedings, the court did not allow the children to visit with their dad. I felt badly about that, but their safety was paramount. Before the school year ended, my attorney and my husband's lawyer scheduled the final court hearing. One of my children's teachers, my three children, and my neighbor were scheduled to attend the hearing. My lawyer alerted me, "The judge who is going to preside at the hearing doesn't want the children to be present." The children had already been granted excused absences from school. I pleaded with God that His will be done. By now, my lawyer realized that I depended on God for everything.

Finally, the hearing date had arrived. My child's teacher, my neighbor, my children and I arrived at the county court-house. We all sat in the waiting room in the judge's chamber. My attorney arrived and went to the judge's secretary to notify them of our arrival. The attorney came out with disbelief on his face. He summoned me to the side, "The judge who supposed to preside over your case couldn't come today. She doesn't approve the children being present." Then he added, "Instead, a male judge will take her place. He doesn't care about you or your husband. The children are his number one priority," he stressed. My eyes welled up with tears.

"I had never stopped praying for what is best for the family," I told my attorney.

Soon everybody was called into the judge's chamber and sat around a large conference table: my child's teacher, my neighbor, the three children, the two attorneys, my husband, and I. After a short introductory statement, the judge asked the children many questions. I recall when he asked them about their dad.

"Our dad acted silly and weird when he drank beer," they replied.

"He got upset when we told him the effects of alcohol on the television and told him to stop drinking," one of the kids told the judge.

I thanked God for His amazing guidance He gave the children. They were Godsent lawyers. They spoke from personal experiences. I didn't have to say anything except verify the facts when I was asked by the judge.

In June of 1991, my youngest child graduated from fifth grade. Even though we were in the midst of bitter divorce proceedings, I invited my husband to the graduation ceremony, and he attended. Now, I have two children in middle school and a son in high school. The final divorce hearing was scheduled for July 1991. The judge ruled that I had full custody and therefore, I would keep the house for a smooth transition for the children. Their dad had daytime visitation. As a mother, my heart was broken; however, the emotional well-being of the children was more important.

I was grateful and thanked God for His everlasting love and peace that surpassed all understanding and for His consistent presence through this tough journey. Although the utility companies and the mortgage company notified me that the joint account was closed, I assured them that I now had my account, and they would get paid. They were understanding and they didn't charge me any late fees. I extended my heartfelt gratitude to my neighbor who accommodated us for two whole weeks, and to my principal for his compassion and understanding. Most of all, I gave glory to the almighty God for His loving presence and peace throughout this challenging time.

The first year after our divorce was challenging. For the next twenty years he was included in all of our family's celebrations either at my house or at restaurants. It was important to both of us that we celebrated holidays together. My ex-husband and his new wife catered Thanksgiving dinner at my house. I cooked his favorite dish for Christmas dinner. Unfortunately, after a long illness, he went to heaven on March 2, 2011. I was by his bedside along with his new wife and his children. We miss him tremendously. May his soul Rest in peace.

CHAPTER EIGHTEEN

FEAR OF A NATURAL DISASTER—
HURRICANE ANDREW
1992

In my third year of teaching (1991-1992), I was assigned to a second grade class with another experienced veteran teacher. My second son had had her in second grade. I had an inspiring, productive, and memorable school year with a great team of educators.

The summer following my third year was my most haunting experience to date. It was a year after my divorce. I had weathered the storm inside my house the year before. Now the storm was outside—Hurricane Andrew. Just a few days before the arrival of the most powerful hurricane of the century, local, state, and national disaster agencies warned the residents of the storm's path and its imminent danger. It reminded me of the scripture when God instructed Noah to build the unsinkable boat to protect his family and animals. I had never seen a hurricane before. "God, you protected Noah and his relatives, you can keep us safe, too," I pleaded with God.

I asked my friends who had experienced a hurricane before for advice. One family assumed that Miami wouldn't be in the path of this forecasted monstrous storm. However, they were compassionate for me and my three children who were then twelve, fourteen, and sixteen years old. They suggested that we protect our front living and dining room windows with plywood, as our house was situated across from a community park full of huge trees. On the rest of the windows, they suggested tape crisscross with masking tape. The couple helped us with all the preparations. Two days before the arrival of this unpredictable storm, we purchased a battery-operated radio, various sizes batteries, and flashlights, just in case the power went out. We stocked up on sufficient bottled water, canned food enough for three days, and filled the car with gas. These were the recommendations back then to prepare for a hurricane. We also had the option was go to a shelter and our school was designated as a shelter. It was on the other side of the park. I didn't know what to expect and none of my neighbors went to the shelter, so neither did we.

After we collected all loose items from the porch and secured them in the garage, on the eve of August 24, 1992, my children and I gathered in our family room. I had important documents such as our house insurance, medicine, and pertinent emergency contact information in a small suitcase by my side. We were glued to the television while there was still power. At about 3 am, we heard the howling of the wind that almost sounded like a train passing by. It intensified. It felt as if the windows were caving in.

While staying strong and trusting in God for His protection, we moved to the living room where the window was secured by a large sheet of plywood. By this time, the weather had gotten worse and we relocated ourselves in our guest bathroom located almost in the center of the house. Some of us sat on the floor while one person sat on the toilet seat. We still had the tub if needed. (A few months later, friends told me that children can lie down in the tub and be covered with a mattress). The lights went out! The wall started shaking against our backs! The kids started crying! I recall reminding them to pray to God as they were taught. I began conversing with God. "Dear God, this morning my daily scripture is reminding me how You saved Noah and his family from the deadly flood. Now you can save my children and me. One more thing, God, you promised that you would not destroy the earth with flood," (Genesis 9:8-17). I pleaded with God. This time my eyes teared. We heard more crashes around the house. The nightmare started at about four in the morning and lasted two hours. I thanked God for His protection over us.

Cautiously, once we heard the storm begin to subside, we went to our family room. My neighbor's curtains from the sliding door in the back were flying back and forth. "Maybe they needed fresh air," I thought. To our dismay, the sliding doors had caved in from the impact of the wind. They had just remodeled their kitchen that summer. I felt badly for my neighbors who had helped us secure our windows. Unfortunately, their property was damaged.

Looking through our front window, the park looked like a war zone. After the "all clear," radio announcement that the monstrous wind had passed Miami, we ventured outside. In the morning we discovered that the plywood on the two front windows was blown against the back fence. Tiles had blown away from neighbors' roofs. Tree debris blocked the roads. During the morning hours, we wandered through the neighborhoods. We couldn't recognize our friends' houses because the trees that served as landmarks looked like bulldozers had run over them. The roof of one of the houses lifted and landed on their front lawn. I'm grateful that electricity was restored within twelve hours. As to the damage to my house, I lost a few shingles and the roofers who came to repair my neighbors' roofs replaced mine free of charge. I was grateful for God's protection. Later on, friends commented that God was with me. Yes, indeed! He has been my companion all my life. I thanked God for protecting my children and our property from danger and destruction. Also, I was grateful to those who assisted me with our preparations before the storm hit.

I was heartbroken when I heard water came in through the second-floor roof of our elementary school and destroyed the books in the media center. Thanks to the generosity of organizations around the country, they were replaced. Many of the employees and families suffered damage to their homes. As a result, many stayed in hotels and with friends. Yet some have lost electricity and telephone services for months.

The Miami-Dade County school board delayed the opening of schools by two to three weeks while clean-up and repairs were made. In some parts of the county, homes and schools were severely damaged. However, we are grateful there was no loss of life.

CHAPTER NINETEEN

THE LONG-ANTICIPATED FAMILY REUNION

It was with mixed emotions that I decided to visit my birthplace during the summer of 1994, twenty-five years after coming to the United States. Visiting my birthplace was both an emotional and an exciting experience. Since my last visit, I have completed my God-planned teaching training, had my family, and taught for five years. I felt it was time to return to my home country to visit. I would have gone back earlier but there had been a change of government, and all the church leaders I had worked under had fled the country. Now I needed to see my family. It was going to be both an emotional and exciting experience.

My two brothers and all my siblings and extended families still lived in the village where I grew up, except for those who had improved themselves through advanced education and had moved to Addis Ababa, the capital city of Ethiopia.

It was an emotional visit because, unfortunately, my mother who nurtured me physically and emotionally was no longer there to welcome me. Every summer vacation when I was young and visited home, she was the first one to arrive at the location where the four-passenger airplane landed. She never stopped hugging and kissing me once she got ahold of me. We both always cried for joy. During these visits, my mother made sure that I ate every food that I had missed during the time I was away from home. Soretti, my sister-in-law, the wife of our eldest brother, had helped to care for me as well. I still missed the special hugs and kisses from my mother. I thanked God that she lived a long life, longer than most of her friends in the village despite the hard living and working conditions there. During my years in the U.S., I sent her some money to buy her the best national clothes, which she wore proudly. This would not replace my presence with her but served as a form of comfort. Unfortunately, she went to heaven six months before I visited. I know she will welcome me in heaven when I meet her. For now, that is the only comfort I have.

It was an exciting visit because the number of people in my immediate family had quadrupled. I wanted to show my appreciation by bringing gifts for my extended family because my older siblings had taken care of me when I was young. In general, people expect gifts from visitors who live in a foreign country, especially America, where they think money grows on trees and everyone is rich. Not only did I live in America now, I taught in American schools and got paid well and married a university professor with a doctorate. I was a stay-at-home mom raising my children.

My siblings had had more children since I left. Some of them were grown up, had gotten married, and had their own children, now. For example, my two brothers had nine children each, and some of the children had their own children. Through one of my sisters, I learned that there were dozens more of my extended family members. This led me to have insufficient money and clothes for all of my family members. So, I borrowed money from the bank against my mortgage.

First, I asked a colleague who was a travel agent to find a reasonable round-trip ticket. My round-trip plane ticket with Lufthansa Airlines, from Miami to Addis Ababa, Ethiopia, was about $2,500.00. I was fortunate to have had a one-day layover in Frankfurt, Germany, to practice my German again after twenty-six years. I departed Miami at the end of June 1994 and returned to Miami at the end of July. This gave me one month to visit relatives in both the capital city and my birthplace.

Now that I'm an American citizen, I had an option to purchase an insurance policy to ship my body back to the U.S., just in case something happened to me while in Africa. I thought this was insane. So did my siblings when I told them. They couldn't believe that people make advance plans for their possible death like this in America. They believed that God is always in charge of everything; therefore, one didn't need to prearrange anything. However, I thought of the saying, *"God helps those who help themselves."* Therefore, I had to do my part. I purchased the insurance.

There were many things to do before I departed for Ethiopia. First and foremost, I had to get vaccinated from a doctor who specialized in tropical medicine. It was interesting that the doctor discovered that I already had immunity to bacteria that are common in tropical countries. She only prescribed me medicine against malaria. I already was taking several vitamins which possibly protected me from common cold viruses and the flu. Sanitation in the capital city was almost similar to that of the Western world. Therefore, I didn't worry. The fact that I had immunity to bacteria was great news because when I visited relatives and friends in the villages, I consumed local food and drank wherever I went. It is in our culture to offer food and coffee to guests, which I enjoy. Sometimes they offered my brother and me homemade honey wine, which I never drank because it gave me a headache.

The next giant chore I had to complete was buying gifts and clothes for my extended family. My sister, Terunesh, who lived in Addis Ababa and knew every family member, gave me recommendations that I solely depended upon. I went to reputable department stores such as Burdines and JCPenney looking for good bargains. I never followed fashion trends or styles. I packed ten medium-sized and large suitcases with clothes. One large suitcase was crammed with my belongings including three light dresses, two pairs of shoes, and a few personal things. I had also a carry-on bag with my devotional books, a Bible, and a few things I might need for my one-day layover in Frankfurt, Germany.

Miami International Airport was not as busy as it is nowadays. My three children, ages fourteen, sixteen, and eighteen years, and my ex-husband accompanied me all the way to the Lufthansa check-in counter. The agent looked at all the suitcases lying around and asked, "How many passengers are traveling?"

"My mom," the children replied. "Yes," my ex-husband confirmed.

"There are limits on the number of bags allowed," I overheard one of the Lufthansa agents explaining. Once I finished with my passport verification and itinerary, I explained to the Lufthansa agent, "It has been twenty-five years since I saw my family. My nieces and nephews have grown up since I left. They too have children and expect many things from me. I'm the only one who has lived abroad."

I started speaking with an agent in German. He was amazed that I knew German. I told him that I lived in Germany for three years before coming to America. By this time, they had compassion for me. I don't remember if they charged me for half of the luggage or not. I was grateful and thanked God that they even allowed me to take everything with me on the plane. I extended my heartfelt gratitude to those at the counter in German. I felt that God showed me a favor even in the most unexpected circumstances. The name "Aster" (Esther) means that I find favor with God. His wishes follow me everywhere I go.

I couldn't contain my tears when I said "goodbye" to my three children and my ex-husband. Then my daughter, the youngest child said, "Why does Mom cry?"

"Because it is the first time your mom will go on a trip for a month and will miss you," my ex-husband said. Amazingly, in those days, family members could accompany the traveler to the departure area and spend time together until boarding time. As I boarded the plane, I waved to them "goodbye."

The airplane was gigantic. Every seat seemed like a first-class seat to me. We departed in the late afternoon. When night came, I tried to sleep. Suddenly, there was turbulence. The pilot announced that we were over the Atlantic Ocean. Even if I could not see it, I could imagine from my knowledge of geography how enormous the ocean was. As usual, I began praying, "*Please heavenly father, protect us from all danger like You protected the disciples when they were confronted with a violent wind. Take me home safely to see my relatives. Please give me peace.*" Psalms: 91 has been my comprehensive insurance all my lifetime and I began to read it. I finally fell asleep.

After nine hours of flying, we landed in the Frankfurt, Germany, airport early in the afternoon. The flight attendants offered us more food than we could eat. I was grateful because I was accustomed to eating Western food and when they served what looked like raw shrimp I couldn't eat it. They reminded me of grub worms from our yard. I had previously arranged for an airport shuttle to take me to the hotel. There were many nationalities on the shuttle. Whenever I heard the driver speak in German, I communicated back in German. I realized that people were pleased to hear someone speak their language.

When I arrived at the hotel, I was amazed to see so many trees and shrubs in the surrounding areas. It reminded me of my birthplace. I loved the scenery because it was all green and quiet. My room was situated on the second floor, and I had a perfect view through my window. Before I ventured into the hotel lobby, I inspected all the safety instructions to prepare myself in my hotel room, just in case. In addition, I made sure I knew where the restaurant was located so that I could eat dinner before I went to bed. As a former home economics major in Germany, I was familiar with the menu. I ordered my meal in German, surprising the waitresses and receiving great service.

After dinner, I realized that some guests were watching the soccer World Cup on TV in the hotel lobby. Soccer is the Ethiopian national sport, and I decided to join them. Most of the spectators were men. I watched until about 2 am. One of the male guests realized that I was the only female watching. He asked, "Why are you the only female watching?"

"It is an Ethiopian national sport," I replied.

Still, he couldn't believe that a female would be so interested in sports.

Unfortunately, after I heard the deadly shooting during the game, I went to my room. What should have been an exciting and fun event turned into a tragedy. During my evening devotion, I thanked God for the safe flight to my destination and prayed for peace during the rest of the game. Regrettably, I couldn't sleep well after the shooting tragedy.

I woke up early the next morning, dressed, and had my morning devotion. I surrendered to God for a safe flight to my home country. Then, I ate breakfast and watched the world news before departing for the airport. The shuttle driver informed me that we needed to arrive at the airport two hours early to give me ample time. So, I gathered my personal belongings and waited in the hotel lobby for the shuttle. I was very pleased with the hotel and the shuttle services.

I arrived at the Lufthansa check-in counter on time. It was great to know the language because workers at the airport appreciated it. The flight was scheduled for early afternoon. I also realized that as a U.S. citizen, I had a preferred entrance after the security verified my passport. The best part was that there was only a one-hour time difference between Frankfurt and Addis Ababa. Still, the flight duration was about seven hours.

The first four hours of the flight were daylight. As we were flying, the pilot pointed out historical sites. I remember flying over the Mediterranean Sea and Italy. I didn't experience the turbulence we had over the Atlantic Ocean. I loved it when my early elementary school geography class came alive. In addition, I noticed that the map of Italy is similar to Florida. He continued giving us air geography lessons, announcing the Red and the Dead Sea until the sun set and it became dark.

As we approached Addis Ababa, Ethiopia, the pilot stated that we would land at about 9:30 pm. My heart started pounding for joy. My sister, Terunesh, who was a well-known business-woman, promised that she would send an important person who knew the airport to meet me when I arrived. I didn't know this man but he was acquainted with my picture from my sister. He helped me with all the suitcases, took my passport, and asked me to wait in line for customs clearance.

The majority of the airport employees spoke Amharic, which I was not fluent in because I did not grow up in a city. Before my sister's friend (the mystery man) came back, it was my turn for the customs agent. In my own country, fear haunted me because I didn't know the person who met me and I needed my passport right then. Then the customs agent asked for my passport in Amharic. I pointed to the direction where the man went and I stumbled with my answer. I answered the female customs agent in English and said, "I have been away from my country for twenty-five years and I didn't speak Amharic in the first place." I could see the surprise on her face and she said, "I'm twenty-five years old, too." Clearly, she didn't understand exactly what I was telling her. Then I saw the man coming from the duty-free store. He came and gave me my passport and I thanked him. Apparently, the customs agent knew where he went. Then she continued asking, "What are in all those suitcases?"

"Clothes for my extended relatives in the villages." I told her. She opened one of the suitcases and found only clothes as I had told her. Lastly, she asked me, "Do you have a video camera?"

"No, I don't own any video camera, only disposable cameras to take family pictures," I replied to her.

She had compassion for me and believed the truth I told her, and then she said, "Close your suitcase and go." I was ever grateful to her and the man who helped me. Most of all I thanked my heavenly father who guided me all the way.

As I looked out at the exit door, I saw my sister who was coordinating everything for me, holding a bouquet and standing beside her grown-up young men whom I had never met. Obosha, my brother, also accompanied her. I was speechless, we just hugged and kissed each other several times and wept with joy. She owned a Mercedes car and my nephew drove her car while another relative drove a different car. I sat in my sister's car along with my brother Obosha and my nephew who was driving. We were conversing in my tribal language, Oromifa, my mother's language. Before I knew it, we arrived at my sister's house. The guard opened the gate to my sister's property. After they took my luggage out, my nephew parked the car in the garage. I don't remember if the other car was parked in the compound or not.

Although it was about 10:00 pm (4 pm Ethiopian time in the evening), my sister had helpers in the house to get the dinner ready. I could eat our food any time because I missed it. My sister is a great cook and she prepared a variety of Ethiopian dishes. Ethiopian food contains several spices and it is very aromatic. About ten people were dining with me.

My brother Obosha slept over since he lived far away. My sister, our family's businessperson, owned a modern house with three or four bedrooms, a bathroom with running water, and a dining and living room. The kitchen was located in the back of the main house by itself.

After I unpacked what I needed for the evening, I took a shower and went to sleep in my sister's room. She prepared a place for my brother to spend the night. I didn't experience jet lag but I had no problem falling asleep.

In the morning when I woke up, my sister had already prepared freshly roasted and ground coffee, and my favorite breakfast, Ethiopian sour flatbread, spread with spiced butter. Our brother, the Reverend Lamessa, offered prayer and thanksgiving for my safe arrival, and her adult boys joined us for the delicious breakfast together.

After breakfast, we discussed my plan to visit Obo, our eldest brother. My brother and sister informed me that a new road leading to my birthplace had been built. Since I had never seen the beautiful scenery in person except flying over it in a four-passenger mission airplane, I suggested we take a bus. My brother Obosha planned to accompany me. My sister suggested that her youngest son should also accompany me to see his mother's birthplace for the first time. I thought it would be an exciting and adventurous journey.

My brother and sister informed me that the first public telephone in the village was installed and functioning the day before I arrived in Ethiopia. My brother and sister commented, "It was welcome news for you," they told me. I was overjoyed and thanked God because I could call my children in America. I planned to spend over two weeks in the village.

Before my departure, my sister and I went through my suitcases to make sure that I gave clothes to those relatives who lived in Addis Ababa. Unfortunately, they were more aware of fashion trends from reading European fashion magazines than I was. My sister assisted me in sorting out and taking with me what was appropriate for the relatives in the village, like the more modest clothing with longer skirts. The adults were pleased to receive money, and the older children were tickled to have American-made jackets and sneakers. I never forgot when one of my relatives asked me whether I had bought a Rolex watch. I had no clue what he was talking about. So, I asked him, "What is it?" He seemed to be surprised that I didn't know after living in a foreign country for twenty-eight years. He didn't ask me again.

Obosha's family invited us to a delicious dinner at their house. My sister-in-law is a great cook. She prepared a variety of meat and vegetable dishes. My sister and her grown-up children attended as well. I don't recall how many of my nieces and nephews were born since I left Ethiopia twenty-five years ago. With my sister Terunesh's assistance, I brought clothes for everyone, including my brother. I enjoyed tremendously the company of my brother who raised me and his family.

Before I left for my birthplace, she advised me to cover my hair because I looked like a foreigner. I'd never worn blue jeans and boots in America, so she helped me buy them. The boots became handy when I was in the village because it was the rainy season and muddy. I'm grateful to her advice.

As part of the breakfast prayer, Obosha and my sister prayed for our safe trip. My sister emphasized about her youngest son who was sixteen years old at the time, "Always keep him by your side and treat him like your son. Let him sleep with you on the same bed," she stressed when we stayed overnight at a motel on our way to the village. I had three children, and my second son was sixteen years old as well. My sixteen-year-old son would never agree to this.

It was a one-and-a-half-day drive by bus, with a one-night stayover, halfway between Addis Ababa and Aira village. We purchased the three bus tickets and were all set to depart in the middle of the week. My sister prepared my favorite nonperishable snack for our trip. I gathered all the suitcases that contained clothes for my siblings and their children in the village. We arrived at the bus station around 5:00 am (11 am Ethiopian time) and the bus was supposed to leave at 6 in the morning. One and a half hours passed. In Ethiopian culture half to an hour delay is normal. Travelers were waiting anxiously. I overheard that the driver was from one of the three major tribes who didn't speak our tribal language. Everyone was wondering why he would be assigned to drive the bus. I knew there had been tribal tensions for a while. The constant waiting annoyed the travelers. Meanwhile, I was communicating with my heavenly father to make the best choice for everyone. After six hours of waiting, the manager replaced the initial driver with someone who spoke Oromifa. At about noon, we were on our way to Aira, Wollega.

The road between Addis Ababa and Nekemte, the capital of Wollega, was asphalt. When I attended high school, I took that road a few times. We drove by a very famous agricultural area being farmed with modern equipment. It was so green it looked artificial. We stopped at the roadside shop and purchased their famous delicious bread, which I now make at my house. Then we passed through Nekemte, the capital of Wollega province. I was scared and surprised to spot military tanks abandoned along the roadside. It reminded me of the movie, *Marsh*, which I had seen on television. My brother told me under his breath that they were the remnants from the civil war in Ethiopia a few years back. What a nightmare! A few miles later, the driver pulled the bus off the road. Two government inspectors walked onto the bus and ordered all passengers to exit while they ransacked our belongings. I'm grateful that I could communicate with God in my heart for our protection and safety. I believe my brother, being a pastor, was also pleading with Him. I was thankful to Him that my brother and my nephew accompanied me. I had no idea what they were looking for. Later on I found out they were looking for guns. It was a horrifying experience in my own country. It reminded me of my experiences when I visited East Germany when I was a student in West Germany. Next, they checked our luggage. Then, they requested us to get back on the bus.

The bus driver and passengers were relieved, and we continued on our journey. We were now traveling through dense forest, and I could also see beautiful mountains and valleys, as well. Traveling by bus allowed me to enjoy God's beautiful creation, which I had never been able to experience before from the air. Before I knew it, we came to an amazing mountain view and down below was a very steep valley. Suddenly, the bus couldn't move. The road was muddy and the additional weight of the passengers as well as the many pieces of luggage added to the problem. The driver then asked the men to get out and possibly help push. I exited the bus with my brother and nephew. I looked again at that steep valley; it was very scary. What if the bus rolled down to the ditch? I thought. Immediately I came to my senses that the same God who protected me all these years would also help the driver get us to our destination. Thank God after several trials, the bus was out of the mud and we were on our way.

Some passengers thanked God that the bus driver was changed before we left Addis Ababa, because the driver we had now was even-tempered and had patience through this whole ordeal. We were delayed by six hours for our departure; however, I believe that God was simply waiting for the right driver for our trip. Later on, our driver shared with us that many cars flipped over and ended up down in the valley at the location where the bus had stopped. It was amazing how God's plan worked. My sister contacted Obo by phone, the first public phone built a day before I arrived in Ethiopia and told him why we were delayed. Our eldest brother, being a prayer warrior and a man of great faith, earnestly pleaded with God for our protection and safe arrival.

It seemed that the driver was knowledgeable about the Wollega province and the roads; he kept driving until late at night. I enjoyed the majestic mountains, valleys, and the beautiful sunset on our way. The driver and passengers decided that the driver needed to rest overnight at a nearby town before reaching my birthplace, Aira. Thank God my brother arranged the hotel for my nephew and me. He slept in another room and my nephew, and I shared a room. I remember my sister forbidding me from talking to strangers as my accent betrayed me for being an American. The Ethiopians might charge me as a tourist. I'm grateful that I had such a wise sister who was knowledgeable in business dealings.

The next morning, after eating breakfast, we were on our way to Aira. I had never traveled by a bus or a car in our province. This adventurous and exciting trip was new to me. When I was in my home village in the mid-sixties, there was no road built from Addis Ababa to where I was born. I had no idea where the bus stop would be from my house. I thanked God I had my relatives traveling with me.

About two hours later, we arrived at the Aira bus stop at about 10 am (4am Ethiopian time). I remember my two nephews from Obo, my sister's son and my grandnephew from Obo's side, were waiting for us. They were all born after I left the country. I didn't know how far the bus stop was from our house. These young men took turns carrying my suitcases; I had no clue how far. We kept on walking on a dirt road through green grass and cornfields. The road became better and better. I spotted a roadside shop.

"Where is this?" I asked.

"Gaba Jimataa," (Friday marketplace) they told me. I looked through the door from a distance and saw toilet paper on the shelf and other modern materials. It was a tremendous improvement!

"Aira should be the capital of Wollega instead of Nekemte. It is cleaner and more beautiful." I told my brother Obosha. He lived in that city for many years when he was a pastor.

He agreed with me and said, "You spoke a prophecy because the community was thinking about it, too." We kept walking down the hill and slightly up the next hill. Ethiopia is full of hills, especially in Aira. Once more, Obosha asked me, "Do you know where you are?"

Then I looked around and saw the giant sycamore tree where my cousin and I brought the cattle to rest after they drank water.

"I know where I am!" I exclaimed with excitement. I pointed towards where our house and our friends' houses were. My brother was amazed. My nephews too were amazed as they didn't know about my childhood experiences. They built many things, including a church and a high school. Almost, after thirty years, it became my landmark and brought back my childhood memories.

Finally, I arrived at home and the absence of my mother overwhelmed me with emotions. My sister and sister-in-law started hugging, kissing, and weeping nonstop. I walked over where Obo was sitting and gave him hugs and kisses. For a while, I kept weeping about my mother. Our eldest brother who was the comforter, encouraged me to stop crying because there was nothing that could be done.

There were about a dozen family members and friends at the house. Soon the family gave us water and soap to wash our hands. This is an Ethiopian custom after a long trip or before and after eating a meal. Obo said table grace and thanked God for bringing me safely to Ethiopia and for protecting me on the bus ride. They served us lunch on two traditional round plates, one for my two brothers, sister-in-law, and my niece who was expecting and the other for the younger nieces and nephews.

It was a humbling experience sitting between my two nurturing brothers for the first time in my life during every meal for the duration of my stay at my birthplace. I'll never forget it. I remember one of them commenting; "You cannot go anywhere." They both loved me unconditionally and raised me after my father's death.

After lunch, with Obosha and my other sister's assistance, I divided the clothes I brought as gifts. I had to purchase more in Addis Ababa with Terunesh's help because there were more relatives than I anticipated. Uncles and aunts I had never met came to visit me. My brothers suggested that I give them small amounts of money as a gesture.

That same afternoon, I visited my mother's burial site. My sister who was a businesswoman and lived in Addis Ababa, had built a tombstone for my mother. I wished I could hug her. Tears were flowing down my cheeks. I told her that I loved her and she had loved me as if I were her only child. I asked her for her forgiveness for not visiting more often. My brother said prayers and I left with a heavy heart but in peace.

Our eldest brother who raised me commented that I was like a bride coming home. He gave me a room where Obosha stayed when they were newlyweds. He slaughtered meat and the family prepared homemade honey wine and other drinks made from grain. However, when my brothers and other siblings drank it, they gave me Fanta or lemon juice to drink. Whenever guests came to visit, they offered them the honey wine, grain beverage, or coffee and sour flatbread spread with spiced butter, a common snack.

I noticed that Obo continued the prayer breakfast he had initiated when I was still in elementary school. He used to walk from house to house with the help of two strong sticks. Now that his muscles were weaker and he was older, neighbors came to the house for prayer breakfast. The spiritual and physical nurturing brought back emotional memories. I shared with my brother that I too continued my morning and evening devotions because of his example. After dinner, we read the scripture and had devotions. The nieces and nephews took turns to do the devotions. One evening, Obo asked me to read the scripture in our tribal language from Psalms 23. He couldn't believe that I still could read it and he was thankful. So was the rest of our family.

The next morning, Obo advised Obosha and me to visit a few close family friends he had known before I was born. Our first visit was to a family whose family members had passed away since I left Aira. It was about half an hour walking distance one way. As it has always been in our culture, the family made coffee and served us with the sour flatbread (injera). There was one unprecedented change I noticed. This friend of ours prepared and served us herself. Before I left my country, the family owned several slaves and all labor was done by the slaves. However, after the change of government, those who served as slaves became independent. It was a wonderful custom just to show up at a friend's house without notice. There were no phones in the homes. One day, around mid-morning, my brother and I made an adventurous walk to another longtime family friend. It was about one-hour walking distance. First, we walked down the valley. There were forests on each side of the road. We crossed the wooden bridge I used cross when I attended the church that was located up the hill from that area. I was grateful the congregation built a new church closer to our house. It was a shorter distance for Obo to walk. While we were walking, I spotted monkeys jumping from tree to tree. I was ready to take pictures. They stared at me through the branches and disappeared. They thought I was going to shoot them. Obosha assured me that there were monkeys around our house. They came to eat the coffee beans Obo planted as well as the bananas.

When we arrived at our friend's house, we were saddened to find out that the husband had been ill for a while, and he became blind. The wife had become deaf. The husband immediately recognized Obosha's and my voice. The wife insisted that we drink coffee and we did. Luckily they had a house helper. The family knew me from my childhood. Before I left, the wife commented: "You used to be skinny and dark, now you're white." I was taken by surprise and I agreed with her. It dawned on me after I returned to America. She was right! In the U.S., we're in an air-conditioned house, then we get in an air-conditioned car. We're seldom in the sun. On the other hand, Ethiopia straddles the equator and while the sun is very hot, the air is dry air. Sometimes it reaches 100 degrees in the villages, while in Addis Ababa the temperature is between 40 degrees in the evenings and above 70 degrees during the day.

After we visited with them for about half an hour, we left and stopped by my childhood dress tailor. He lived a short distance from the house of our family friend. They told us that he had about five or six children. We were in shock because they never had children. My father took me to his house to have my dress sewn while we waited for it to be finished. I had never forgotten the smell of freshly sewn clothes. The tailor was very good. He never used patterns. He just measured the length, chest, and waistline. In those days, Obosha lived far away for pastoral training, and therefore, he was not with me.

On our way home, we stopped at my elementary school classmate's house. She now had a family. We hadn't seen each other for more than thirty-two years. She, too, prepared coffee and the famous sour flatbread (injera) spread with spiced butter. It tasted so delicious with coffee. We spent some time reminiscing about our early childhood together. Despite eating everywhere we went, I didn't gain any weight because we walked up and down the hills everywhere. I didn't have walking sneakers; I used regular comfortable shoes and boots.

Every day family members and friends from far and near visited Obo to congratulate him for my visit. I was amazed how Obo created a beautiful outdoor seating area surrounded by fruit trees. I was surprised to see my childhood playmate who was deaf and mute. She came for a visit in the pouring rain. I had no idea how she found out that I was back for a visit. Growing up, we created our sign language. I found out that she had a son who became a medical doctor. We were excited to see each other again. We were able to communicate many things through body language or total physical response.

On Sunday, I attended the newly built church. My nieces and nephews led the way.

Obo couldn't accompany us due his difficulty in walking. I loved walking on the trail that led to the church through the cornfield, fenced with a variety of pole beans. The pastor of the church, Obosha, and the pastor I was engaged to in Germany had been classmates. He was excited to see me after almost twenty-nine years and introduced me to the congregation. Again, it was an emotional reunion with many of my childhood friends. Some of them came to visit me at home during the week. It was an unforgettable experience.

The pastor invited my brother and me for dinner at 7 pm (1 pm Ethiopian time). "It is an American time, exactly on time," he stressed. We laughed. I assured him that my brother and I would be there on time. In Ethiopian culture, people never arrive on time and usually arrive at an event at least an hour late. The dinner was at one of the church elders' houses. It was wonderful to walk through the cornfields at night with the help of flashlights. I was humbled and honored to be in the company of such distinguished leaders of the church. I enjoyed the variety of meat and vegetable dishes I had missed for so long. I drank Fanta, which was widely available then. I wasn't bashful eating as many Ethiopian women are who pretend they are not hungry and eat very little. I thanked the pastor and the elders for the warm welcome and the dinner.

My godparents also invited my brother and me for lunch. My godfather was the first pastor that I remember. He spoke fluent German and traveled to Germany many times. At the time I visited, he was retired. My godmother prepared all the food and is considered the best cook in the village. My brother and I relished the food. We drink coffee for dessert. There is no dessert in Ethiopian tradition. Instead, we drank coffee brewed with a pinch of salt. In the cities, they may use salt or sugar. To this date, I don't serve desserts unless it is a holiday or birthday, or I have guests.

I had relatives who walked half a day's journey to come and visit. One was the eldest sister of my childhood cousin. A young boy accompanied her because it was a long distance to walk. I was overjoyed to see her. At that time, her youngest brother, who was my shepherd companion, had been in America for twenty years. I knew she wanted to know about his well-being.

I shared with her that he was doing great and he had been a university professor for a while. I told her that we didn't see each other often because it takes about three hours by airplane. Her other brother lived about half a mile from our house, separated by a cornfield. She stayed overnight at his house before returning home. There were relatives from my sister-in-law's side who came from a longer distance. I was grateful to have so many loving family and friends.

Our eldest sister, Ade Gaalitu, invited Obosha, my nephews, nieces, and me for lunch. This was the furthest walking distance of any of the places we had visited so far. Somewhere between our house and my sister's house, there was a river. People placed tree logs across the river during the rainy season to cross it. Ironically, before I left the U.S., I dreamed that I encountered a river and couldn't cross it. I shared this dream with my relatives. We arrived at this river. There was no way I could jump like my brother and nephews with long legs. Obosha, turned towards me and said, "This was about your dream." Then they looked for a log and put it across the river. Obosha and my nephew held each other's hands and then held my hands, one on each side, and finally, I crossed the river carefully stepping on the log. Soon we were on our way up the hill where my sister and her extended family lived.

I always felt bad for our eldest sister because she had never attended school. She got married very young. She had five children: two boys, one who died during the civil war, the other son burned while he was conducting a project. He was a science teacher. I recall that her daughters attended school. One of the girls became a nurse and had been working at the hospital in the village. She took off from work to help my sister prepare food for us. My sister prepared everything Obosha and I enjoyed eating. I treasured the food and the company of her extended family.

Later on, relatives told me that this sister took care of me because I refused to stop breastfeeding. But somehow, I managed to run away from her and came back to my mother. I have no idea how I traveled that distance in the world. I treasured our eldest sister and her family when I visited her.

The time was flying because I was constantly on the go, visiting families, friends, and places before I returned to Addis Ababa. My next visit was to the high school that was built in Aira after I left my country. It is within walking distance for all students who live in the village. Now students don't need to travel hundreds of miles to attend high school after they complete elementary school. One of my nephews was a science teacher at high school. He gave my brother and me a tour. Although it didn't have all the science equipment, teachers taught with the limited resources they had. Students learned through note-taking and memorization.

At my sister Terunesh's request, my nephew who accompanied me needed to see a doctor at Aira Hospital. I met my nieces who were nurses, a brother-in-law who was a pharmacist, my sister a nurse assistant, and an elementary schoolmate who specialized in eye problems. I also found out that another elementary schoolmate was the hospital administrator. We had memorable conversations about our elementary school years. Later, his daughter was married to one of my nephews. My nephew received great care. His mother (my sister Terunesh) was a nurse at this hospital before she moved to Addis Ababa and started a pharmacy business.

It was an exciting event to have dinner at my second sister, Dessie's, house.

Although she had never finished elementary school, she worked at the German Mission hospital as a nurse assistant where she met her husband. She is considered the kindest sister by many of our relatives. She was the one who slowly made me aware that bleeding every month was not a curse but God's way of transforming girls into womanhood. She washed my undergarments. I am ever indebted to her.

Yet another relative, our eldest sister's sister-in-law who is about my age, invited us for a meal. She attended the same elementary school I attended. She stayed with us because my sister's house was about an hour's walking distance. I didn't know how far she pursued her education, but she was working at the hospital when I visited my birthplace. However, she got married to a pastor. Her husband came to the U.S. for pastoral training for about a year. He visited me in Miami before he returned to Ethiopia. We had a delicious meal and enjoyed each other's company.

In the middle of enjoying the company of my relatives and friends and eating delicious food, I was thinking about my three kids back at home. I knew they were in God's hands and in the care of my closest friends. My daughter, fourteen years old, stayed with a very close friend, whose daughter was the same age. We were neighbors when she attended the same school as my daughter. They slept overnight at each other's house frequently. My friend also has an older daughter. My two boys, sixteen and eighteen, stayed at our house under the watchful care of a dear friend, who lived three houses away from ours. For several years, we always celebrated holidays. I designated her as an emergency guardian for the three children. My husband and I had been divorced for three years at that time and I had followed the court's guidelines to provide adult supervision at all times. I also gave my two friends my ex-husband's contact information. I cooked their favorite foods and put them in the freezer to enjoy while I was gone.

I was so grateful for the newly installed public phone in the village. The phone station was about five minutes' walking distance from Obo's house. Because there was a seven-hour time difference, I called them in the evenings, U.S. time. It was quite the sight at the phone station. People lined up to make calls. I observed an elderly man who used a phone for the first time. He held the phone in front of him and bowed to the person on the phone on the other side. He believed the other person could see him. Bystanders constantly reminded him to hold the phone correctly. I could not contain my laughter silently. I went with one of my nephews. Here I am an Oromo woman talking with my children in the U.S. in English. They stared at me as if I were crazy. I charged the calls to my telephone carrier. When I returned to the U.S., the bill for these international calls was over five hundred dollars. However, I was grateful just to hear their voices.

My time in the village became shorter and shorter each day. About three days before returning to Addis Ababa, I started making a list of what I would bring back with me to the U.S. to show my children and my students, such as coffee beans from my brother's coffee farm, and cotton from the field. I knitted my first sweater by spinning that cotton into yarn.

My sister-in-law, Soretti, and my sister Ade Dessie prepared my favorite snack for eating on the road. It was made with roasted, ground wheat, and mixed with spiced butter. My sister, Terunesh who lived in Addis Ababa, prepared a variety of meat dishes, vacuum sealed and frozen. She had advanced kitchen equipment and was an expert in preparing them. God knows how these would go through the customs, especially in U.S.

Instead of taking the bus back to Addis Ababa, my brothers and I suggested another alternative. This time, I would travel by car to the nearest city that had an airport. There were Ethiopian airlines that flew to Addis Ababa. My nephew who came with me and another nephew, Obo's son, accompanied me on the plane. The question was where do we get a car to the airport? It took about two hours one way. I was sure that Obo with his great faith had already been guided by God. His youngest daughter, who was a nurse, had a Norwegian colleague and friend, who visited us frequently while I was there. She was good friend of Obo's family. She came to our rescue and borrowed the car from the mission.

Before we departed, we ate lunch with about a dozen family members. Obo read a scripture and prayed for a safe flight. The farewell was overwhelming. Hugs, kisses, and weeping. I remember my brother reminded me not to wait another twenty-five years to visit. Unfortunately, as of today, it has already been twenty-four years since I last visited.

My niece's friend borrowed a jeep from the mission and she drove my nieces, nephews, and I to Dembi Dollo airport, which is about a two-hour drive. There were about six people in total. We stayed at the hotel overnight. I booked the tickets for my two nephews and myself. We ate breakfast with everyone and thanked our Norwegian friend for her kindness. Everybody accompanied me to the Ethiopian Airlines. This was the first time I had ever flown on this airline. My two nephews went through security without a problem. But when they did all my scanning, it beeped. A female security asked me if I had a wire in my bra, which I had. I took off my bra and left my shirt on. It still beeped. Then she ran the scanner down my legs and it beeped, again. She then realized that the beeping was a result of the stockings I wore.

Finally, I proceeded to the plane. It carried about fifteen passengers and was very clean. The pilot and the flight attendants spoke Amharic, but I was able to communicate with them anyway. It was a comfortable three-hour flight. When I exited, I thanked the Ethiopian pilot in English for a great and safe flight. He appreciated the compliment, but he was surprised that I didn't say it in Amharic.

My sister Terunesh and her son met us at the airport by car. We arrived in Addis Ababa late in the afternoon. My sister prepared coffee and more food to eat before dinner. She asked me what I needed to bring back to my children and friends. Twenty-five years ago when I traveled to the U.S., it was only for one year. Therefore, I took only a few souvenirs. Now, I would take everything I could possibly carry on the Lufthansa airplane. My sister identified a few marketplaces in Addis Ababa where I could shop. Before we left the house, she warned me because she was a pro in bargaining.

"Don't open your mouth about the cost of things. Merchants might escalate the price sense that you talk like a foreigner." I recalled selecting a beautiful Ethiopian national dress with glitters. The price started at about $400.00 Ethiopian birr (dollar). She offered the shop owner 100.00 birr. He refused. My sister walked away while I was still looking at the dress. There was a line of other shops and she stopped at one of them. The man followed her and told her that he would sell for the price she offered him. Finally, she paid even less than the previous price she offered. We found embroidered shirts for my children and even for my ex-husband. I also purchased a medium-sized breadbasket woven with colorful tinted reed. In addition, I purchased small round colorful baskets for storage and other souvenirs and memorabilia to give to my friends who took care of my children. We also found colorful embroidered tablecloths with matching napkins.

After a couple of days of shopping with my sister, I concluded that she is indeed a professional bargainer. As for myself, I needed to attend a bargaining school and learn the language, too.

My brother Obosha and my nephew arrived in Addis Ababa by bus two days later. They told us that the government officials stopped the bus, searched, and found a gun. I didn't remember if they confiscated the gun or not. We thanked God for a safe ride home. I knew Obo back in Aira was praying for his brother and son's safety.

Before I returned to the U.S., I worshipped at the Evangelical Lutheran Church Mekane Yesus, where the pastor and the elders of the church had faith in me and selected me for the scholarship that first brought me to St. Olaf College in the U.S. Unfortunately, the pastor and the church leaders responsible for my scholarship were no longer there. I was not sure if they were traveling out of the country or somewhere else. I am forever indebted to them.

I was excited and grateful to be invited by my first niece's (Sara) family for dinner. My sister Terunesh and her sons accompanied me. She is Obo's first child and I was about nine years old when she was born. When I left Ethiopia, she was in her early teens. Since then, she has become a registered nurse, gotten married, and had two boys. My niece prepared a variety of Ethiopian food for us to enjoy. She is a great cook. I was grateful to see her and her family, and for the delicious food.

I was also honored and humbled to be invited to a dinner at the former church school principal's house after twenty-five years. He was one of the possible candidates to receive the scholarship, but it was offered to me. He reminded me about the scholarship with laughter. The family is now my sister's neighbor. His wife prepared a wide variety of both Western and Ethiopian dishes just in case I had forgotten to eat Ethiopian food. I extended my heartfelt gratitude for their hospitality.

I had a special celebration lunch at my niece's house. She had given birth to her first son two weeks before I visited Ethiopia. He was my sister's first grandchild and my grandnephew. The day I departed for U.S., my niece invited family and friends to this magnificent, fit-for-a-royal family lunch for her son's baptism. I wished I could taste from every dish, but instead, I took a picture of the display of food. Occasionally, when I get homesick for our food, I look at that picture.

To my best memory, my sister Terunesh packed three suitcases, one with food, the other two were packed with clothes and souvenirs. Everyone was praying that we would pass through the security easily with all of these items in tow. The Lufthansa flight was scheduled to depart at about 10:00 pm. The day of our departure, my sister Terunesh invited all our relatives who lived in Addis Ababa to her house. She served some of my favorite food and coffee to everyone. My brother Obosha, Terunesh, and the rest of the family members prayed for my safe return to my family back in U.S. It was a somber moment as everyone was weeping. After I hugged and kissed everyone, we departed for the airport.

Three to four cars in procession accompanied me to the airport. My nephew drove the first car, my sister's Mercedes, with my sister, my brother, and me in it. The second and third cars carried other family members. I knew my luggage was in one the cars, but I didn't know which one. There were probably more cars, but I don't remember for sure. My sister followed me to the luggage check-in counter. To my recollection, the agent asked me to pay extra money for the extra luggage. There was some disagreement as to which currency to pay with. In the end, I paid the required amount and boarded the airplane with more weeping. I'm not sure why, but we stopped in Rome for half of an hour and then continued on our route to Frankfurt. After seven hours of a relaxing flight, we landed in Frankfurt around noon. There was about a four-hour layover. I ordered lunch at a German restaurant in German. I ordered sauerbraten with a side dish, kasekuchen (cheesecake), and coffee and sat down at a table that could seat four people.

Two middle-aged men were looking for a place to sit. They asked me, "Can we join you?"

"You're welcome!" I replied. They pulled extra chairs and sat down at the table. They asked me whether I understood the German menu, to which I replied "yes." When the waitress served my meal, I held the fork and knife in each hand and silently looked down. Then one of the men said, "Amen!" I thanked them. When the waitress brought their food, they prayed out loud including a request for my safe return to the U.S. They shared with me that they were from New Jersey and on their way to do mission work in African countries. I thanked them for their service. I thanked God for prompting me to pray the way I did. I didn't want to feel hypocritical by praying in public.

I called my children in the U.S. and informed them that I was on my way home. I confirmed the scheduled arrival time in Miami. It took ten hours because we were flying against the jet stream. I prayed to God for protection throughout our flight. This time I realized there was hardly any turbulence as we crossed the Atlantic Ocean. Therefore, I slept most of the time. I was awakened when the pilot announced that we were in a different time zone; we had, just crossed the prime meridian. The appearance of the sun was majestic. For a while I tried to nap but couldn't because I was anxious to see my children. About an hour before arriving in Miami, the flight attendants passed security checklists to the passengers. I started filling it out. The male passenger next to me made a comment, "You're checking off that you carry food in your suitcases."

"It's better to tell the truth. It will set us free," I replied. He didn't say anything else. We lined up to check out through customs. They had only about three checkouts. The line was backed up. Then it was my turn to check out. A lady came and said, "Do you have food in your suitcases?" I responded, "Yes." She then said, "Just exit."

I didn't know how God sent his guardian angels to let them know that I had brought food from my country after twenty-five years. I thanked God for His constant presence with me everywhere I went. My three children and my ex-husband were waiting at the door. My family couldn't believe it when they heard about my experience of going through customs. I couldn't wait to get home and call my sister and Obo and tell them what God had done. I called them at midnight, which was morning in Ethiopia, and they were amazed.

I was touched by the love and care our family members had shown me during my visit. I was grateful for their existence and extended my heartfelt gratitude. In addition, I wanted to extend my sincere gratitude to the friends who invited me to their homes and who visited me at my brother Obo's home.

The minute I returned to Miami, my children were excited to hear about my trip to my birthplace. I gave the embroidered Ethiopian shirts to my boys and my ex-husband, and a dress for my daughter. I also brought souvenirs for those who looked after my children. I brought coffee beans, cotton, and wooden artifacts to share with my students. I couldn't wait to share the souvenirs I brought from my country.

Once I returned from my home country in the summer of 1994, I resumed my teaching profession with more enthusiasm. The academic year 1994-1995 was very exciting. I taught second grade for five years, two years of regular students, and three years of advanced classes called TEAM (Teaching Enrichment Activities to Minorities). After I shared with them that I was from Africa, they were so curious.

"Do you live in a tree house?" they asked. These students were so curious they dared to ask daring questions.

Without being offended, I replied to them. "Yes, I shared bananas with the monkeys." We all laughed. I assumed they pictured Tarzan jumping from tree to tree.

CHAPTER TWENTY

REGIONAL TEACHER
OF THE YEAR FINALIST

In the fall of 1999, something beyond all expectations happened to me professionally. It started when one of the teachers on the Teacher of the Year committee approached me and said, "Would you like to run as one of the nominees for teacher of the year for our school? You're an excellent teacher and we want to nominate you," she added. I was perplexed.

"What do I need to do?" I asked.

"The committee will compile information about why you're the best candidate," she replied. "The winner from our school will compete against winners from forty-five schools in the region."

"Teachers are recognized for doing their work?" I was perplexed. Why me?

The day of the election arrived. The other candidates had been teachers longer than I had been. I think there were four of us nominated. All employees at the school were encouraged to vote. I received the most votes and was overwhelmed with joy. I didn't have enough words to express my gratitude. I thanked God and my colleagues for believing in me. The staff was excited for me.

I was given a questionnaire I had to complete. It included my personal information, questions about why I was the best candidate, my teaching assignment, special teaching techniques, and my school and community involvement and leadership. I needed references from my principal, a United Teachers of Dade Steward, and recommendations from two parents. All forms had to be typed professionally. I know we purchased an Apple computer in 1984, but for some reason, I spent every evening at a friend's house typing and printing because I didn't own a printer. After I completed all required documents, I assembled them in the order it was suggested, with the cover sheet beautifully decorated with pictures of students' work in collage form. All completed questionnaires from the winners from forty-five elementary, middle, and high schools were hand-delivered to the regional office. My colleague drove me there. One of the employees collecting the packages looked at mine, especially the cover, and seemed to be surprised. It included a colorful collage of students' class activities. I told God that I completed what I needed to do. The rest I trusted in God's hand. I went home.

About a day later, I received a call from the office. I walked up to the principal's secretary, and she handed me the phone. I had no clue what I was about to hear and was nervous.

The regional chairperson for the teacher committee said, "Congratulations! You're one of the top five finalists out of forty-five schools in the region."

"Thank you! Thank you so much!" I said it repeatedly and my eyes welled up with tears. "Refine what you've already written, complete the additional questionnaire, and return it as soon as possible," he stressed.

When I left the principal's office, everybody congratulated me. Soon the office staff made a banner to hang in the office. It read: "The Year 2000 Teacher of the Year, Region VI Finalist, Congratulations! Aster!" I was overwhelmed with joy and amazement to be one of the top five finalists out of forty-five elementary, middle, and high school teachers.

One of the veteran teachers remarked as I was leaving the office, "Finally, the right person is selected."

"What do you mean?" I asked.

"It is the first time in twenty-five years of the school's history, that any teacher of ours ever received this top honor," she stated.

I thanked her for the kind words. Most of all, I thanked God for all He has done for me.

The next step was for a committee to visit my classroom and observe me while I was teaching. This was followed up by an interview. Both the classroom observation and an interview at the region office were scheduled on the same day. The committee was comprised of about ten members, including regional personnel, teachers, teachers' union representatives, and community representatives.

Something unexpected happened leading to the day of the observation. That year I had an advanced class with twenty-one students in my first grade class. During the course of the year, when I noticed that students needed to be in the gifted program, I recommended them to the administration and school counselor with supporting evidence. Parents must consent for their child to be tested for the gifted program (I was one of the first three teachers certified in gifted education in my school). By the day of the observation, about four students had made the program. Then only seventeen kids remained in my class. Normally, I would get additional students, but everything happened so fast. I would accept whatever was in God's will. The day of the observation, three more students were absent due to illness. Now, I had only fourteen students. The room was almost empty. I followed my conscience and remained truthful to my profession, regardless of what the committee might think.

Prior to the committee's arrival, I placed enough chairs around the room for them. The committee members were escorted to my room and they sat wherever they wanted. They were given students' work folders in alphabetical order and color coded by subject. I handed out color-coded lesson plans that reflected my master lesson plan. It had every lesson plan for every subject from the beginning of the school year.

When the visitors were seated, some of my students asked, "Are these high school students?"

"They are special visitors and they have come to observe our class," I replied. A few weeks back, I had had students from the Design and Architecture School who came to help our class with our neighborhood project. I didn't tell my students about expecting special guests to visit our class that day. I wanted them to act and obey class rules just like it was any other school day. As I always have done, I trusted in God's hand.

I followed my daily class schedule and taught mathematics. After the committee observed how I presented the skills being taught to the students, how I interacted with the students, and how they were actively involved, they went around the room and talked to the students. In addition, they saw students' work displayed on the wall as well as around the classroom. The most significant project was the class neighborhood, built in collaboration with high school students, and decorated for Christmas. On the wall, a map of the world identified where each student's family came from, connected with black yarn, to cut-out figures. It resembled a spiderweb.

I wonder what went through the committee members' minds when they saw unusual projects completed by these few students and who were so smart. I didn't let the committee know why I had only thirteen students that day. I knew that God would provide the opportunity to share with the team if I was asked. The total class observation was about an hour.

That afternoon, the same committee members scheduled an interview with me at the regional office. It was about twenty-five miles away. The administration assigned someone to watch my class while I was gone.

When I arrived at the region office, another finalist was being interviewed, so I waited in the lobby until it was my turn. Meanwhile, I was communicating with my heavenly Father to guide my mind and words for the proper answer to their queries, that His will be done. Then one of the committee members came out and took me to a conference room where everyone was seated. They asked me to be in the hot seat, the head of the table. (In my house I never liked to sit at the head of the table because it makes me feel like I'm in charge. I like to sit where I'm close to the kitchen). Although I knew most of the committee members from my involvement in the school community, they introduced themselves following proper protocol.

The first question they asked me was about my teaching experiences. What qualifies me to be the best candidate for teacher of the year from our region? I had written on paper why I was the best candidate; however, it was intimidating to brag about my accomplishments, involvement, and recognition verbally. This was against my culture's nature. The whole process was like defending a thesis. Their inquiries were based on what I had written in the package I submitted. I was excited when they asked me about the class size. This was a great opportunity to share why I had a smaller class. I shared with the committee that some of my students performed high on their SAT scores. When I confirmed each student's ability and could determine that he/she belonged in the gifted program, I recommended that to the administration. So far, four of my students have qualified. I also informed the committee that on the day of the observation, three students were absent due to illness. They were satisfied with my responses.

The region held a luncheon banquet in honor of the five regional finalists. Administrators, United Teachers of Dade Stewards, teachers, parents and family members of the five finalists were invited to the banquet. Unfortunately, my children didn't attend because I didn't receive the invitation from my school in time. A few elected officials and district school board members attended the celebratory event.

My district school board member who knew me from school and community involvement stopped by our table and made an intriguing comment to me, "I knew you were a great politician, but I didn't know that you're a great teacher. Congratulations!" I thanked him for his kind words. In 1988 and 1989, he was in attendance when I received the Exemplary Volunteer of the Year certificate.

The winner of the five of us finalists was announced at the luncheon. She would go on to represent our region at the district level. I was grateful to God, humbled, and honored to be one of the top five finalists out of forty-five schools. We all received beautiful plaques.

CHAPTER 21

APPOINTED AS A
DELEGATE TO CHINA

Sometime during the fall of 2000, I received a letter of appointment from the director of the National Board Certification Office to join other elected public officials, school board members, and national board-certified teachers from around the country to attend a symposium at the invitation of the Ministry of Education in the People's Republic of China.

The main purpose of the trip was to compare the educational standards of the two most industrialized nations, the United States and the People's Republic of China. The trip took place in April of 2001. I was surprised at the invitation. I was not a national board-certified teacher. Similar to my journey in the past, I shouldn't be surprised by what was in God's plan. I trusted in His guidance. I knew that one or two teachers at our school were national board-certified, but they were not invited. I wondered who had recommended my name and why. I wanted to know who was behind this mystery appointment. I picked up the phone and called the National Board Certification Office to inquire. I still didn't get an answer. The national office assured me that I would receive a detailed package about the itinerary and the financial obligation this would require. Immediately I shared the news with my supervisor and she congratulated me for the invitation. I shared with my colleagues too, they were overjoyed, and some offered their support if I needed help.

A few weeks later, I received the trip package. Along with my personal information, they advised me to enclose about one-third of the trip expense. The total charge included five-star hotels in Beijing, Nanjing, and Shanghai, food, transportation to and from the educational symposium, sightseeing of historic sites in Beijing, climbing the Great Wall, the Forbidden City, and much more. The duration of the trip was two weeks.

I thanked God that I was invited with this elite group of elected national officials, school board members, and national board-certified teachers. In the past, God provided me with everything I needed for my education without asking Him. I had faith and trusted in Him and His providence that He would bring people in my path who would help me with the trip. *"And my God will supply every need of yours according to his riches in glory in Christ Jesus.* (Phil.4:19). *"And without faith it is impossible to please him, for whoever would draw near to God must believe that he exists and that he rewards those who seek him."* (Heb.11:6). Therefore, I mailed my personal information and the down payment. At that time, I wasn't sure if the departure date coincided with our spring vacation. However, I was determined to follow God's lead.

After Christmas vacation, I contacted a pastor who then oversaw the Evangelical Lutheran churches in Miami-Dade and Monroe County. I had never met him before. He assured me that he would ask a Christian organization to contribute to my trip. I was grateful to my colleagues who also contributed to my trip. The National Board instructed all participants where and how to apply for visas through their sponsor. I had been through this many times and I completed the paperwork promptly.

Throughout my preparation for this trip, I suspected that I would encounter obstacles; however, by the grace of God, I knew I could overcome all hindrances. After Christmas vacation, I realized that my trip didn't coincide with the spring vacation. That meant I had to take two weeks leave of absence. There was a discussion about whether I should be granted personal (without pay) or professional leave (with pay). Although my trip had to do with an educational trip, my supervisor denied me professional leave with pay; I took two weeks' leave without pay because I was determined to attend this historic event. I completed all leave of absence paperwork, signed by the principal and myself about two weeks before my departure. *"What, then, shall we say in response to this? If God is for us, who can be against us?"* (Romans 8:31)

About this same time, we heard that twenty U.S. Air Force personnel were being held hostage by the Chinese government. I had no idea how this might impact the trip, but I had peace and the situation didn't deter me. Just before I departed for my trip, on my way to the principal's office, I met my supervisor halfway. "I came to say goodbye," I said.

"Are you still going?" was the response.

"Yes, I am ready," I replied.

"I wish you a safe trip!"

I flew from Miami International Airport to Los Angeles, California, where the entire delegation met. After a brief meeting with our team leaders, whom we had never met, the delegation leader informed us that we would meet our roommates in Hong Kong. There were about one hundred U.S. delegates, and a few came with their spouses. We boarded this massive airplane from Cathay Pacific Airways that resembled a mansion filled with about twenty-seven Asian flight attendants. This was different from the previous jumbo jet I had flown in the past. The flight duration from Los Angeles to Hong Kong was sixteen hours. There was a giant wall-sized television that displayed our location during the trip. When it was safe, we got up and walked around. Wow! There was no shortage of food. I didn't know which of the three meals we were offered was best; breakfast, lunch, or dinner. Then we took another airline for three hours to Beijing, where we stayed for five days. I met my roommate in Hong Kong for the first time. It was amazing how the government orchestrated our luggage; when we arrived at the five-star hotel, our luggage was already in the room. We were amazed at their hospitality. Throughout our trip, our Chinese host took care of our luggage.

My roommate was an elementary school teacher, national board certified, and had received teaching performance awards. She was from the Midwest and was very friendly. Once we were settled, I shared with her that I'm a Christian and have daily morning and evening devotions. I asked her whether she preferred to get ready first in the morning or not. It worked perfectly. I showered first while she slept. Then I was able to have my morning devotion while she took a shower. In the evening, we followed the same routine. I was cognizant that China is a communist nation, but that didn't deter me from taking my Bible and two devotional books. Like the American Express commercial: "*Never leave home without it.*" I never leave my house without my devotional books and Bible if I have to spend anywhere overnight.

We ate an elegant dinner at the famous Beijing's Peking Duck Restaurant. The host told us this was where former President H.W. Bush, Yasser Arafat, and Fidel Castro dined. The delegation sat at a giant round table. In the middle was a revolving lazy Susan, decked with roasted duck and a variety of Chinese vegetables. The presentation of the food was so glorious that one could dive in. For utensils, they offered chopsticks, forks, and knives. The restaurant owner was amazed at how well the U.S. delegates utilized chopsticks.

I discovered some similarities between the Ethiopian and Chinese cultures. After dinner, guests were supposed to leave food on their plates, otherwise, they would be considered greedy. When greeting anyone, the individual bows as well when giving or receiving something, including business cards. One needs to use both hands and a bow. I was amazed to find out that the word for tea in Chinese is *cha* which is almost the same sound as in Ethiopian *shai*. During the two weeks I spent in China, I felt at home. I had many Chinese friends in the United States but they never shared with me the cultural differences or similarities. Before traveling to China, I learned a few Chinese phrases from the father of one of my colleague's students. I could say Xièxie (sshyeah-sshyeah) for thank you; "Nǐ hǎo ma?" (nee-haoww-mah?) for how are you? Food is delicious; "*Hao*" with a thumb up; and (zài jiàn) for see you again.

Coincidently, that same father was in Beijing for a business trip at the same time I was there for this trip. He came to visit me at the hotel where we were staying. When he saw me in the hotel lobby, he hugged me. Our tour guide informed us that Chinese people don't hug. Maybe this family lived in the U.S. and they were Westernized. I didn't know how he knew that I was a Christian, but he showed me the most beautiful Catholic church in Beijing. He also took me to a very large exhibit displaying all of the many different types of food they would be serving during the Olympics, as well as to the site where the 2008 Olympics would be held. My roommate couldn't join me so I had a private tour. I was grateful for his hospitality. I was able to forget about the hostage crisis just for a little while because a Chinese parent from my school in America had made me feel at home. During dinner, my roommate shared with the other delegates about my private tour and they were amazed too. To this day, I am still very grateful for this extraordinary opportunity.

The following day, after our arrival, we visited the University of Beijing for the symposium. Before we departed, the hotel served us a colorful, elegant, and delicious breakfast: It included a variety of meat including fish, fruits, vegetables, and beverages. There were a few buses that transported the delegates from place to place. Each bus had a delegation leader; ours was the state representative from New Mexico and he accompanied us everywhere we visited. I was fortunate to sit with the director of the National Board Certification in the front row of the bus. There were other officers with us, as well. Our bus had a young dynamic Chinese tour guide with a sense of humor, who had worked at Disney World in the United States. She advised us that there is no hugging in the Chinese culture. In addition, she warned us not to be offended by the most common questions the Chinese ask visitors: "How old are you?" and "What is your salary?"

Once we arrived at the university, our Chinese counterparts gave us a tour of the facilities in small groups. The university auditorium seating arrangement with its headphones and staging area reminded me of a picture of the United Nations Assembly. The National Board Certification office compiled information in Chinese and English on each delegate.

Elected officials from around the U.S., the director of the National Board Certification and her staff, national board-certified teachers, the individuals who were scheduled to make a presentation, and those in the audience were introduced. Our hosts, the Ministry of Education faculty of the People's Republic of China, introduced representatives from the Ministry of Education. Everyone put on the earphones to be connected to the translation device. Sometimes this caused an inconvenience when switching back and forth. The main focus of the symposium included: 1) How teaching in the United States is delivered and assessed, and 2) How teachers are trained and evaluated. I learned that certain states in the United States didn't enforce compulsory education, which amazed me. Our Chinese counterparts were flabbergasted to find out the discrepancies in the American educational system; each individual state administers its own state assessments instead of using a national test. The People's Republic of China has one form of assessment. In one of the schools we visited, students' test scores were posted in the hallways. Their scores ranged from about ninety to one hundred percent. In my country of Ethiopia, there is one national examination administered to all students in the country scored by percent. At an early age, students and parents are required to take education seriously. Before the school year begins, Chinese teachers visit their students' parents' homes, making sure everything is ready for the school year. Parental support is critical for the student's success.

In the United States, teachers' training and evaluation is advanced. In 2001, the Chinese Ministry of Education began to improve their teacher training program. Contrary to teacher evaluation methods in the United States, parents participate in the teacher selection process in the People's Republic of China. I was astonished that students' discipline wasn't an issue. In a fourth-grade science class, there were about forty students. Each student's desk was separated by glass barriers. With a clap of the hands, the teacher initiates an activity: After ten to fifteen minutes of loud discussion, a single clap ceased the activity and immediately their eyes were turned to the teacher. The American educators were amazed at the sight. Looking back to my home country, Ethiopia, students' discipline wasn't an issue either. However, unlike the Chinese parents, the parents in the village were illiterate and parental involvement was unheard of. Therefore, it was the responsibility of the school to educate and discipline the students.

Similar to the United Nations Assembly, there was a group photo of the United States delegation and members of the Ministry of Education from the People's Republic of China following the symposium.

The city of Beijing is rich with significant historic sites. Some of these were included in our itinerary. We visited the Forbidden City, Tiananmen Square, the Summer Palace, and, my favorite, the most recognized symbol of China, the Great Wall. It was begun in the third century BC and was constructed over several centuries, claiming the lives of thousands of builders. As our bus approached the location, we witnessed this magnificent highway, which seemed to reach the blue sky.

"There are two ways; both of them lead to the top, to the visitors' viewing site," the tour guide stated. "The left route is easier and not as steep as the one on the right," she added. The right wall is steep and is challenging. My roommate and I were standing together, I turned to her and said that the Great Wall reminded me of biblical text about the narrow and wide gates. *"Enter through the narrow gate. For wide is the gate* and broad is the road that leads to destruction, and many enter through it." *(Matthew 7:13)*. Every time I encounter remarkable events in nature or with people, it reminds me of biblical verses. I remember she looked at me with disbelief on her face. I'm grateful we both decided to take the right, the more challenging route. We had our water and comfortable sneakers. I was stunned at the Asian women wearing high-heeled shoes to hike the path. My roommate reminded me of a hiker with her book bag on her back climbing ahead of me with confidence. I had a medium-sized purse with water and a copy of a local newspaper the editor had provided me to take to the Great Wall of China and have a picture taken with it.

We began our expedition up the wall, encouraging and supporting each other until we reached the visitors' viewing location. It was an amazing view from the top and peaceful with all the greenery in the surroundings. We saw God's marvelous creation as far as we could see with our naked eyes. No wonder Jesus went to the mountain by himself or with His disciples to pray. *"After six days Jesus took with Him Peter, James and John the brother of James, and led the up a high mountain by themselves. There He was transfigured before them. His face shone like the sun, and His clothes became as white as the Light...Peter said to Jesus, 'Lord, it is good for us to be here. If you wish, I will put up three shelters—one for You, one for Moses, and one for Elijah.'"* (Matthew 17:1-13). I didn't dare to look back down the way we climbed the wall. It reminded me of the story of Sodom and Gomora when God ordered Lot and his wife to flee, *"But Lot's wife looked back, and became a pillar of salt."* (Genesis 19:26). Sooner or later we'd have to go back down, but for now, I just enjoyed the view. It was an excruciating journey, but worth it to reach the top. We stopped to rest for only a minute or so because we didn't want to block each other. It was one way, ascending, and descending.

Some of our colleagues suffered injury to their feet. I have never forgotten the sight when the Chinese soldiers carried one individual down the steep route. I was grateful to experience the helping hands of our seeming adversaries, in the midst of a hostage crisis, who had compassion for us visitors.

Our next stop was the city of Nanjing, known for its beauty and cleanliness. Every year, there is a contest between the various cities to determine which city is the cleanest. In 2001, when we visited, Nanjing, which was once the capital of China, was the winning city. During our visit, we visited schools as well as families.

Bicycles are the major means of transportation. Both in Beijing and Nanjing, an oversized bicycle lane, parallel to the main streets, is dedicated to cyclists. It is an awesome sight to see businessmen in suits and women in suits and high heel shoes, riding on bicycles. There are huge parking lots for bicycles.

On our way driving to Shanghai, the traffic with cars was bumper to bumper.

Advertisements in English on high buildings resembled that of New York City. We spent a day or two, visiting various silk, pearl, and elegant carpet factories. According to our tour guide, many women work long hours for minimum wage. Each delegate purchased whatever souvenirs they wanted to bring back to the U.S. depending on their budget. I was grateful to get some souvenirs for those who helped me with the trip.

During my trip, many of the US delegates as well as the director of the National Board, had read my biographical background information. They encouraged me to be certified by National Board. They suggested that I register with the state of Florida Education Department when I returned, to complete the required portfolios and rigorous assessment.

Upon my return from the People's Republic of China, the editor and publisher of the *Kendall Gazette*, Miami's local newspaper, wrote an extensive story about my trip which was placed on a full-page front cover of the newspaper. I'm grateful to the publisher who had written several stories on me in the past. The paper has recognized me three times during Women's month, and other times for my accomplishments as a community and school advocate. After I returned from my trip, the same pastor who supported my trip financially invited other Lutheran congregations in Miami and hosted a reception with special cake and refreshments at my home church following my presentation on my trip. I didn't have words to express my gratitude for his support. A few weeks later, I received a heartwarming official proclamation from our group team leader, New Mexico State Senator, Senator Carlos R. Cisneros.

CHAPTER 22

GOD LAID ME ASIDE

During my trip to China, my colleagues encouraged me to register with the Florida Department of Education for the National Board Certification. According to them, I had the qualifications but needed to go through the process for certification. I was humbled by the encouragement from these accomplished professionals and was excited to pursue it when I returned to my school.

The state department paid for about two-thirds of the fee, and I paid the remainder. Then I received all the materials and sequential guidelines to complete the certification process. Elementary school teachers follow the guidelines for the general education certification. After reviewing all the materials, I embarked on this enticing and prestigious project.

Why in the world am I going through this process? Didn't God let me travel along with those who already earned their certification? Is it the additional money I would receive after earning the national certification? I was perplexed. Didn't God provide me with everything I needed without asking for it?

As Christians, we face many trials, some of which we bring on ourselves. I listened to colleagues' praises instead of dwelling on God's abundant blessings. I embarked on this enticing journey, only to find out that this wasn't in God's plan.

I have never forgotten what happened on December 6, 2001. It was about 7 am, and I had assembled all the National Board Certification materials and was on my way to the school to work with those who had taken the National Board. Other teachers and I had scheduled our meeting early in the morning before school started. I parked my car and began walking carefully towards the school. I held the materials tight in my left arm, protecting them as if it were a baby. The sidewalk to the school building was wet as it rained the night before and it was covered with some leaves. Suddenly, I slipped and fell on my right hip and shoulder still holding the materials tight to prevent them from falling on the wet ground.

Thank God one of the parents passing by saw me and assisted me up and walked me to the cafeteria. I didn't know the extent of my injury. With the help of my colleagues, they called 911 and the paramedics arrived immediately. As much as I tried to lift my body to sit on a stretcher, I couldn't move an inch due to excruciating pain in my lower back. Finally, the paramedics lifted me up and put me on a stretcher and wheeled me to the emergency vehicle. I overheard students asking if the fire truck was part of career day. While in the emergency vehicle, the paramedics took my vital signs.

They asked me, "Move your legs."

I couldn't believe I couldn't perform this simple task; after all, every morning I did one hundred sit-ups after I read my devotional. My oldest son met me at school.

The paramedics brought me to the emergency room at of one of the largest private hospitals in our area, and left me in the hallway, filled with other patients. They reported to the nurse's station. My oldest son was standing by me. I felt like screaming because of the pain in my back and hip. However, suppressing pain during my circumcision was something that I inherited from my culture, which still haunted me. As I was laying on the stretcher, I glanced around and was surprised to see my other two children and my ex-husband standing there. I was overwhelmed with emotions and my tears welled up. (My husband and I had been divorced for ten years; however, we had established a positive relationship about our families.)

"How did you find out so fast?" I asked. "Eba (eldest son) called us," they replied.

I thanked them and told them that I was glad to see them. I advised them to go back to workplaces as it would take a while to be admitted to a room. My son would inform the others. I was grateful he was working from home.

After a while, the nurse wheeled me to a semi-private partition. She came and took my vitals. Soon an emergency department doctor came and ordered an X-ray. They told me that the damage to my hip and back was not visible because of all of the swelling. However, the doctor ordered medication to reduce the inflammation. He also ordered some kind of muscle relaxer. I told my son to take a break and go home. After I had taken the medication, the nurse came to check on me.

"How are you feeling?" was the question.

I was mumbling, my tongue was tight, and I couldn't get a word out.

The nurse realized that I was allergic to the muscle relaxer. She took my vital signs repeatedly. Then the doctor prescribed another medication, which I assumed to counteract the previous one. Soon the nurse came back. This time I was able to talk. Then the nurse shared with me a shocking fact: "We almost lost you!"

"What do you mean?" I asked.

"Your blood pressure dropped."

To this date, I'm extremely sensitive to medications. Even extra-strength Tylenol makes me light-headed. I recalled my gynecologist prescribed Tylenol with codeine for pain in 1992 after a major surgery. Soon, I began hallucinating; my bed was spinning. My doctor stopped that medication and I requested a regular Tylenol, which relieved the pain.

A month later, I received a check for $130.00 from the hospital. I immediately called. "There must be a mistake. Usually, you send me a bill, instead I received a check from your department."

"You didn't finish the Tylenol with codeine your doctor prescribed. You're refunded for the remainder." I thanked the individual and I learned something new.

As to my injury status, the emergency room doctor wanted to keep me under observation for twenty-four hours. I was so grateful that my son brought me my devotional book and the Bible. He knew soon it would be morning, and I had to have my devotion. I had no idea what time of the day it was. I thanked him for thinking of me.

Before sending me home, the doctor ordered Vioxx for pain and inflammation and sent me home in excruciating pain. He advised me to make an appointment with worker's compensation doctors. I had never heard of worker's compensation. I had never been injured on school property. With the assistance of the school secretary, she provided me a list of doctors. When I called the worker's compensation doctors, they told me that there was no opening until the middle of January 2002, almost a month after my fall. Meanwhile, I developed an adverse reaction from the Vioxx. When I lay down, my heart started pounding. It felt as if someone was playing basketball under my bed. I stopped taking it. Instead, I used regular Tylenol and ice for the pain and inflammation. I thank God that my eldest son, Ebadut, was still living with me. My car was a van and it was painful to raise my body to sit in it. I was so grateful that my son had purchased a sports car with a low seat. He was my caregiver and drove me to my doctor's appointment. I was forever indebted to him for the care and love he showed me.

My sister and her family who lived in Minneapolis, Minnesota, at the time of my injury, came to visit me. I was grateful to see the family in this difficult time. I couldn't get up because of the pain in my back and hip and their help was invaluable. I couldn't believe my eyes when I saw my brother-in-law and their three grown sons purchase the groceries and start cooking. I had never seen my brother-in-law cook. My sister supervised him and her sons. The food they prepared tasted so delicious. I was forever grateful to them. I was grateful too to my son because he had been buying my favorite foods. My sister was amazed at my son's generosity and hospitality.

My sister remained with me through the Christmas holiday while her family returned to Minneapolis. I was so exhilarated that my sister joined me to attend Christmas Eve service, which has been my favorite holiday since I was a child.

She was great moral support as she had been a nurse and owned pharmacies while she was back in Ethiopia. In the late seventies, my husband had visited my sister's family on his way to Southern Sudan. When he returned, he shared with us that he had received a royal welcome. As a gesture of his gratitude, he prepared a spectacular dinner and barbecue and invited my sister, our three children, and me. My ex-husband was an expert in barbecuing. In general, men don't cook, but they all seem to like barbecuing. I was grateful for his thoughtfulness during this trying time. My sister was so indebted for his effort to entertain her. By that time, I was using a walker to get around.

After one month of waiting, I finally saw one of the worker's compensation doctors. They reviewed the X-rays taken at emergency room which I had brought with me. He discovered that I had herniated discs and a fractured sacrum. Seeing the natural smile on my face, they assumed I was faking because I also didn't scream when they were raising my feet. They had no clue the cultural suppression of pain that haunted me forever. Later on, I shared this experience with my friends and they told me that many people fake injury to collect benefits.

"Why in the world would anyone pretend to be injured?" I asked. "Unfortunately, that's the way some people collect benefits." This idea infuriated me. Next, I was referred to an orthopedic doctor.

Through my adversity, the cultural barrier was broken. My brother-in-law and his sons prepared meals for me at my house and my ex-husband cooked and invited his sister-in-law to his home. I was grateful and thanked God for the rare opportunity. I know that God makes all things work together for those who trust in Him. *"And we know that in all things God works for the good of those who love him"* (Rom. 8:28).

At this time, I had a worker's compensation attorney whom my neighbor recommended. Although I was informed that the worker's compensation doctors were not patient friendly, I thank God for two doctors, a neurologist and an orthopedic doctor, that He placed in my pathway during this challenging period. The orthopedic doctor, whom I considered sincere, viewed my back and hip X-rays. He confirmed that I had a herniated disc and fractured sacrum. All these medical terms, even though they are parts of my body, became stranger every time.

Then, the orthopedic doctor asked me. "Did you ever have a bone density test?"

"What is that?" I questioned.

"To check whether your bones are porous. It is done with a special X-ray. When you're able to lay down flat on your back, ask your gynecologist to order this test for you," he added. I was amazed that bones could be porous like a sponge. Then he gave me a referral to the neurologist whose office was in Hialeah, Florida.

I'd never been in Hialeah before. It didn't have a good reputation. The traffic is a nightmare and so are the road signs. Thanks to my son who was a mechanic, he somehow found his way around. The doctor's office was about twenty-five miles away. Once we arrived, there was another form to complete, even though I carried around my previous medical information. Then, the nurse called me in to the neurologist's office. An older doctor was sitting in a recliner, with a cigar in his mouth. Wow! I'd never seen a doctor smoking before. I was in for a surprise. My son was sitting in the waiting room. I started praying that God give this doctor wisdom. Then, he pulled out the X-rays I brought and placed them against a viewing machine to examine the damage to my discs and lower back. He pointed out every detail of my injury on a plastic model of the human spine next to his desk. As the saying goes, "*One cannot judge a book by its cover.*" He was a great doctor.

He then said, "I don't recommend surgery to correct the herniated discs. It might not be corrected and you may have more problems. I will recommend therapy," he said. He prescribed for me to see a worker's compensation therapy provider close to my home. I am ever grateful for his ingenuity in saving me from having back surgery.

I'm indebted to the orthopedic doctor who suggested a bone density test. I followed his recommendation and also shared previous X-rays with my gynecologist at my annual checkup. At that time, I was able to lie flat on my back. The bone density X-ray revealed that my bones were in bad condition, especially my left thigh. God was walking alongside me when I fell. I couldn't begin to imagine what would have happened if I fell on my left side.

I thank God as long as I live and am grateful for giving the neurologist and the orthopedic doctors the wisdom for their decisions. To this date, I'm receiving the treatment I need to make my bones stronger. Something good came out of a tragic event. I'll always thank God for watching over me even when I was not following His lead.

The National Board Certification activities must be completed while I am actively engaged with my students. Therefore, I had to return the National Board Certification materials to the Florida State Department of Education, in its original package immediately. I had to explain the reasons and include possible doctors' notes so that I would be refunded the fee I paid for the certification. My worker's compensation doctor recommended that I take disability leave for a few months. As a first grade teacher, I needed to be on my feet all day, which would mean I would be in constant pain. In addition, I couldn't use my right hand due to the injury when I fell on it. I had shoulder muscle damage, as well. Thanks to my worker's compensation attorney who insisted that I have an X-ray taken of the right shoulder. Finally, it was approved. Eventually, it has gotten better after several therapy sessions.

My attorney contacted the Miami-Dade County Public Schools Worker's Compensation Department regarding disability payments. He told me that I would be paid two-thirds of my salary while on disability leave. "How will I pay my mortgage and bills? The devil was testing my faith in God. The same God who supplied all my needs in the past would also provide me now," I assured myself and kept trusting in God. However, I had to see for myself. I logged into the household budget program on my computer and started entering the income and expenses for the next five and half months. One column was red, indicating that I didn't have enough income to cover all the expenses. I continued to pray to God that He remove those red columns. I have never forgotten the devotional text I read on March 20, 2002, that same week. The theme was, "From Red to White," from the prophet of Isiah, ". . .though your sins be as scarlet, they shall be as white as snow" (Isaiah 1:18). This was my third month since I took disability leave. Although it talked about the blood of Christ cleansing our sins, the Holy Spirit also revealed to me that God would erase the "red" negative balance I previously calculated. Immediately, I was reassured and had complete peace. To my recollection, my attorney told me if I returned to teach before my sixth month, the Worker's Compensation Department might reinstate the one-third salary they deducted during the disability leave.

As always, I continued with my daily morning devotions and scripture readings, which gave me strength and comfort for the day, while my evening devotions gave me complete peace and protection throughout the night. *"At present, you may be temporarily harassed by all kinds of trials. This is no accident. It happens to prove your faith which is infinitely more valuable than gold."* (1 Peter 1:6-7). I also read from Pastor Rick Warren's devotional, which states, *"The things you wish were most removed from your life are often the very things that God is using to shape you and make you into the believer of character He wants you to be."*

With the help of God, I returned to teaching by May 2002, before the end of the school year. I was excited to see my first graders and their parents, and so were they. I extended my heartfelt gratitude for their compassion. I received many get-well cards, and visits from my students, parents, and colleagues. Especially thanks to my room mom who constantly stopped by and visited me. During the time I was on disability leave, my amazing first grade colleagues were so creative that they held a grade-level meeting at my house and warmed my heart with refreshments. I extended my gratitude for their thoughtfulness. This was my most memorable event.

Before I was nationally board certified, God provided me the opportunity to travel with some very respected people to China, and I came to my senses that earning this prestigious honor was not in God's plan. I asked God for His forgiveness and had perfect peace since then.

For the period of the 2003-2004 academic year, I served as first grade level chair elected by my first grade colleagues. Subsequently, from 2004 to 2006, I served as primary grades department chairperson elected by my colleagues in the primary grades and served as a liaison between the administration and primary grades (kindergarten, first, and second) teachers. I was grateful for their trust in me to represent them.

Now that I had the divorce behind me with God's help and the individuals He put in my path, I encountered a new road-block in my teaching profession. My principal informed me that the enrollment in our school was decreasing because relief schools that were being built were now dispersing students to these other new schools. Therefore, teachers with less teaching seniority must transfer. I was one of them. This happened about a year after my divorce, the worst possible timing. My school administration assigned me to a school where our former assistant principal was then an administrator. I had worked with her when I was a volunteer leader. She was the most compassionate principal any employee could wish to work for, except the school was about twenty-five miles away from my house.

My principal and his assistant were very sympathetic to my situation. I recalled conversing with the assistant administrator in the cafeteria. "There was nothing that we could do for you," she commented. *"Nothing is impossible for God,"* I replied, and my eyes filled with tears. I knew it was the district office that was responsible for the transfer of teaching staff. I had scheduled an appointment with my soon-to-be new principal for an orientation.

On the day of the orientation, the principal gave me a tour of the school, introducing me to most of her staff. When we met in her office, she offered me some kind of leadership position since she had known me for several years at the previous school. Coincidently, the school was the same model as my neighborhood school, with open classrooms. I extended my heartfelt gratitude for her warm welcome and for making me feel at home in this difficult time.

I was teaching summer school at my neighborhood school and received a call from the principal's office! I had no indication what it was about. When I arrived at my principal's office, both the principal and his assistant were seated. Then the assistant principal said, "Do you remember what you said when we were conversing? 'Nothing is impossible for God.'"

"It happened." At that moment my eyes teared. Both administrators continued, "One of your colleagues is transferring to a school close to her home. You would be the right person to replace her. Therefore, you will remain at the school." Those days, the school staff needed to be racially balanced and I fit the profile. Tears rolled down my cheeks with joy and gratitude. I thanked both my principal and his assistant and gave them hugs. I thanked God for reopening a door and an opportunity to be close to my kids' schools and my home. I trusted in God that something good would come out of this as He promised in the scripture. *"And we know that in all things God works for the good of those who love him, who have been called according to His purpose,"* (Romans 8:28). Next, I contacted the other principal who made me feel at home at her new school and thanked her for her compassion and for the warm welcome.

I recall the time, the academic year 1992 to 1993, when I was given a regular second grade class. However, in the following three years, from 1993 to 1996, I was granted a dream second grade class with students who earned high academic grades but were not yet screened for the gifted program. The program is called TEAM (Teaching Enrichment Activities to Minorities). Although I had already earned a gifted education certification, I needed special training to work with these students. They needed challenging activities in all academic areas, particularly mathematics and science.

During spring, primary grade students learned about plants and animals. I decided to grow sweet potatoes from seeds. I intended to incorporate this with sustained silent reading, which was recommended. Prior to planting the seeds, we discussed that plants need food, water, air, and sun. I also heard that plants grow when one talks to them. I realized that my students were restless when they came back from lunch. Every student labeled their plant seeds and placed them in a common area. As soon as they arrived from lunch, each student picked a book and their plant and placed it on their desks and read to the plant silently for half an hour every day. I, too, read silently. People came to my class and couldn't hear a pin drop. As each plant sprouted and grew, students learned the different parts of their plants. However, the students began complaining about the size of their plants.

"My plant was not growing as big as my friend's. I read to it every day. It is not fair!" One girl argued.

"Did you provide all that the plant needed?" I questioned. "Yes!" was the response.

We discovered that some students overwatered their plant. We concluded that too much of anything is not good. Finally, they were convinced. They enjoyed measuring and comparing the heights of the plants with that of their classmates. This then incorporated their mathematic skills. I was also proud how well they cooperated when they measured their plants and compared them to each other. They were looking forward to reading to their plants until the end of the school year. Then they took them home.

One year I had well-behaved advanced second grade students. I challenged them with an assignment. I had heard or read somewhere that "*It takes nine or more positive people to overcome or change one negative person.*" Towards the middle of the school year, the administration enrolled a male student in my class who had behavior problems. The students took on the challenge to apply this theory and be positive. It was as if I had a magical wand to change him. Our class did many hands-on activities. I requested a group of boys include him in their group for the rest of the school year. They accepted the challenge and included him in every activity, including eating and playing with him. They had a positive influence on the new students. He too enjoyed being with the group.

At the end of the school year classroom teachers nominate individuals for academic excellence in various subjects who have turned around academically or in behavior. This time, I asked the whole class to individually nominate a student and explain why. Then, I collected their nominations. To my surprise, the students unanimously nominated the new student who had enrolled with bad behavior. They stated that his behavior had improved tremendously. I thanked the group who welcomed him into their group and those who nominated him. I was in tears of joy and the new student was overwhelmed for being nominated as the Turnaround student by his classmates. When I gave out the end-of-the-year awards, I shared with the audience this touching experience.

I have always enjoyed challenging young minds. Sometimes I invited parents who worked in the science field. I recall inviting a dad who brought in various caged insects to the classroom. The kids had an in-house field trip without leaving their classroom and paying for the buses. They were mesmerized at the displays.

Another time, the curriculum called for studying neighborhoods in social studies, and odd and even numbers in mathematics. I decided to incorporate these skills in real-world experiences. Each student built a model of his or her house. Parents were allowed to assist. Before the end of the grading period, they brought their projects to the classroom. I had a large classroom with long tables I could use for displaying their models. Meanwhile, I invited magnet high school students who were studying design and architecture, to help in the planning of our class neighborhood. The mother of one of the students was an educator at the architecture school. My students implemented the concept of even and odd numbers in numbering homes. Also as a class, through brainstorming, they decided the different components of a neighborhood, such as roads, a school, a hospital, and a playground.

Students were introduced to the vocabulary associated with building a neighborhood. My students had an amazing day being mentored by older students. It gave them a hint as to what they might become when they grow up. There is nothing more exciting and rewarding than teaching different grade levels and diverse student populations.

While enjoying the diversity of my students and helping them to gain the knowledge they needed, I also encountered an embarrassing moment. I always let my students sit in groups of four or six according to their given assignment. One day, in my first grade, everyone was engaged in completing their work.

Suddenly, a boy came to me and said, "Someone touched my wiener." "Why would bring your wiener to school?" I asked. "Where did you put it?" I asked.

Then, he pointed to his private part. The boy grinned and the whole class burst into laughter. Having lived in Germany, I only knew "wiener" as a hot dog. As to the behavior of the students, I reported it to the administration and met with the parents. This incident was both an embarrassment and teachable moment. Because of this incident, I emphasized the importance of sharing proper words with their children when I presented workshops for the families at the district level.

After teaching second grade for ten years, I had the opportunity to share my advanced teaching experiences with the district teachers who were selected to teach TEAM classes. The Miami-Dade Public Schools advanced academics department observed my teaching style and delivery when I was teaching advanced second grade class. In 1998, 1999, 2001, and 2002, I was asked by the advanced academics department of Miami-Dade Public Schools to provide teaching enrichment activities to minorities in professional development sessions to all teachers in the district who were selected to teach the TEAM classes.

As a member of United Teachers of Dade County, the union board requested me to provide professional development on two types of training during the summers of 1999-2001. The first training was to help new teachers begin a successful school year. It included general ideas on how to set up their classrooms and prepare color-coded lesson plans and grade books. I brought my own samples, which the union representatives had seen and approved prior to this.

Organization and classroom management is the foundation of successful teaching. I provided them with general tips to help them start a school year with positive experiences. My general philosophy was to reward students at the end of the school day for good behavior with stickers or put stars next to their names on the board to give them tangible incentives. This system worked best for me throughout my teaching career.

The second professional development was entitled "Been There, Done That," and it was for select teachers who were in their third year of teaching. This training was more of a networking experience and I facilitated the conversation and provided them with more proven classroom strategies.

As the diversity of our district students increased, teachers in our county needed to be trained to serve those students who spoke languages other than English. I received my training in ESOL (English for Speakers of Other Languages) now called ELL (English Language Learners) in 2001 and added that endorsement to my Florida state certification. I was now qualified to teach students in grades one to twelve, whose primary language was not English.

Many Spanish-speaking and even Japanese students were enrolled in my class. Since I didn't speak Spanish, I used total physical response (hands and feet) to teach the students the same way I learned German. I paired them with English speakers. I also suggested books on tape from the public or school library.

In 2014 while walking around the neighborhood park, a young lady stopped me. "I was in your first grade class. You helped my mom and me to read and write English when we first came from Cuba," she proudly stated. She refreshed my memory of who she was. I remembered the name. I was so grateful to hear that she's a high school social studies teacher in the county. She reminded me of the activities we did when she was in my class. We exchanged phone numbers and addresses.

In 2015 and 2016, when I ran for Miami-Dade County School Board, District 7, she and her friend were great assets.

I hope and pray that some of my former first and second grade students become United States presidents one day. During the election year, I introduced my students to presidential election politics without any party affiliation based solely on qualifications. Whoever won, he or she would be the teacher's helper for one month. Since there are nine months in a school year, each winner becomes class president for one month (equivalent to four years). A winner could run for a second term.

Students were permitted to nominate a classmate or themselves. I posted the list of all nominees on the board. Then the class selected the top six candidates to run for president through tallies. After one day, each candidate gave a speech to their classmates why he or she would be the best candidate. After that, the class voted. The one with the highest votes became the president, and the second highest became the vice president for one month. The day after the election, the parent of the winner showed up with a pizza party for lunch. When I asked why the pizza luncheon, the mother told me that her son had promised to give a pizza party if his classmates voted for him. I shared with the class that it is called "bribery" if one promises a reward in exchange for a vote. This was a teachable moment. The mother was my room mother and both boys were good students. Students copied all the votes (tallies-concept and skills being taught at that time) for mathematics. After I provided some examples, students created word problems for homework using class election tallies.

The following year when a female student ran for president and won, the boys were infuriated. They were not ready for a female president. This was second grade students, and took place about twenty years ago. Later in the year, there was a press conference, where the students interviewed the class president on the actual qualifications of the United States president. They learned a candidate must be born in the U.S. and be at least thirty-five years old.

While performing my duty as an educator, I was also involved in my church as preschool vice president (1998-2002) and president (2002-2003). I also served on the church council as vice president and president from 2004-2006. In the early years of my leadership at Lord of Life Lutheran Church, a giant Costco warehouse was built about a hundred yards from the church preschool. The company wanted to sell alcohol. The company's parking lot was close to the church preschool. After discussing with the preschool board and the church council, I suggested that members of the council and the preschool attend one of the commissioners' hearings to oppose the sale of liquor. I was humbled that the president-elect of the council and our church pastor accompanied me and others to the hearing. The sale of alcohol was put on hold temporarily. A few years later, the store voluntarily relocated their company to a more appropriate location.

I also became a member of the Miami-Dade Police Hammocks District Citizens' Advisory Committee in 1986, and I was vice chairwoman and chairwoman from 2004-2006. I am still on that committee today. Long before I became a member of the advisory committee, in the early 1980s, I recall spotting a suspicious person along the neighborhood walking trail. I was taking a walk in the early evening with my daughter who was still in a stroller. As I walked a couple of times around the park, I noticed the suspect changed his location. Immediately, I returned to my house and called the police. They came promptly. I also alerted the neighbors. I was in disbelief to find out from the families who lived around the park that their girls had been followed a few days before as they walked home from school. According to the police report, the child predator lived only a few blocks from the school. Although, the slogan, "*see something, say something*" was not implemented until after the 9/11 terrorist attack on the World Trade Center, when I saw the suspicious person, I immediately reported it to the proper authority.

During the last six years of my teaching profession, in addition to other roles I held, I was also a member of my school's Educational Excellence School Advisory Committee (EESAC) 2000-2006) and chairwoman of the same committee (2003-2006). I was grateful to the school community who elected me as their chairperson to this worthwhile committee.

After my retirement in 2014, I was asked to be on the PTA board at my granddaughter's school where I had previously taught. I became the president of the board as a grandmother and worked with amazing young officers. Automatically, I became a member of the EESAC committee. After my term as president ended, the administration appointed me to serve as a business/community representative.

Obo, our eldest brother, walked with the support of two long and strong sticks after he suffered muscle weakness as a result of polio when he was in his teens. But he accomplished more than a healthy person: he walked miles to attend church, walked to teach at the German Mission school, conducted prayer breakfasts in the villages every morning, planted more fruits and vegetables and trees more than any villager, and most of all had the largest coffee plantation. He thanked God for his physical disabilities. It made him work harder and appreciate the fruits of his labor. My sister told me that the German missionaries marveled at how much God heard Obo's prayers and answered them.

It reminded me of my own life's journey. Many people often wondered why I am always happy with a smile on my face. Like Obo, I, too, had mishaps in my life. However, my heart overflows with gratitude for what God has done for me throughout my life. My brother became the model of my faith. Therefore, I choose to count my blessings and smile.

"*The smile on my face doesn't mean my life is perfect. It means I appreciate what I have and what I have been blessed with. I choose to be happy,*" says Charlie Brown.

During my teaching career, I got my students' attention by frowning at them when they got into trouble. They were used to seeing me smile and they would stop what they were doing to get that smile back.

CHAPTER TWENTY-THREE

AMAZING BLESSINGS
BEYOND THE CLASSROOM
2006-2008

"The Lord bestows favor and honors no good things
does he withhold from those who walk with Him."
(Psalms 84:11)

For more than seventeen years, God blessed me with teaching American children and serving others in my community. He brought me from chasing cattle in Ethiopia to educating children in an industrialized world. He guided and placed me in the Miami-Dade County Public School system, the fourth-largest school district in the nation. He helped me to help children reach their potential as I reached my potential. I never could have anticipated any of this.

Sometime during the third grading period in the 2005-2006 school year, my school principal asked me to attend an annual countywide professional development conference for a school committee I had been a chairperson of for the last three years. The keynote speaker was an individual known for her advocacy for families in the Miami-Dade County Public Schools. I considered her an acquaintance, as we were on a few committees together. Before the conference started, I went to greet her and we had a productive conversation. At the end of our conversation, she asked me how I was doing in my teaching profession. I confirmed that I was grateful; everything was going well. She then mentioned that she had applied for another district position called Office of Parental Involvement (OPI) and would be interviewed that day. I wished her good luck because she deserved it. In addition, I thanked her for the exceptional trainings she had given the participants over the years. Finally, I mentioned to her, "Please remember me when you get the job."

"Do you want to leave the teaching profession?" she inquired.

"If it is God's will, I will follow His lead," I expressed to her.

"Contact me in three weeks," she said as she gave me her contact information.

A few weeks later, I contacted her at her new department. She advised me to prepare my resume portfolio and bring it to the school board administration about twenty-five miles away. The guidelines for the position were posted on the district's website. I recall that being bilingual (English, Haitian-Creole, and Spanish) was one of the requirements as well as previous experiences working with families/parents. I had extensive experience working as a volunteer and leader. Knowledge of word processing and other computer skills were also essential.

I prepared my application according to the job description posted on the district's website. Each section of my application was separated by a color-coded divider. I was pleased with how everything came out. All of the contents of my binder were supported by my technology experiences. When I hand-delivered my resume binder, the supervisor was impressed. The candidate was to be selected by the district committee members appointed by the supervisor. When I was called into the conference room, I knew most of the committee members from my involvement in the local and district volunteer and leadership roles. After a brief self-introduction, I felt at home. Each member of the committee asked me questions on what I submitted in my portfolio. It almost sounded like defending a thesis. I left the outcome to God.

God had already equipped me with the skills that I needed long before I had ever imagined. The scripture tells us, *"Now to him who is able to do immeasurably more than all we ask or imagine, according to his power that is at work within us"* (Ephesians 3:20).

Back in 2001, one of our school colleagues offered a series of professional development classes on "Intel Teach to the Future and Enhancing Education Through Technology." I registered for the course to enhance my teaching delivery. I was intrigued by how technology brought learning alive. Even though I took technology courses at one of the local universities long before I started teaching, it became more meaningful now that I was teaching. In this course, we created technology-based instructional strategies to enhance the delivery of education. In addition, I created a webpage for web-based projects, linked to educational sites. My webpage was linked to school-related information to enhance communication between the school and parents. I also posted students' assignments. At the end of the course, we received credits and a monetary reward for successful completion.

I had no idea that my prior technology training in 2001 would become my strongest asset for the next six years, until my retirement. I defied the old saying, *"You can't teach an old dog a new trick."* I'm grateful to my supervisor for believing in me. She assigned me to maintain our department's webpage in collaboration with the district's Information Technology Services (ITS) supervisor. I met with the department technician periodically to update our department webpage.

I was hired as a teacher/counselor in August 2006, which was a full-time position. I now had twelve months of employment instead of ten months as a classroom teacher, which meant more salary. Soon after taking on this new role, on September 17, 2006, I was also blessed with the most adorable granddaughter, my first grandchild, from my second son.

From 2006 to 2008, I coordinated districtwide volunteer of the month activities for the Office of Parental Involvement (OPI). My supervisor had selected about six parent leaders from the school community. Every month, schools send applications to selected outstanding volunteers of the month based on the criteria established by our department. Each month, the committee reviewed the applications and nominated one volunteer of the month for the district. As a district staff member, my responsibility was only to facilitate the process—I had no voting rights.

At the end of the year, the department honored all the winners at a very exclusive luncheon. The committee prepared gift bags for each of the recipients. In addition, I requested certificates from the mayor of the Miami Dade County office (he had been the major of the Kendall district police department when I joined their advisory committee twenty years ago). The mayor graciously provided about nine framed certificates, proclaiming the service of each volunteer. In addition, a large proclamation was presented to our department. The mayor sent one of his staff to present them at the luncheon. I was ever grateful to the mayor for his kindness. I have never forgotten when the local newspaper scheduled an interview with me at my home for an article entitled, "Who You Know that Counts," during my early involvement in the school system and the community. From this experience, I learned that *establishing relationships with important people is a key component to accomplishing things in life.*

In addition, I developed and implemented the first Constant Contact e-newsletter for the Office of Parental Involvement (OPI) department at the district office. When my supervisor and I met with the district's internet technology service administrator, she too encouraged me to go forward with the project. Every month, I compiled a series of family/parent activities, training,

and announcements posted these on our webpage, and distributed these to all stakeholders through the Constant Contact
e-newsletter. The e-newsletters were reviewed and edited by
three of my colleagues, my supervisor, and her supervisor, and
verified by their initials. Then, I was given a "GO" post signal. I
recall calling Constant Contact main office and inquiring for any
updated information. They constantly updated their services. I
felt as if I grew up with the company. I continued these projects, in another department until my retirement in 2012. My
supervisor's boss directed me to pass on the knowledge to my
colleagues before I retired. I am thankful for this opportunity
He has given me and for the confidence my supervisor(s) had
in me. I was the oldest among thirty staff members. However,
I never felt old in God's eye; *"Who satisfies your desires with
good things so that your youth is renewed like the eagle's"* (Psalms
103:5). Again God promises us in Isaiah, *"But those who hope
in the Lord will renew their strength. They will soar on wings like
eagles; they will run and not grow weary, they will walk and not
be faint"* (Isaiah 40:31). What a wonderful assurance to have!

CHAPTER TWENTY-FOUR

FROM TEACHING STUDENTS TO TEACHING THEIR PARENTS
2008-2012

During the summer of 2006, before I applied for teacher/ counselor position in the Office of Parental Involvement at the district office, I was one of the many teachers from across Miami-Dade County Public Schools (MDCPS) selected to attend a free weeklong and all-day conference called "Leading from the Classroom." The participants were selected based on their educational awards and leadership roles in their schools. I thank God I met those qualifications and more. Guest speakers from around the United States were invited to deliver the methods and skills necessary to teach adult students.

For the next four years, from 2008 to 2012, I was assigned to The Parent Academy Department (TPA). It was a free, year-round, parental engagement initiative of Miami-Dade County Public Schools, helping parents become full partners in their children's education. The goal of this program was to provide educational excellence for all of our children by informing parents about the importance of their roles. The program had various strands, including basic computer skills for families, internet safety, Parent Portal, and the constantly changing FCAT/FCAT 2.0 (Florida Comprehensive Assessment Test). All training was delivered in English, Haitian Creole, and Spanish.

One of my favorite and most successful technology initiatives was the Parent Portal. It is an online site where parents can log in to see up-to-date information about their child's progress. Once my colleagues and I were trained on Parent Portal delivery to the parents, we were each assigned to different parts of the county. I was assigned to a region that had more affluent parents. The majority of families/parents spoke English. It had about sixty or more schools. These schools were close to where I lived so as to not waste time traveling.

The workshops took place in each school's media center (library) or computer room. My responsibility was to log onto the district's website, and then to the Parent Portal. Parents followed along as I demonstrated how to create a personal account and access their children's classwork. Each parent created their account using their emails and child's information. The parents were surprised to find out how technology connected them to their children's classroom without leaving their home. I provided them with my office phone number in case they needed further assistance. This training was for parents of children in kindergarten through twelfth grade. I find that this is the most effective technology ever created to monitor students' progress and be able to communicate with the teacher through emails.

A short while later, I was assigned to alternative schools on the other end of the county conducting the same workshops. The families in these schools were economically and educationally disadvantaged. I started conducting workshops on Saturdays from 9 am to 11 am. The PTA (Parents and Teachers Association) provided refreshments. Many families/parents, often twenty to thirty, attended. I was overwhelmed at the turnout. One day one of the parents expressed her frustration as I was about to present the parent portal.

"I never get any progress report on my son. He is in middle school. When I asked him where his report card is, he insisted he didn't get it."

"From this day on, you'll know all his daily classwork. You'll view his progress and report card before even your son sees them," I assured the mother.

After the mother had created an account and logged into the parent portal account, she realized that her son was failing most of the subjects.

"I'm upset at his work," she exclaimed. "Thank you for this training. From now on, I'll check on his progress regularly. If he tries to tell me he doesn't have his progress report or report card, I'll tell him that I've already seen them." After delivering several workshops to the families/parents, I realized that the families/parents just needed information tools like these to help their children. I came to the conclusion that all parents, regardless of their education and economic background, love their children. They only needed the tools and skills to help them.

Florida State Department of Education has created many standardized assessments using various names. The Florida Comprehensive Assessment Test, or the FCAT/FCAT 2.0, was the standardized test used in the primary and secondary public schools of Florida. The first time it was administered statewide in 1998, it replaced the State Student Assessment Test (SSAT) and the High School Competency Test (HSCT). Again, in spring 2015, the Florida Standards Assessments (FSA) replaced FCAT. Unfortunately, parents were not aware of these constant changes.

I'm ever grateful to my department supervisor for continually challenging my mind and for her trust in my ability. She asked me to develop a presentation for families so that they may have a glimpse of what their children were going through. I graciously accepted the challenge although I'd never taught a class where the various state assessments were administered.

First, I researched the Florida State of Education testing department. Also I called a toll-free number to get further information on the various subjects. In addition, I contacted the district's test distribution center to inquire if they had test samples administered to the students. When I called the department, the person who answered my call was a mom of a former first grade student from many years ago. We both recognized each other on the phone. What a coincidence! I had no idea she worked in that department. I was grateful to meet her again.

I gathered all the information and created a family-friendly PowerPoint presentation on Florida assessment for the families/parents of Miami-Dade County Public Schools. Then with my supervisor's advice, I shared it with the testing director for approval. It was a humbling experience when it was approved and ready for presentation.

The various workshops were created by professionals in the field. I delivered Internet Safety workshops to the families/parents in the region I was assigned to and the alternative schools. Being with the local police citizens' advisory committee gave me added knowledge. Sometimes, we had guest speakers at our meetings who presented beneficial information on cyber safety.

On May 6, 2010, after one of my workshop presentations, I received the good news that my grandson was born. I was so excited that now I have a granddaughter and a grandson. The next day, I visited my adorable grandson and his parents.

I also created an online survey asking for parents' feedback on the department's workshop delivery and its effectiveness. I monitored the feedback and shared the results with our department. I also continued to maintain our department's webpage in collaboration with the District's Information Technology Services for six years (2006-2012). Likewise, I continued to create and implement the Constant Contact e-marketing program to disseminate school community information to all families and stakeholders in the district from 2006 to 2012.

During my last six years at the Office of Parental Involvement and The Parent Academy, God provided me with incredible blessings beyond my expectations. I began volunteering at my children's schools for six years before I started teaching. At the end of my teaching profession, I was able to help families/parents. I'm forever grateful to God for all He has done for me.

<head>CHAPTER TWENTY-FIVE</head>

RETIRED FROM TEACHING AND ENGAGED IN POLITICS

I have been always interested in and involved in school and community politics. Therefore, my retirement from the teaching profession in May 2012 meant I would now have more time and energy to give to my community and politics.

In September 2011, a representative from President Obama's reelection campaign invited me to an organizational meeting at a volunteer's home. The retired couple had been in charge during the 2008 campaign. After meeting a few times, the campaign organizer realized the need to expand the geographical area and split the volunteers. I agreed to be a volunteer team leader for my community, which consisted of sixteen precincts. At that time, I was not sure of all of the details. However, I was willing to accept any challenge. Initially, we met once a month on Saturdays for two hours in the morning or afternoon. A few months before the November election, the volunteers met at my house twice a month. As the election date approached, the volunteers met every week. One of the most exciting and rewarding activity was "GOTV," Get Out The Vote. Starting two weeks before early voting, volunteers assembled at my house from 9 am to 9 pm. The campaign organizer(s) briefed everyone on phone banking, canvassing, and messaging strategies. Then they practiced on each other before going to the voters. I had volunteers with data input experience who entered the results of phone banking and canvassing (knocking on doors). During early voting and on Election Day, I was a staging location director, overseeing the volunteers who were canvassing, phone banking, and training new volunteer captains. It almost sounded like working with a military.

An inconceivable thing in my life occurred in June 2012 before the election. While campaigning, I received a call from President Obama's campaign organizer.

"You're invited to greet President Obama when he arrives on Air Force One, at Miami International Airport," he told me. It sounded like a voice from another world. "I emailed you two attachments explaining the detailed information like where to park and protocols to follow." I was in shock. Is this a dream or real? I had dreamed three times of meeting the president in the last few months. "The president will arrive tomorrow at about 3:00 pm." That was the next day, June 26, 2012.

Immediately, I logged into my computer, shaking with excitement. I located the email that the campaign organizer sent me. I called him back. "I see the two letters," I told him.

"Can you imagine shaking hands with the president of the United States?" he exclaimed.

It didn't seem to be a reality yet and then I answered, "Yes!"

Then he told me, "I'll call you back and go over some security details to be turned in."

The night before, I had to go through a preliminary security clearance by phone. I was so excited I could not sleep. I called my son who lived in California and he in turn told other relatives. The first thing in the morning, I called my previous coworkers and told them. "Do not bother to buy President Obama's poster for my birthday. I will see him in person tomorrow." They didn't believe me. I had retired from Miami-Dade County Public Schools and the school board administration on May 31, 2012, just a month earlier.

I had earlier shared with my colleagues that I dreamed that I met the president three times. That was why they were determined to order the president's poster in full size for my birthday. No one believed that a dream like this could become a reality. Later on, I shared with my colleagues that I actually met the president six times, and three of those were handshakes and a hug. They could not believe it.

The following day, I took copies of the letter to present to the Secret Service as directed. I anxiously drove my car to the event, parked at the designated parking space outside of the Miami International Airport, and proceeded to the Secret Service check in point. After verifying the letters I brought with

321

me, I then went to another security person. At that moment
he directed me and other guests to a special air-conditioned
big bus. It was full of invited elected officials and volunteer
leaders from other parts of Miami-Dade County.

The Secret Service offered everyone cold water while we
waited for the president's arrival. It was the hottest and windiest
day. As Air Force One was landing, all guests exited the bus
and lined up behind a staging area draped in red, white, and
blue. One of the Secret Service agents briefed us on what to do
when the president came around to shake our hands. The Secret
Service gave us specific guidelines about when to take pictures.

What an amazing sight to watch as President Obama exited
the plane without his jacket, his tie was flying because it was a
hot and windy day. After a photo op with officials, he jogged
towards us. As he went around shaking hands, I waited for my
turn. He shook my hand and said, "Thank you." I was speechless! Once he greeted as many volunteers as he could reach, he
thanked everyone and waved goodbye, and boarded Air Force
One. One more wave and he left as fast as he had come. We
all were excited to meet him in person and sad to see him go.

I overheard one volunteer suggest, "Don't wash your hand,
the one you used to shake the president's hand," We all laughed.
When I returned home, I shared pictures and all the excitement only with my family and friends. I wasn't social media
savvy in those days.

The First Lady, Michelle Obama, also came to one of
the high schools in Miami-Dade for her husband's reelection

campaign. This time, I took my six-year-old granddaughter to the event. The setting was different and many of us, including the elderly, waited in line in the scorching sun for hours. We were lucky to find a seat in the gymnasium where the event was held. My granddaughter leaned against me to take a nap while we were waiting for the First Lady's arrival. We could see the podium and the First Lady from where we sat.

Then she said, "Ako (grandma) wake me up when 'Michelle' arrives."

"You call her, 'Mrs. Obama,'" I reminded her. "And you'll know when she arrives."

Soon, cheers erupted as the First Lady entered the gymnasium. "Go! Obama!" she joined the crowd. "Obama for president!" She continued cheering. I was so proud of my granddaughter. She sat through the whole speech and joined the crowd with cheering. Although we couldn't meet the First Lady in person, my granddaughter was thrilled to be part of the historic event. My granddaughter was just two years old when President Obama first became president. I wasn't involved with his campaign at that time, because I was working at school board district office. However, I used to cheer, "Obama for president!" My granddaughter couldn't pronounce "Obama" and she would say, "Bama for president," over and over again. She loved him so much. So did her Ako (grandma).

Two weeks prior to the general election, the volunteers met at my house every day for phone banking and canvassing. My house was conveniently located in the community across from a park with plenty of parking spaces. In addition, I hosted presidential debate events for the extended community. I always served refreshments with homemade baked snacks. To this date, each of those volunteers have their favorite snacks. Some enjoyed sweets, while others preferred spicy. Some volunteers also helped with refreshments. Sometimes, I attended team leaders training to acquire various strategies of campaign messaging and working with diverse campaign volunteers. With the assistance of campaign staff, I recruited volunteers for phone banking, canvassing, and data entry. Volunteers helped in three-hour shifts.

My leadership experiences in the school and neighborhood community benefited me tremendously. I had volunteers from diverse networking groups such as school, neighbors, church, and the gym where silver sneakers gather to work out. I knew many individuals with leadership skills who were willing to be a part of this historic reelection of an African American president. I always asked for volunteers or donations whether it's for church, school, or other nonprofit organizations. I heard a saying, *"No is better than not asking at all."*

I was to meet President Obama a second time when he visited the University of Miami that same year. Many volunteers were invited to meet him. Luckily, the campaign organizers gave me a VIP ticket to line up in front of the podium where he stood. The secret service came around and reminded us how to greet and take pictures when he came down from the podium. Selfies were not allowed. After his speech, he stepped down from the podium to shake hands.

When he came to me, I hugged him and whispered, "I love you and I'll pray that you win the second term."

"Thank you," he responded.

For weeks, those words echoed in my ears.

My house was designated as a staging location and resembled a campaign headquarter. It was decorated with President Obama's both huge and small campaign signs. During Halloween as children were trick-or-tricking, I heard them commenting: "This is Obama's campaign office."

"Can we vote?" they asked.

"Check with your parents." I told them. Parents were waiting for the kids on the sidewalk. I knew most of the families from the community and school.

During the week leading up to the general election, volunteers met at my house 9am to 9 pm. Three dedicated volunteers from California helped during the early voting and stayed with campaign host families. On Election Day, my porch was designated for canvassing. Canvassing volunteers knocked on voters' doors and had a face-to-face campaigning. It was very effective. There was enough water and clipboards with voters' list along with messaging script for the sixteen precincts. My living and dining rooms were used for welcoming and briefing the volunteers on phone banking and for refreshments. My big family room was utilized for data input. I have never forgotten on election night about midnight, someone from Denver, Colorado, called me and complained, "What is that we hear? There is a long line at your place."

"This is a volunteer leader's house." I told the individual. "It is not a polling site."

Then I contacted the field organizer for our area. He told me to come over to the closest and busiest polling station to see the chaotic and amazing site. A giant bus with President Obama's signs on it was roaming through the gigantic parking lot. I was overwhelmed with emotions, tears rolled down my cheeks. Voters lined up around the building in double lines like at Disney World. Volunteers were offering water, pizza, and snacks to all voters who had been standing in line for hours.

At about 1 am all our volunteers returned to my house to watch as the votes came in. Some of my volunteers didn't dare to watch with everyone else. Instead, they went to their homes to watch from the comfort of their homes. Many stayed at my house watching in the living and family rooms. The rooms were decorated with patriotic balloons, streamers, and posters. We had food, a special cake, a flower centerpiece and refreshments that people had brought to share. Once President Obama was declared the winner, cheers erupted and volunteers started crying for joy. We celebrated until 3 in the morning. For those who were too nervous to watch with everybody else, I prepared dinner the following day. I'm grateful to God that the volunteers' friendship lasted beyond Election Day. Everyone has experienced the most memorable time of his or her life.

In the summer of 2013, months after the election, I was invited to Washington, D.C., along with all volunteer leaders from around the country. Everybody went through security clearance before we gathered in a large conference room. I was stunned when one of the Secret Service men remembered me from Miami when I volunteered at a fundraising event. "I know you're a schoolteacher," he stated.

After all other elected officials and campaign advisers spoke, President Obama laid out his agenda for the next four years. Those who spoke included: Minority Leader Nancy Pelosi, Minority Leader Senator Reed, the president of Planned Parenthood, and many other nationally recognized leaders who planned to advance his agenda. The one-day event was most inspiring and everyone was ready to begin the work on the president's agenda.

Then we each went to our community to share the president's goals and vision. I had about fifty volunteers from different parts of Miami-Dade County gathered at my house. Major topics included climate change, affordable healthcare, and sequestration and how to deliver to the voters. To this date, I am part of Organizing for America and participate in the monthly volunteer conference call for updates on various topics.

Before I returned to Miami, I visited with my nephew and his wife who live in Virginia. The evening before my departure, they invited me to an elegant Chinese restaurant in D.C. I enjoyed eating the food as well as its presentation. For the next day for lunch, I was determined to indulge in the Ethiopian cuisine. D.C. has a variety of Ethiopian restaurants. I missed eating from a beautiful round basket with my fingers. It's unfortunate that the only Ethiopian restaurant we had in downtown Miami was closed. Although people enjoy eating our food, there are hardly any Ethiopians in Miami.

Oftentimes, while waiting in line at a supermarket, people ask me. "Where are you from?"

"Why do you ask?" I inquire.

"You have an accent."

"Everyone in Miami has an accent," I respond.

"You have a unique accent," they reply.

"Are you from the Island?" they question.

"Outside of the islands," I challenge them. "About eight thousand miles," I give them a clue.

They guess as far as India and South America (Guyana).

"Where did all Black people come from?" I give them another clue.

Finally, when I mention, "Where did the greatest marathon runner come from?" "Oh, Ethiopia," they respond.

"You're the first Ethiopian I've ever met," they tell me.

"Thank God, I came to Miami," I assure them.

My last VIP ticket to meet the president was during the 2016 presidential campaign in Miami for Hillary-Kane. Again, I got my VIP ticket along with other volunteers and stood in the first row for two hours until he arrived. It was worth it. No matter how many times I meet him in person, I am eager to shake his hand. This time as he came around and reached me, I hugged him with a kiss and asked, "Would you be our president again?" "No," was his answer. I thank

God for allowing me to volunteer for our first African American president whose father was born in Kenya, a neighbor of Ethiopia. During his last four years of presidency, I was humbled to receive Christmas greetings and thank-you cards from the Obamas, which I cherish.

As I was sharing my meetings with our first African American president, the most respected and loved public official in the world, I was thinking how much more excitement would it be for the Christians to meet the son of God on the last day. No VIP ticket is needed except washed by the blood of Christ and saved by grace.

Again, in 2014, I was a volunteer team leader for a Democratic congressional race for about sixteen precincts. This time there were different campaign field organizers. I had the same volunteer activities as for the presidential reelection. Many volunteers were involved in phone banking and canvassing (knocking on doors). There were two campaign offices within a two-mile proximity. I called volunteers to report and help at any of the designated locations. We provided snacks and refreshments at one of the campaign offices. In addition, I hosted a big campaign event at my house for the congressional candidate, volunteers, and the news media.

One of the congressman's platform was to support and advance the Affordable Healthcare Act. One day, one of his communication assistants emailed me that a professional television commercial photographer would contact me to meet with me at my home. Probably on the same day, I received a call from the individual who would interview me. I found out he was coming from New York City. I thought one of the organizers would accompany the individual.

At about 3:00 pm he arrived at my house alone. He handed me his business card. I offered him water and cinnamon rolls I was baking from scratch. It is a part of our culture to be hospitable. Meanwhile, I was earnestly communicating with my heavenly father for his protection and peace. He commented how he enjoyed the baked goods. He then began assessing the lighting from the porch to our large family room and living room. Once he completed the source of lights in the house, he departed, telling me that someone from the campaign would contact me. When I offered him the cinnamon rolls, he thanked me for the hospitality and asked if he could take some with him. I gladly offered him some. After he left, I thanked God for his protection from someone I'd never met. A day or two after the gentleman was at my house, the campaign office called and asked me to report at a business office in an upscale neighborhood about midafternoon. It was about fifteen miles away from my home. I still didn't know what it was all about, except they told me not to wear certain colors.

Once I arrived at the designated location, I saw a few people who volunteered for the presidential reelection. Soon I was pulled aside by a makeup artist. I'd never worn makeup, even on my wedding day. When I studied cosmetology, my colleagues tried to practice on me. I looked in the mirror and I looked like a clown. As she was taking out all kinds of makeup, I didn't know what she was taking out of the large-sized cosmetic bag, I told the makeup artist: "I don't wear make-up!"

"I have to put some on you. The photographers will take pictures for campaign commercials," she stated. "Several pictures will be taken outside. It's sunny outside," she stressed.

For the next half hour or more, she scrubbed my face as if I had dirt on my face. She put on more of this and less of that. Then she said, "You look great!"

As the saying states, *"Beauty is in the eyes of the beholder."* I almost recited to her Psalms 139 that God made me beautiful already.

Then she took me outside where cameras lined up as if it were some kind of breaking news conference. It took almost two hours to shoot a thirty-second video commercial. Light reflector lenses: wide angle, clear protective lenses, Polarizing lenses, Zoom lenses. All the hundreds of pictures were videos without words, only actions. I was supposed to show an "angry face." They had to photograph me over and over again because I couldn't make a good "angry" face. After several trials, finally they got what they needed.

After about two hours of being videotaped for a thirty-second campaign commercial, I was exhausted. But I'm grateful that I was able to volunteer to protect affordable healthcare. I couldn't wait to go home and wash off the makeup. I felt like a different person.

After about two weeks, the commercial was televised on prime time on major local TV channels. Friends, parents, colleagues, and acquaintances started telling me.

"We saw you on TV!" this went on for about two weeks.

"When and on which channel?" I questioned.

"We saw your angry face," they stated. Finally, I requested the link from the campaign organizer as I could never catch the ad. I still didn't see it.

One evening, my granddaughter yelled, "Look! Ako, you're on TV!" she exclaimed. Finally, I saw a glimpse of myself on TV.

Some friends told me, "We recognized you by your back hairstyle" and "the purple clothes you're wearing." I was amazed at how people notice every detail of a person. For weeks, people were commenting on my television commercial. Many thought that I was paid for the commercial. However, I only did it as part of my volunteer work for this worthwhile cause.

As for showing an "angry" face, I remember my sister telling me that I would be smiling when I die.

CHAPTER TWENTY-SIX

More Community Involvement

Organized a Petition Drive to Save Miccosukee (Kendale Lakes) Golf and Country Club from becoming a Tribal Trust Land

A s soon as I completed volunteering for President Obama's reelection campaign, God had another assignment for me. In January of 2013, right after the successful presidential election, the community I have lived in since 1976 faced an astronomical challenge. Every resident who moved to the Kendale Lakes community was assessed a fee to maintain the club and to have access to this most beautiful facility. It had two Olympic-size swimming pools where the neighborhood children learned to swim and compete in competitions. It also had tennis courts and a stunning horseshoe-shaped 27-hole golf course for those who paid an additional fee. For decades, joggers and cyclists enjoyed the scenery. In the early 70's the fee was five dollars, but by the 90's it had climbed to twenty-five dollars. But we were about to lose all of those amenities and instead have a gambling casino bringing with it the crime and drugs that often follow.

The Miccosukee tribe purchased 230 acres of land in the heart of this Kendall suburb in 2001. Within two years, they asked the federal government to designate it part of the reservation. The Bureau of Indian Affairs in 2012 finally agreed to make the golf course part of the reservation. Unfortunately, the residents and the county authorities were unaware of this decision.

At the time the golf course was established, the county officials put into place a 99-year zoning restriction that requires the property to remain a golf course. Under this restriction, only the county commission and three-quarters of the neighbors could approve a change.

The long-time board member and former Kendall Federation of Homeowners Association Inc. president contacted me to organize a petition drive. I did so on behalf of the Kendale Lakes community. I'm grateful that I was acquainted with several residents from the presidential campaign. I called on them to help me get this issue out to the community. When the residents found out that the country club was put into a tribal trust, they were enraged for many reasons. First and foremost, the addition of gambling brings crime to the neighborhood and nearby schools. The traffic would be overwhelming for the residential roads over which the county officials have no control.

I'm grateful to the volunteers who stopped by my house to pick up petition forms and made more copies. One of the volunteers translated the written directions for the petition in three languages: English, Haitian Creole, and Spanish. The volunteers went door to door in the surrounding area of the country club two by two. This reminded me of when Jesus sent out his disciples to preach. I was humbled and filled with joy to see these same residents volunteer to go around their own neighborhoods and collect signatures. I was surprised to reunite with a former friend from my school who I learned lived just few yards away from the country club. The news of the Miccosukee intention to change the zoning had never reached these residents.

We were grateful to the major newspaper, the *Miami Herald*, for sending a reporter to write about the residents' alarm and their effort to stop this change. In April of 2015, the reporter came to the Miccosukee Golf and Country Club to interview some of the residents who were collecting petition signatures. Here were some of the comments made by the volunteers that were published: "It's the centerpiece of the whole community," said longtime resident Ted Baldyga. Said another longtime resident, Aster Mohamed: "I really enjoy the scenery. It's really a beautiful place in the center of a residential area." "Nobody has any objection if they keep the property the way it is, as it's been operating," said Mohamed, 70, the Kendale Lakes activist who was mounting another petition drive opposing the tribe's request. "They purchased it. However, if it turns into tribal trust land, they have to the right to build anything on the property."

The reporter also took a group picture in front of the property. The group asked me to stand in front of the group and show an angry face. I tried my best.

My neighbor and I met with a priest from a large Catholic church whose parish is located right across from the country club. The intention of our meeting was to obtain permission to collect signatures after their church services. They, too, realized that making the country club into tribal trust land would bring more traffic congestion and possibly bring crime and drugs. The priest granted us permission to collect signatures on a weekend. We collected over twelve hundred signatures on one weekend.

Furthermore, I challenged myself to create an online petition signature opportunity called Change.org. One of our neighborhood school's former students suggested it as I was collecting signatures. I googled online and sure enough, I found the link with directions. It was amazing how quickly our neighborhood issue became a national issue. Individuals who had encountered similar problems began posting their comments online. The online petition created an awareness of the issues facing our community. I downloaded the online petition signatures along with the comments and shared them with the community at the town hall meetings. One individual, who was the most dedicated canvasser during the presidential reelection, created a webpage called "Save Kendale Lakes." For more visibility, he linked this to the webpage of the country club we were trying to prevent from becoming Miccosukee tribal trust land for more visibility. The total petition signatures collected from door-to-door, religious institutions, and online petition, was over three thousand.

This petition drive would have not been successful without the encouragement to initiate the petition and support of Mr. Miles Moss, president of the Winston Park Homeowner's Association. He scanned all petition signatures and forwarded them to the authorities. He was a pioneer of the Kendall Federation of Homeowner Associations Inc. when I joined the board in 1983, and we are still members. As a result of the residents' opposition to the country club from becoming Miccosukee tribal trust land, the project has been on hold. Should the Miccosukee Tribe try to change the zoning request without the knowledge of the residents and the authorities, we are ready to fight back with the help of God.

God created heaven and earth and He wants us to take care of the earth. The prophet Isaiah declares God's intent. "You shall not pollute the land in which you live, …You shall not defile the land in which you live, in the midst of which I dwell…" (Numbers 35:33-34).

CHAPTER TWENTY-SEVEN

Was My Running for School Board in God's Plan?

W hy did I want to run for Miami-Dade County public school board district 7 in 2016? "I know and believe that God has created me wonderfully in my mother's womb" (Psalms 139:13-14). Would this be in God's plan? "You've been given work-related gifts that have been chosen specifically for you" (Rom.12:6-8). I was a former educator, seventeen years a classroom teacher, and six years a parent educator at the district office. In addition, I had advocated for the students and their parents, as well as for the community at large, for more than thirty years. I had all the experience I needed to be the best school board member for this large district. Furthermore, colleagues and friends encouraged me to run. They told me, "No one is more qualified than you." I thanked everyone for his or her encouragement and kind words. Then I took their advice and encouragement and decided to run.

Now that I'm retired and my kids are grown up, and my two grandkids are attending school, and with my extensive experiences in the educational field, if it's God's will, I'm ready to serve my school community on a larger scale. I also assumed that a school board position is the least political office because it is a nonpartisan position. The seat I was running for had been vacant and was filled by a Florida governor's appointee until the 2016 election. I checked the Miami-Dade election website and discovered that two individuals had already filed to run for the same position. Both candidates were educators and one of them was a former elected official. I downloaded the several pages of guidelines set for local and state elections. Before filing for candidacy, I needed to have a treasurer who kept accurate bookkeeping. The treasurer recorded and reported income from donations by businesses and individuals and expenses for the campaign on a monthly basis. I attended about three campaign finance and ethics seminars to make sure my treasurer and I followed the proper protocols. The same election officials delivered the presentation at all seminars.

In the midst of this, in April of 2015, my oldest son informed me that he was planning to marry a beautiful girl whom our family had already met. However, he realized that family involvement in their marriage was critical. He arranged for me to meet his future wife's parents in San Jose, California. I was proud of my son that he thought to do this as a sign of respect to both of our families. I spent a couple of days visiting my son and getting acquainted with her family. Although her parents are from another part of the world, we share similar customs. While I was there, her parents and I, along with my son and his fiancée, agreed upon the wedding date of June 11, 2016. Her parents had already identified the most beautiful wedding venue that resembled a Hollywood movie, with its mountain views in the background. My son and his fiancée gave me a tour of the wedding location. It was magnificent.

I thank God my two children and two grandkids were invited and arrived in San Jose the week of the wedding. My two grandkids were in the wedding party and they were thrilled. The bride's parents planned the most elegant wedding and food menu fit for a royal wedding. I'm grateful to the in-laws and thanked them for their hospitality and generosity during the wedding celebration. It was a memorable event.

On August 4, 2015, I filed to run for Miami-Dade County School Board, District 7, the largest of the nine districts. Prior to my filing and registering with the election department, my campaign treasurer and I had to identify a bank to deposit campaign donations. My treasurer and I had each signed campaign forms. Then all forms were posted on the election website for public record. The next morning after I filed, the appointed incumbent filed, too. Now there were four candidates running for the same office. Each month, all money raised and accrued expenses were posted online for the public to view.

In addition to being a treasurer, I had two individuals who were campaign strategists. They designed my business cards and palm cards with my information and platform on it for distribution to voters. To accomplish all of this and more requires financial backing.

My campaign advisors suggested we plan fundraising events in the fall of 2015. This was inconceivable to me. I'm confident in asking for donations for church projects, schools, and nonprofit organizations. However, I was not ready to ask for donations for my own campaign.

"Give us a list of names starting from your immediate family," they suggested.

"I cannot ask my families and friends to donate to my campaign," I contested.

"The money is not for you, it is for the children in your district," the advisors assured me.

They requested that I make a list of at least a hundred people. That was easy because I have many network groups of people that I have known over the years through my involvement in the community.

Reluctantly, I gave the names of friends who are familiar with campaign donations.

I shared with close friends that I was running for the school board for our district. They were overwhelmed with joy and willing to help. Two fundraising events were scheduled in the fall. My campaign advisors sent the invitation to my friends electronically and by U.S. mail. The first campaign kickoff was on October 20, 2015, at one of our association's clubhouses. I'm grateful to the president of the association and the board members for allowing me to use it.

I was overwhelmed with joy to see about fifty of my immediate family and friends including prominent former school board members. A longtime friend who attended the elementary school where I taught owned an Italian restaurant in the neighborhood. He contributed the food as in-kind donation for all the guests. In addition, the following week, October 27, we had another "meet and greet" event at his restaurant. He provided food for a few more events during my campaign. I'm forever indebted to Mike's Restaurant and grateful for all he did for my campaign. The donations at both events helped to defray the initial cost of campaign materials.

In addition to raising campaign funds, my friends, former students, and their parents helped me collect signatures from registered voters in my district. I extend my heartfelt gratitude to them for collecting as many signatures as possible. To be on the ballot in August 2016, I had to have enough valid signatures or pay a fee from the campaign fund. The election department had to verify the accuracy of signatures, places of residence, birthdates, and voters' registrations. Many voters were surprised to hear that a candidate had to pay to be on the ballot. Many voters were reluctant to provide their birth dates and addresses. I'm grateful to one of the local church pastors who is not affiliated with Lutheran churches but was so willing to help. They have a big congregation and it is one of the largest polling stations. He introduced me to the members at both services, provided me a space to stand and get signatures from those who live in my district. On Election Day, the pastor allowed me to put up my campaign sign. I was touched by the kindness of the pastor and the members who welcomed me with open arms. I had never been to that church before. After all of my efforts, unfortunately, I didn't have enough signatures; therefore, I had to pay a fee from the campaign fund to be placed on the ballot. I will always be grateful to those who contributed to my campaign, helping me to finish the race.

A few months before the election, two candidates dropped out of the race. The incumbent, the governor's appointee, remained on the ballot. Now it became a race of who raised the most money. Right from the beginning, I wasn't excited about raising campaign money. I depended on my grassroots supporters that I have known for many years to vote for me. On the other hand, my opponent raised ten times as much as I did. Therefore, I considered myself David, the shepherd, and my opponent as Goliath with a lot of money.

Although I recall the saying, "money doesn't buy happiness," it is important to hire poll workers at various polling sites during early voting and election day. I'm grateful to all my friends for their friendship and volunteerism in many areas. I have never forgotten standing on my feet for nine hours a day for two weeks and on Election Day, for twelve hours. I was overwhelmed with gratitude when voters I'd never met before, came to me and said, "We voted for you because reading about you, you're an honest person." "If it is God's will, you'll win, if you don't, He has something better for you." I was touched by their comments.

344

About a month before the election, I met a couple who were hosts of a Christian radio station at a Christian organization breakfast. The husband immediately advised me to get in touch with his radio station. A week later, I contacted his office to make an arrangement to record a commercial about who I am and my platform which would be aired to the targeted voters during the early voting. This was also an in-kind donation. I was ever grateful to the couple for their generosity.

In addition, I also met a dynamic Haitian-Creole radio and TV personality, and a motivational speaker I had known from previous campaign volunteering. She too invited me to video-tape my platform for the Haitian Creole community, as there were several voters living in the district I was running in. She donated her service to my campaign as in-kind. All these individuals were truly Godsent and I'm indebted to them forever.

Since there was a large number of Spanish-speaking population in the district, there was a need to translate my campaign flyers into Spanish. I was acquainted with a Spanish lady who owned a translation company whom I met when I had volunteered for a campaign in which she ran as lieutenant governor for Florida. When I approached her, she too donated the translation service as in-kind. I am forever indebted to her. If I didn't get involved and volunteered, I would have not met these individuals. I recalled the saying, "If we give, we'll in turn receive."

On election night, on August 30, 2016, I felt so much at peace that I didn't look on TV as the polls came in. However, I received texts and emails from friends congratulating me for finishing the race. The following morning, I found out that I received twenty-one percent of the votes. I thanked God for giving me peace even though I didn't win, for the wonderful people I met along the way, and for their continued friendship even after my campaign was over. I might not have won the election, but I won the hearts of thousands of people.

I think some voters were suspicious of my last name "Mohamed." Perhaps God has a plan for me in the years to come as the voters suggested during my campaign.

Acknowledgement

Above all things, I thank God for giving me a chance to live on this earth and for opening unfathomable windows of opportunity. As with everything in my life, my memoir would not have been possible without the encouragement, help, and support of several people God put in my path. My acknowledgment may look long, but please understand that without the individuals and organizations listed herein, I would not be the person I am today. *"It took the whole world to educate me."*

I wouldn't be on this earth without my mom and dad's determination to give birth to me after losing two young boys just before I was born. To my mother, my loving gratitude for always looking out for me. I am forever indebted to you. However, I ask for your forgiveness for not visiting you more frequently before the angels called you home.

I am grateful to my eldest brother, Obo Deressa, for naming me (አስቴር) Aster (Esther in the Bible) and for nurturing me spiritually, taking care of me like his own daughter after my father's death, when I was just nine years old. I am forever indebted to him for chronicling my life's story from birth through my adulthood. Above all, for being a model of my Christian faith to this day.

My deepest gratitude to my second older brother, Obosha (the Reverend Lamessa), for his unconditional love by assisting our eldest brother while he was away on pastoral training. Friends, relatives, neighbors, and especially I admired his inspiring singing voice and laughter.

To our eldest sister, Ade Galitu, for comforting and taking care of me. To my two older sisters, Ade Dessi, Ade Terunesh, and my sister-in-law, Soretti, for preparing all the meals and working on the farm while I babysat missionary children or knit when I wanted. Particularly many thanks to my third sister, Ade Terunesh, for updating me with our family's stories.

To the German Mission, thank you for the beautiful hand-me-down clothes you provided me with during my early years.

My heartfelt gratitude goes to Ms. Robin, director of the German Mission school, for seeing in me the potential that I could learn and succeed from the moment I entered first grade and for paying grades 1-8 tuition. Additionally, for securing full scholarships for my high school board, room, and tuition at the most academically prestigious Christian high school and to study in Germany.

My heartfelt gratitude to Reverend Ezra and the elders of the Evangelical Church Mekane Yesus in Addis Ababa, for starting me on this most wonderful journey that I never could have imagined in my lifetime. For granting me the scholarship to the U.S. that opened my calling to the teaching profession, and for providing me a place to live while I worked at the church. To Reverend Ezra and his wife, Ade Gannet, my gratitude to you for providing me lunch while I worked at the church. To Obo Tamasgen, director of the Mekane Yesus elementary school, thank you for your dedication, and sacrifice, and for the opportunity to work under your leadership.

I extend my sincere gratitude to Dr. Olson, a professor from Saint Olaf College in Minnesota, and his students for worshipping at the church I worked at during their visit to Ethiopia, which opened a door of opportunity to one of our church members to study organ at St. Olaf College in the U.S. I am indebted to Dr. Olson and the St. Olaf College Community for their generosity for sponsoring me for another year.

My heartfelt gratitude to Ms. Joel, the registrar at Augsburg (University) College in Minnesota, for welcoming me to continue my calling, the teaching profession at Augsburg College where I received my teaching degree. Thank you for hosting my graduation party at your residence.

Many thanks to the American Lutheran Church Women for the unexpected scholarship grant for my master's degree in educational administration at the University of Minnesota

To the Reverend and Mrs. Flachman, for making me feel at home in a strange country. I thank Naomi, Rev. Ezra's sister, for introducing me to your family. My heartfelt gratitude goes to the Flachmans for presiding over our wedding ceremony at your church and for hosting a reception.

Every step of my life reflects my name *Aster* (finding favor with God and the people He placed in my path). I had never forgotten Easter Sunday 1975 when I attended South Miami Lutheran church. After searching for a Lutheran church for several months based on two criteria: a preacher that preaches to my heart and a friendly congregation. That day I found both of my wishes, a dynamic preacher and my friendly Miami American family, the Musaus. They later became my children's adopted grandparents.

To, my husband, Dr. Dominic, for searching for the best and safest neighborhood to raise our children, and for his courage and insight to live in an only white neighborhood.

Thanks to God he had a doctorate degree to teach at FIU that earned him the respect he deserved.

My heartfelt gratitude to the Kendale Lakes neighborhood for their warm welcome with coffee and refreshments a month before we moved in (Just stay home moms) along with Donna, who moved to the neighborhood one month before we did. Two months later, we were acquainted with most residents with a progressive dinner; I volunteered to be one of the three hosts, introducing my neighbors to Ethiopian cuisine while assimilating into the American culture.

My gratitude to my Kendale Lakes American sister, Donna, neighbor, and a prayer partner for life, for her hospitality by allowing my children and I to stay with the family during the most difficult transition of my life, my divorce.

Without the encouragement of my two community activist friends, Marie and Dorothy (may she rest in peace), I would have not been active in the various community organizations, assimilated in the American culture, and become an educated and informed citizen in the democratic process of politics and services. Marie, I thank you for listening to my story and for encouraging me to write and read it, moreover, for writing the inspiring Foreword of my memoir.

Special thanks go to my first employer in my teaching profession, Mr. Leonard Greenbaum, and his team, for valuing and welcoming me into an affluent neighborhood school, Kendale Lakes Elementary. I want to extend my gratitude to the Parents and Teachers Association board who saw the potential of leadership in me and appointed me to this board. I express my appreciation to all my colleagues for their support during my teaching career.

To my Christian family, Lord of Life Lutheran Church for over thirty-five years, for welcoming and encouraging me and my children to participate in leadership roles which have strengthened my Christian faith. I will always appreciate you.

My heartfelt gratitude goes to my district supervisor, Ms. Anne Thompson, director of the Office of Parental Involvement and The Parent Academy, for uncovering my hidden gift of working with technology, to defeat the old saying, "*You cannot teach an old dog a new trick.*" Thank you for the amazing opportunity you gave me for the last six years I served the families in Miami-Dade County Public Schools.

My appreciation to the Kendall Federation of Homeowners Association board, especially Miles, Marvin, and Art Simon, former Florida State Representative board member, for encouraging me in many leadership roles on this board. For helping me to understand and to experience firsthand what the real American democracy means through my participation. Miles, thank you for encouraging me to lead my neighborhood petition drive to keep it a safe place for our residents.

I am forever grateful to my family and relatives, especially my grandchildren, former students, their families, and my friends for encouraging me to run for the Miami-Dade County School Board District 7. I would have not been able to do it without the many hours of volunteerism and financial support. I am indebted to Mike's Pizza, a family restaurant, for providing in-kind food services for my campaign. Sincere gratitude to the individuals who promoted my campaign through the radio, television, and translation. My heartfelt gratitude to my campaign treasurer, Dr. Douglas Smith, for the countless hours he spent balancing campaign donations and reporting to the election department. Although I did not win the election, I won the hearts of thousands of people.

My sincere appreciation to the South Florida Writers Association (SFWA), for inspiring me to write my memoir during the 2017 conference. I thank Jeff, a board member, for extending the invitation to attend.

I extend my heartfelt gratitude to my three children: Eba, Tac, and Adi for their consent to the reason for my divorce from their dad to be included in my memoir.

My heartfelt gratitude to Louise Farnworth, a church friend and a retired high school English teacher; my memoir would not be what it is without her continuous dedicated efforts. Her critique, expertise, and suggestions during the process of writing this book are incredible. Many thanks to Louise's husband for his expertise in photo captions.

My gratitude to my friend Wendy Coen, Coen & Company Public Relations, for editing my first memoir draft and encouraging me to continue writing my story.

Special thanks to my nephew, Reverend Dr. Dinku, a missionary pastor, for translating my brother Obo's journal from our tribal language Oromifa to English.

My sincere appreciation to Ms. Ashild Berg, a family friend and a missionary nurse to Ethiopia, for sharing a photo of a thatched grass roof hut with mud walls, the kind I lived in with my dad, mother, and five siblings during my early years through social media when I visited in 1994. I am also grateful for her visiting me in the United States in 2019 after reuniting on Facebook twenty-five years later.

My gratitude goes to Dr. Janis Jordan, a former Miami-Dade college library director for recommending *The Chicago Manual of Style, Seventeenth Edition, The Essential Guide for Writers, Editors, and Publishers 2017*. It is the most beneficial and comprehensive handbook for writers. However, in order to benefit from the guide fully, I should have taken a college course.

Lastly, many thanks to hundreds of friends, neighbors, parents, and students who spot me and inspire me everywhere I go, reminding me that I was their teacher in the first and second grades. I am always inspired by their kind words.

APPENDICES

TRANSLATION OF A LETTER FROM ASTER'S BROTHER, DHERESSA BATO

To my sister Aster Bato,

How are you and your family doing? How is work going?

We are all fine, thanks be to God. Even though troubles and worries of this life continue to engulf us, we shall not be moved while we have the Lord on our side. Last time [we heard] that your country [America] suffered a strong hurricane [in your area]. We prayed for recovery and hope that God will make the situation better for you.

In June 2004, I received your letter and warm greetings [gift] through Rev. Lamessa. May God bless you.

In your letter, you asked me to write and send you your life story. Thus, I have tried to write it up to the best of knowledge and ability. And here I send it over. However, since I couldn't read and comprehend what I earlier wrote and archived due to my [dwindling] eyesight; I kept on postponing the writing until today. Please accept my apologies.

The following is what I've tried to write about your life story:

You were born on May/Ginbot 27, 1937 [1944] in Aira Lalo [Chaliyota] in the vicinity of the German Compound. The year you were born, I was struck by a serious illness that left me bedridden. Sick in bed, I was reading the story of Esther from the Bible, which was so pleasing to me to name you after.

At age nine, in 1946 [1953], you entered school. From grade one to eight, you were ranked in the top three of your class and received awards. You pursued your education with great enthusiasm and completed eighth grade in 1954 [1962] when you sat for ministry [National Middle School Examination] at school in Nadjo.

You passed ministry [the national exam] with flying colors. On Pagume 4, 1954 [September 9, 1962], you set out for Bushoftu to attend ninth grade, that begins in September [Meskerem]. That day I accompanied you on board as we flew from Aira to A/A [Addis Ababa]. What surprised and amazed me back then was the fact that I was able to escort you to school even though I was physically weak. I praise the Lord for enabling me to do that [for you]. On Meskerem 18, 1955 [September 23, 1962] you started ninth grade in Bushoftu, Debre Zeit. During your stay there, Rev. Yohannes Lawnhart looked after you on my behalf.

From 1954-1957 [1962-1965], you pursued your education in Debre Zeit. In the month of Megabit [March], when you were a junior in high school, you received a scholarship from Germany where you left for on Megabit 14, 1957 [March

23, 1965]. This time God has accompanied you to your new destination as I couldn't make it like I did when we traveled together from Aira and Addis Ababa. Tsige Gemeda and Miss Ravin also traveled with you to Germany. You were 20 years, nine months, and fifteen days old when you left for Germany.

While doing your training in Germany, you received another scholarship to study in America [U.S.]. After the completion of your studied in the states, you got married, started a family of your own, and secured a prestigious job. Praising the Lord for being with you and guiding you hitherto, here I conclude the account of your life story that I wrote to the best of my recollection. You may want to add to it and expand on what is missing. And with this, I would like to ask you to send me a copy of your memoir when you complete it. Rev. Tadesse Birreti has assisted me in writing this document.

May the peace of the Lord be with you and your family.

Please read 1 Sam. 2:1-9; Psalms 103:1-5.

When you write your life story, I remind you to include this letter as an Appendix.

—Your brother: Dheressa Bato (signed)

ORIGINAL LETTER FROM DHERESSA BATO

March 17/2005

3. ቀዳሚዉ፡ንዑ፡ነገወቴ፡እን፡ወደእስተ፡ወ፡ደነበቴ፡ኔፑት፡መሕከነፀም
ቴ፡በፈየስን፡ሦቱ፡ስልጋኒ፡ኩቴፈይ፡ዼ፡ይ፡ሮ08.4/1954
ኩኑ፡ኡ/ኢ፡ተጋትሮ፡ሺይ፡ሪን፡ወኔን፡ኡኔ፡
የወርስ፡ንንበኒ፡ዮዼንኒፈ፡ነገወቴ፡እ፡ኡን፡ደ፡ሲ፡400፡
ፈየኔ፡ፀኳ፡ተኡተንፁኒ፡ኃኩኩነፀን፡ተወንክፀጸእ
70ኜ፡ሺ6ኡነፉ፡ወምቱን፡ንንንተፈ2ኒ፡ኩፕስ ፀ፡
ኔፑት፡መሕከነፀም፡18/1955 ቴ፡ሁፚፈኪ፡ይ፡ስንፚዼፈ
በፈየስን፡ኡቱ፡ስስጋኒ፡ዼ፡ስ፡ተስፀ፡
የወርስ፡ንንኳጐ፡ኩኒን፡ስፚ፡ኩስስ፡ኩንፀ6ን፡
ኩስ፡ቀምፀኪ፡ስወንፈፈ፡ደ፡ስ6ን፡

4. በሲ 1954 – በሲ 1957፡ ይ፡ስሲ ዛፈ ፈቱ፡ ህን፡ፅ
መንጋ፡ፈ ቴ፡ ኑቱ፡ 114፡ በሲፕ፡ ኩቴ፡ ፀ፡ ሮ፡ 6ዓ ኒ፡
ንይ፡ፈ፡ወወ ዼ፡ በፈየ፡ኃ፡ዼ፡ ኩ፡ ኩፀ ን፡ መ፡ንጀ ኡ፡ 14/
.1957 ኃ ይ፡ፕ፡ወወ ዼ፡ ዼ፡ ኃ ፡ኗ ፀ መ ፡ ን ፡ ኒ ፡ ኽ ፀ ኒ፡ ህ ን ፡
ኩ ኒ ኽ ፡ ን ፡ኒ ን ን ፀ ፉ ፈ ፡ ኩ ፚ ፀ ፡ ወ ም ፀ ፡ የ ወ ር ስ ፡ ን ፡ የ ፡ ወ ወ ዼ
ኩ ን ፡ ፀ ፡ ወ ን ፡ የ ወ ፡ ኩ ኽ ፀ ር ፡ ነ ገ ወ ኡ ፡ ወ ፡ ደ ኩ ስ ፡ ሲ ፚ ፀ ፡ ፈ ፡
ማ ወ ፡ ሱ ን ፀ ኽ ፡ ዮ ፡ ወ ር ስ ፡ 20 ፡ ዼ ፡ ኪ ፡ ወ ፡ ኡ ፡ ወ ፡ ወ ፡ ን ፡ ወ ፡
ኪ ፡ ኡ ፡ ስ ፡ ስ ፈ ፡ መ ሕ ከ ኒ ፡ →

5. በ የ ፡ ኡ ፡ ወ ዼ ፡ ኡ ፡ ኡ ፡ ፀ ፡ ፀ ር ፀ ፡ ወ ፀ ፈ ፡ በ ፈ ፡ ይ ፡ ስ ፡ ን ፡ ይ ፡ ኒ ፡ ወ ፀ ፡ ጐ ፡ ን ፀ ፡
ኽ ፡ ር ፡ ፈ ፡ ኽ ፡ ር ፀ ፡ በ ፀ ፡ ፀ ፡ ስ ፡ ኩ ፀ ፡ ፀ ኽ ፡ ወ ፡ ን ፡ ይ ፡ ስ ፈ ፡ ፈ ፈ ፡ ፈ ፡
ወ ፡ ፀ ፡ ፡ ይ ፡ ኡ ፡ ፀ ፡ ህ ፀ ፡ ስ ፡ ፀ ር ፡ ኪ ፡ ተ ፡ ስ ፡ ኩ ፀ ፡ ፀ ፡ ህ ፡ ር ፡ ፀ ፡
ህ ፀ ፡ ፀ ፡ መ ፡ ስ ፀ ፡ ኡ ፡ ፀ ፡ ፀ ፡ ተ ፡ ኽ ፡ ኡ ፀ ፡ ፀ ፡ ስ ፡ ኡ ፡ ፀ ፡
ወ ፀ ፡ ን ፡ ፀ ፡ ኡ ፀ ፉ ፡ ኡ ፀ ፡ ፀ ፡ ን ፡ ኡ ፡ ፀ ፡ ህ ፡ ወ ፡ ን ፡ ኡ ፡
ህ ፡ ወ ፡ ን ፡ ደ ፀ ፡ ፀ ፡ የ ፡ ወ ፡ ን ፡ ፀ ፡ ኽ ፀ ፡ ኽ ፀ ፡ ም ፡ ኪ ፡ ፀ ፡
ፀ ፡ ኡ ፀ ፡ ኽ ፀ ፡ ን ፡ ኡ ፡ ፀ ፡ ፀ ፡ ን ፡ ኡ ፀ ፡ ፀ ፡ ኡ ፀ ፡ ፀ ፡ ን ፡ ኡ ፡ ፀ ፡
ፀ ፡ ኡ ፡ ፀ ፡ ፀ ፡ ፀ ፡ ፀ ፡ ፀ ፡ ፀ ፡ ፀ ፡ ፀ ፡ ፀ ፡ ፀ ፡ ፀ ፡
በ ስ 409 ፡ ን ፡ ን ፀ ፡ ን ፡ ን ር ፡ ር ፡ ን ፡ ስ ፡ ን ፡ ስ ፡ ወ ፡ ኡ ፀ ፡
ፈ ፈ ፀ ፡ ን ፡ ስ ፡ ወ ፡ ቴ ፡
ን ፀ ን ፡ ወ ፡ ሱ ፡ ኩ ፀ ፡ መ ፡ ወ ፡ ፀ ፡ ወ ፀ ን ፡ ህ ፡ ቱ ፡ ኡ ፡
ፀ ፀ ን ፡ ወ ፡ ፀ ፡ ፪ ፡ 4 ፡ ር ፀ ፡ 103 ፡ 1–5 ፡ ይ ፡ ን ፡ ፈ ፡ ኡ ፡
ኩ ፀ ን ፡ ፀ ፡ ፈ ፡ ኡ ፡ ፀ ፡ የ ፡ ወ ፡ ን ፡ ን ፡ ፀ ፡ ን ፡ ፀ ፡ ኒ ፀ ፡ ፀ ፡ ን
ወ ፡ ኡ ፡ ኡ ፡ ፀ ፡ ፈ ፡   ኩ ፡ ኡ ፡ ኽ ፡ ፡ የ ፡ ፀ ፡ ፀ ፡ በ ፡ ፩

TRANSCRIPTION OF A LETTER FROM ASTER'S TWELVE-YEAR-OLD GRANDDAUGHTER, JOHANAH
(As written)

3-30-18

Dear, Ako

You are the women of my life. You care for me like I'm the only thing in the world. I thank you for always caring for me no matter what. Every time I'm feeling low you are always their to make me feel better. You let me cook with you. Sometimes okay I'm lying all the time, I eat some of the dough and/or the batter. I can't help myself from doing it. Your batter is just so good especially since you made it. You are like my guardian angel you gard me and stand up for me. You also do amazing things, that's why your my role model. You have so many accomplishment, and know so many people. You are friends with the president. That's a huge honor. You ran for the school board member. Even though you lost it was probably a huge honor. You are probably really proud of yourself, I know I am. When I grow up I want to be like you. You have always been there for me, like a cow and a calf. Happy Easter to you a wonderful women. I hope you know how amazing you are, because everyone loves you. Who ever thinks otherwise is CRAZY. I know you have heard this so many times but I deeply mean it. I love you to the moon and back there is positively nothing you lack. You will always be close to my dear heart. I will always remember you til the end of time.

Love,

Your little angel (Johanah)

ORIGINAL LETTER FROM JOHANAH, ASTER'S GRANDDAUGHTER

3-20-10

Dear, Ako

You are the women of my life. You care for me like I'm the only thing in the world. I thank you for always caring for me no matter what. Every time I'm feeling low you are always their to make me feel better. You let me cook with you. Sometimes okay I'm lying all the time, I eat some of the dough and/or the batter. I can't help myself from doing it your batter is just so good. especially since you made it. You are like my gardian angel you gard me and stand up for me. You also do amazing things, thats why your my role model. You have so many accomplishment, and know so many people. You are friends with the president. Thats a huge honor. You ran for the school board member. Even though you lost it was probably a huge honor. You are probably really proud of yourself, I know I am. When I grow up I want to be like you. You have always been there for me, like a cow and a calf. Happy Easter to you a wonderful women. I hope you know how amazing you are, because everyone loves you. Who ever thinks otherwise is CRAZY. I know you have heard this so many times but I deeply mean it. I love you to the moon and back there is positivly nothing you lack. You will always be close to my dear heart. I will always remember you til the end of time.

Love,
your little angel (Johanah)

(My granddaughter, twelve years old wrote this letter and gave me for Easter).

About the Author

Aster Bato Mohamed has lived an extraordinary life. Her strong faith, instilled in her by her brother Obo Deressa sustained her throughout her remarkable life's journey that has taken her around the world. Born in the small Ethiopian village of Aira, Aster's odyssey has taken her from Ethiopia to Germany, and finally, to America. Dedicating her life to education, Aster has been honored with multiple prestigious awards for her many achievements inside and outside the classroom throughout her long career in the Miami-Dade County Public Schools system. Now retired, Aster continues to live in Florida and is the proud mother of three successful children and a loving grandmother.

www.ingramcontent.com/pod-product-compliance
Lightning Source LLC
Chambersburg PA
CBHW070902120626
46546CB00001B/98